DATE DUE

AG 7 '97			
OC 1 '97			
AP 7 '99			

DEMCO 38-296

TOURISTS

Tourists

HOW OUR FASTEST GROWING INDUSTRY
IS CHANGING THE WORLD

Larry Krotz

Faber and Faber
Boston · London

Library of Congress Cataloging-in-Publication Data

Krotz, Larry, 1948–
    Tourists : how our fastest growing industry is changing the
world / Larry Krotz.
        p.   cm.
    ISBN 0-571-19893-7 (cloth)
    1. Tourist trade.   I. Title.
    G155.A1K76   1996
    338.4'791—dc20   96-14821
                                                             CIP

Jacket design by Leslie Styles
Printed in the United States of America

To my mother

Contents

Acknowledgments

The author gratefully acknowledges research support from the Manitoba Arts Council, without which this book would have been very difficult to produce. I want to thank editor Valerie Cimino at Faber and Faber for her helpful and patient work and Ed Knappman for his support.

Also, I would like—in no particular order—to salute those whose ideas made contributions to this book, as well as those who have been good-spirited traveling companions or who, over the years, have taught me to enjoy travel. Neil Webster, the late Dale DeMarsh, Helen Koepke, Bonny Fraser, Nancy Embry, Jane Stuart, Charles Wilkins, Hugh McCullum, Rebecca Garrett, John and Andrea McCullum (who have been my hosts twice in Africa), Cheryl Albuquerque, Katherine Medland, George Cella, Rob and Isabel Mainor, and my daughter Sarah Krotz.

1

The Travel Bug

I was once invited to a travel party. Some parties have food themes or costume themes or old-movies themes; but at this one it was world travel. The price of admission was participation in a lottery. Each guest brought $200 and the name of some place in the world they wanted to visit. Our money was taken when we arrived and placed in a little metal strongbox. The names of the dream destinations, the places we most wanted to visit, were written on a piece of paper, read out to the rest of the group, and placed in a hat. The names of all the guests were placed in another hat. We wanted to go everywhere; Paris, Rome, Alaska, Turkey, Portugal, Ireland, Kenya on a Safari, Easter Island, Iceland. One person wanted to go to Las Vegas; two picked Machu Pichu in Peru. The destinations mirrored the table of contents of six month's worth of *Travel & Leisure* magazine.

The host, who had dreamed up this idea, had been all over the world either as a tourist or in connection with his profession as a teacher. He had worked in South America for several years for CUSO, the Canadian University Services Overseas. The travel bug was deeply ingrained in Neil, and he had returned to various parts of Latin America dozens of times as well as making trips to the Middle East, Europe, Britain, Ireland, and to places throughout North America. He was a frequent-flyer plan's dream; he never came back from one trip without plans for the next one firm in his mind. And he loved to share his stories and adventures.

The evening progressed through small talk and food and slides of one

of Neil's recent trips, preliminaries craftily stretched out to allow a seductive anticipation to build. The rules for the lottery were simple: the
name drawn from one hat would get the money, all $3,200. But that win-
ner had to agree to leave within two weeks for the destination drawn
from the other hat. At last no one wanted to wait any longer. We hung
together through the tantalizing seconds during which every possibility
hung open; any one of us might be packing his bags for anywhere on
the globe. Neil then reached into the hat and withdrew the name of a
young woman. Everybody looked at her for a moment, hating her. The
prize was Turkey. The young woman appeared panic-stricken and confused; the waiting and fantasizing was now over, and she had to act. She
protested that she had wanted to go to Ireland; no one was sympathetic.
Rules are rules. So off she went, on her adventure.

The rest of us went home. It had been a memorable party (though a
bit expensive). But somehow it was more than just a unique evening's
entertainment. The governing assumption of that evening recognized a
monumental revolution in the possibilities of human history. Behind
the sport of our lottery loitered a set of possibilities for experience that
would have been too astonishing for any generation preceding our
own even to contemplate—yet we were casually able to take them for
granted. Up until that time I had barely gone anywhere. But this little
party brought forward the most profound possibilities and made me
consider aspects of our time that make it different from all other times,
and me and my contemporaries different from all other peoples in history. We have an obsession with travel, and it is astounding how casual
we can be when considering it. It is possible to travel to any place in the
world within a day. Such travels are possible not only for an elite of
wealthy, able adventurers, but also for "normal" people—for every one
of the very ordinary, unremarkable human beings, for example, who
were gathered that May evening in a middle-class living room in an
apartment building in Winnipeg, Canada.

Being well traveled has long been a mark of superior sophistication.
Synonymous with *worldliness,* it traditionally put the traveler, whether
an explorer of the Arctic or the jungle, or a partaker of the "grand tour"
of the culture spots of Europe, a head above the ordinary rabble. But
that was predominantly the case when travel was a luxury, reserved
for those who had money, time, and a mighty sense of adventure.
What my friend's party demonstrated is how much the world has
changed. Gathered there were not wealthy people with a lot of time on

their hands; they were teachers and social workers, lawyers, and lower-level professionals. One was a student. We were adventurous, to the degree that each was willing to wager $200. The winner had to be the kind of person willing to be a good sport about spending two weeks somewhere that was dictated by the luck of a draw. But we didn't have to be Odysseus or Christopher Columbus or Henry Morgan Stanley or Vanderbilt. Any one of us could be as casual about packing our bags for a journey to Istanbul as our grandparents would have been about a trip to the next town. We could, what's more, make such an undertaking with a minimum of disruption to our existing lives. We could be gone a mere two or three weeks; our jobs, friendships, family structures, everything would remain intact during our absence. We could go to the ends of the earth and not miss a rent payment at home. At worst we might need to arrange for someone to come in and water the plants once or twice and perhaps board the dog or the cats. We would return with stories, experiences, perhaps a sunburn or a lingering case of upset stomach, and then, without missing a beat, promptly resume lives left such a brief time before.

Within our lifetimes, with technological developments such as six-hour flights between America and Europe, increased leisure time, and burgeoning disposable income, travel—at least for many of us who live in North America, Western Europe, Australia, and Japan—is no longer a luxury. Some people consider it a right. In 1989 more than one billion people, one in five of the world's population, boarded airplanes to fly somewhere.

This makes us very different from our ancestors and doubtless will make our children different from us. In the 1980s I started to travel, and in the decade since I have been on two lengthy trips to Africa, seven trips to Europe, and six journeys into Latin America. My father, who died in 1958, barely left home. He made one trip as a young man from Ontario to visit his brother who lived in Alberta. Because he was the wrong age, he missed the major expedition for young men of his generation, which was to cross the ocean and fight a war. In contrast to both of us, my nineteen-year-old daughter has been to France, Scotland, Mexico, and Germany; has lived for a year in England; and crossed the Atlantic by herself when she was eleven.

This book distinguishes travel for pleasure from travel for business, or travel for immigration, or travel to wage war, or many of the other kinds of roaming around that have historically moved people from one place to another. Hence the title *Tourists*. The word "tourism" or "tourist" is a charged one. It is quite open to snobberies and disdain and is frequently used as a pejorative. Author Paul Fussell, who wrote about British travel between the wars, complained: "I am assuming that travel is now impossible and that tourism is all we have left." It seems he could barely spit out the word. In the snobbery hierarchy, travel is on one level; tourism on another, much lower spot. I find that whenever I'm called a "tourist," regardless of its truth, something inside me recoils. My self-image doesn't quite want to accept the designation. The word conjures a caricature somewhere between a naif and an ignorant buffoon; an unserious passer-through. I'd much rather be a traveler. But as is the case with all loaded words, neither term, "tourist" or "traveler," gets quite adequately defined. They become mutually exclusive as if, like enemies, the tourist is destroying the world for the traveler in the same way shopping malls destroyed the world for corner shops, or cars destroyed it for the horse and carriage.

The word "tourist" originally came into the language to describe the transient groups of visitors who moved through Europe in the early 1800s visiting museums. Collections of antiquities were the rage, and museums at the Vatican in Rome, the Louvre in Paris, and others in England, Germany, and the Netherlands were springing up to house them and display them to the curious and the interested. The popularity of the displays attracted groups of people who had both the time and the money (not to mention a well-informed interest) to move from country to country, city to city, museum to museum touring, as "tourists." Mass tourism, or travel for pleasure by great numbers of ordinary people, is more recent and largely a function of our time and our generation. It was not until the 1960s that working-class Britons and Germans were able to travel freely more than the distance that a train could cover in half a day. And it was not until 1964 that ordinary Japanese were even allowed to travel abroad for pleasure, and then they were limited to one trip a year. Now those working-class Germans and Britons are found in overwhelming numbers in Greece, the south of Spain, and the Caribbean islands; the Japanese tourists are everywhere. These three national groups, within a span of thirty years, have become travelers in astonishing numbers.

The word "travel" has the same linguistic root as "travail," to work or struggle or endure hardship, which means it has never been considered an easy undertaking. The great travel stories of mythology are all essentially stories of adversity, triumphs over hardships by characters imbued with stupendous courage and endurance. Homer's Odyssey kept Odysseus away from home for twenty years and included thirty-six months of being blown around the Mediterranean by storms, seven years marooned on the island of Ogygia, and a trip to the Underworld. (This was perhaps the first image in literature that travel could be hell). The journey of the Children of Israel from Egypt to the Promised Land required most of the life and all of the strength and patience of their leader, Moses. The Crusades sucked years and the youth out of most of Northern Europe's finest knights and adventurers. The journeys into Africa by Burton and Speke, by Henry Morgan Stanley and Joseph Conrad, among many others, bubbled under with danger, tedium, discomfort, and fear.

Because of the full menu of dangers and hardships, it usually took a promise of riches or fame (or both) to get even the most intrepid and adventuring spirits out on the journey: Marco Polo, Christopher Columbus, Giovanni Cabot, Vasco da Gama, Sir Francis Drake, and all the other explorers from the fourteenth to the eighteenth centuries, including those who perished for their troubles on ill-fated searches for things such as the Northwest Passage and other treasure routes. Ordinary people embarked on longer journeys only because they had to. The common sailors crewing the ships of the great adventurers were there, in the main, because they had little choice. Some of them—hiding-out criminals or victims of Lord Nelson's press gangs (hapless characters would be given lots to drink and then, when they sobered up, would find they had signed on for the Royal Navy)—had no choice at all. The same lack of choice faced the hordes of peasants forced on migrations to new lands and territories by famine, war, and political or economic hardship. Few of these had a very happy time of it on the journey. There was little comfort, no security, and the vulnerabilities to accident, sickness, and death that faced them constantly in their wretched lives were, during travel, at their highest.

Even with today's comforts and predictabilities, travel is not easy. Ask anybody who's made a thirty-six-hour junket from Northern Europe or North America to Australia or New Zealand. Not even the amenities of first class can begin to ease the fatigue and jet lag that assaults the body from such an undertaking. True, it is not the thirty-six weeks that such a voyage might have taken by sea a century or two ago, but it is still hard work.

Because it was such hard work, travel required the excuse of purposeful activity to get it started; a migration, a war to fight, a pilgrimage to make, or treasures to locate and exploit. It was not meant to be fun. Dr. Samuel Johnson defended it as importantly connected to the quest for learning. "The use of travelling," he stated, "is to regulate imagination by reality, and instead of thinking how things may be, to see them as they are." Others were not so sure. Roger Ascham (1515–1568), a private tutor to Queen Elizabeth, was skeptical and highly critical of "aimless travel abroad, especially to Italy," principally because he perceived such roaming to have a harmful impact on the use of, development of, and education in English language and culture.

Until the coming of railways in the 1830s, methods of land travel had stayed basically unchanged since antiquity. If one wanted to go somewhere, one went on foot or, if lucky, on horseback or by horse-drawn carriage. The literature of the time tells us how reluctant people were to travel, and understandably so, because of the hardships and dangers of the journey. Jane Austen's character, Mr. Knightley, in her 1816 novel *Emma*, frets about the "evils of the journey," and the "fatigues of his horses and coachmen," as he and his family are about to set off on a trip from London to Highbury. The distance that causes this trepidation is not an oceanic or a continental crossing but a little jaunt of sixteen miles. Yet, given the conditions of the day—bad roads, weather, and the dangers of highwaymen—it was not an experience to look forward to or to undertake without planning and waiting for the best possible moment. The trip over rutted bumpy roads in a rocking, jolting carriage equipped only with rudimentary springs would have taken four to five hours. It would leave the travelers stiff, sore, dusty, muddy, and probably more weary than a trans-Atlantic flight would leave us now. It was not undertaken frequently, demanded a good excuse, and, once done, usually required a week or two in order to rest up for the return trip's travails.

With the advent of railways all this began to change. Witold Rybczynski, in his book on leisure time, *Waiting for the Weekend*, tells how by 1841 British trains were taking people on weekend pleasure excursions from Birmingham, for example, to the sea. The outings were day trips, or sometimes over-nighters; the travelers would make the venture out on Sunday, spend the night in a hotel, and make the return trip on Monday. As they evolved, these weekend holiday excursions inaugurated methods that would become honed and perfected over time into the systems we are familiar with in modern tourism: the outings were aimed at working people rather than the rich, they spoke highly of the value of recreation and refreshing body and mind, and they depended heavily on advertising to sell them. "Eight hours at the seaside for three-and-sixpence," promised contemporary ads. Soon the ventures came to have such broad appeal and promise that tour companies dedicated solely to the organization and promotion of such travel were formed. One of the pioneers of mass, cheap, travel for working people in the mid-nineteenth century was a young English printer with an entrepreneurial bent named Thomas Cook. The modest travel business he inaugurated later burgeoned into the massive, worldwide, vertically-integrated enterprise that still bears his name. The start of Thomas Cook's great travel empire came through his pioneering cut-rate railway tours in England in the 1840s, which he expanded a decade later with tours to the Continent. Vacation resorts such as Blackpool sprang up to handle the traffic and cash in on the popularity of the craze. The rudimentary infrastructure of the present-day travel industry was struck.

The package vacation tour for middle-class and working people was organized with typical efficiency by the Nazis in Germany ninety years later. Rybczynski describes the undertakings of the *Kraft durch Freude* (Strength Through Joy) organization set up by Dr. Robert Ley, director of Hitler's Labor Front. "Ley established special seaside and ski resorts, yachting and riding schools, and even operated a fleet of ten cruise ships that sailed the Baltic and the Mediterranean. Thanks to such initiatives, one German worker in three was able to take part in some sort of vacation travel. Between 1932 and 1938, [such] tourism doubled."

There was no problem with the public's appetite for travel. It was there, created in large part through a literature filled with the adventure and exotica of hitherto unseen places, people, and experiences. What was needed, and what became available through the efforts of Thomas Cook and ultimately through companies such as Club Med, was the organization, the framework within which ordinary people could live out the fantasies, presented in literature, that had been reserved for the rich or the extremely adventurous. Cook promised his customers a holiday trip for the equivalent of a day's pay. That, remarkably, is what we still have. When Americans make their annual winter trips to Mexico or the Caribbean or Hawaii, though it is not now a train journey of a hundred miles to the sea but an airplane flight of perhaps three or four hours over ten or fifteen times that distance, the price of the flight remains very close to an average day's pay. Thousands of Canadians migrate south every winter to the balmy coasts of Florida (where they drop $2 billion into the state economy). What lures them, other than sunshine and sand, are airfares from Toronto or Montreal that can be as low as $149— an average day's pay.

Turning travel into an industry had several mixed results. In a later chapter we look more closely at Thomas Cook, Club Med, and other forces that have turned recreational travel or tourism into a full-blown industry. The immediate impact, though, was to change the way the world was looked at and the way people behaved toward it. Suddenly the distant and the exotic became available. The means to visit places that had been unreachable not so long before was brought within reach. Just as suddenly the prevailing desire became to take the edge and danger and strangeness away from what had recently been exotic. Safety, predictability, and convention came to be greater values than unpredictability and surprise. Holiday Inns are securely part of an honored pattern developed as part of that predictability when they advertise "no surprises." When travel became the business of tour promoters, and the masses became the customers, certain guarantees started to be demanded—and provided. The new group of travelers might want their adventure, but it seemed they didn't want surprises or uncertainty; they wanted assurances that they could undertake their adventures within the realms of predictability and with some safety. As I write this, a Canadian couple, a lawyer and his wife, are suing their travel agent because, during a 1993 trip to Rwanda, they were caught in the middle of guerilla gunfire. This was still a year in advance of all Tutsi-Hutu hell breaking loose in that tiny, mountainous middle African country, famed until then for its mountain gorillas. But the Canadians claim they were not warned of danger, and during the trip "felt certain of their imminent death," and have since suffered post-traumatic stress. Theirs is a uniquely late-twentieth-century and Western response. One thinks of the likelihood of Dr. Livingstone or Captain Richard Burton filing post-trip lawsuits to compensate for their stress.

Modern tourism's mass appeal speaks also to the fragmented nature of contemporary culture. In an essay entitled "The Rites of the Tribe," Jack Kugelmass points out that there is ample evidence tourism was "quite prevalent before the invention of the postcard. Romans were every bit as intrigued by the pyramids as we are. . . ." But a change in modern times and in present-day society is nonetheless fundamental.

"Whereas early travellers were cognizant of their own exceptionalness," states Kugelmass, "modern tourists, aside from a relatively small proportion of adventure travellers, go in order to do what others have already done, afraid, perhaps, that not to do so would be a sign of lower social status." Traveling, or going somewhere as a tourist, has become, like the viewing of annual sports and cultural events—the World Series or the Academy Awards—one of the things that we do in order to share in our culture, in order to be tied together. "Sightseeing," writes Dean MacCannell, "is a kind of collective striving for a transcendence of the modern totality, a way of attempting to overcome the discontinuity of modernity, of incorporating its fragments into unified experience."

This is where "tourism" gets its knock from the snobs. This is where those of us who are loathe to think of ourselves as conformists want to jump off the bandwagon. According to writer John Dunn in an essay in the *Globe and Mail*, the ugly or undesirable side of the "collective striving" has turned tourism into "the sleazy god of ritual conformity." For historian Daniel Boorstin, the lemming-like, slavish adherence to tourism's rules and patterns maps out the differentiation between "travel" and "tourism," traveler and tourist. Travel, argues Boorstin, is the journey into the unknown, a sometimes dangerous ordeal with no guarantees but many promises. Tourism, by contrast, is a different state of mind, expectant of an "antiseptic, pleasant, relaxing, comfortable experience." "We go more and more where we expect to go. We get money-back guarantees that we will see what we expect to see. . . . We look into a mirror instead of out a window, and we see only ourselves."

Why do we travel? When I asked people, I received a variation on a simple set of answers. To escape the humdrum routine of everyday life. To seek adventure and romance. To find home, but home with sun, sand, and heat. Because we can. Because our culture tells us we must. Travel in our culture is a symbol of many things—it is a symbol of our freedom to take control of our own time and movement, and it is a symbol in part of our status. It is also a sign of an enduring and increasing restlessness.

Over time, subtle shifts have occurred in how we realize and appreciate travel. As the 1980s turned into the 1990s, a Lou Harris poll for *Travel & Leisure* magazine identified a shift in the trends and tastes of travelers from what they called "escapism to enrichment." The desires for luxury resorts declined, as did demands for things such as a "good night life," expensive cuisine, and having a lot of readily available places to drop cash without much thought or much return. Priorities were changing. On the increase were desires to do things such as experience a completely different culture; gain a new perspective on life; learn more about nature or cultural, historical, and archeological treasures; and visit places that tourists had never been before. In one respect these trends closed the circle in ways that might have pleased, say, Thomas Cook. In *Cook's Tours*, Edmund Swinglehurst describes the incredible hunger for education and self-improvement that were the motivating drives behind Thomas Cook's 1850s British working-class tourists. "The idea of making travel easily and cheaply available always carried with it ethical undertones. Possibly this is because the pioneers of travel for the millions were nearly all motivated by religious and social ideals (Cook was an avid temperance activist) and also because the early tourists felt that the enjoyment of leisure required some justification." It took a full century, until the end of the Second World War, before people felt free to indulge in uninhibited pleasure and hedonism in their travels and consider these as defensible virtues.

For the people surveyed by the Harris poll, the desire to travel itself remained high. Nobody expressed a weariness with it all and a desire to stay home instead. In fact, despite the worldwide economic recession of the early 1990s, the impulse to travel did not diminish, and the numbers showed barely a dip. In the early 1990s, travel was still growing at a rate of about 4 percent annually and was expected to continue as population, leisure time, and discretionary income levels increased while the cost of travel itself decreased. Worldwide air travel, according to the International Civil Aviation Organization (ICAO), was growing at rates of 6 to 7 percent a year in the early 1990s and was expected to continue to grow. If there was a shift, it was to the Far East; passenger traffic on Asian and Pacific airlines was by now leading the way in the numbers game. As holiday travel moved from being perceived as a luxury to being perceived as a right, tour operators allowed only that economics made customers more discriminating and drove them to shop more carefully for better deals: the general volume of tourism continued unabated.

Of all the phenomena that have become part of life and our world in the last fifty years: nuclear power, television, computers, recreational sex, and mass travel, in the final analysis I believe mass travel will be the one that will most change the world. It is huge. Making use of the stupefying numbers that dazzle us through their stratospheric unreality, the scorekeepers now call tourism a $3 trillion industry. Actually, in 1995, according to the World Travel and Tourism Council (WTTC), it was a $3.4 trillion a year business, up from $2.9 trillion in 1990 and $1.9 trillion in 1987. (If patterns hold, it is on its way to a predicted $7.2 trillion by 2005.) Travel for pleasure accounted for two-thirds to three-quarters by volume of all world travel and for a much higher percentage to certain holiday destinations like the Caribbean or Greece. Domestic tourism, or travel by citizens within the borders of their own country, exceeded by both volume and expenditure international tourism; ten times the volume and seven times the expenditure according to a United Nations agency, the World Tourist Organization (WTO). In the developed world, travel for pleasure is the third largest household expense, after food and shelter.

Within one generation, tourism leaped to become the biggest employer and fastest growing industry in the world. Travel and tourism accounted for 7.5 percent of capital investment in the world in 1995, and for one out of every nine jobs. It was a major industry in more than 125 countries. In some regions it was almost an economic monoculture. The thirteen countries that make up the English-speaking part of the Caribbean community receive about six million tourists a year, a number that exceeds their combined local population. On some islands tourists have come to vastly outnumber the local people. In 1990 the Bahamas had fourteen tourists for every local person; in Sint Maarten, it was twenty-four tourists for every native. The economics of this are of considerable importance, since tourism earns these islands about $7 billion a year. In 1990 developing countries as a whole were earning about $55 billion dollars a year from tourism. The potential for continued growth seemed astronomical and dazzling. Long-term forecasts by the WTTC predicted that travel and tourism's contribution to the world gross domestic product would grow by more than 100 percent by the year 2005, that capital investment would increase by 80 percent, and that employment generated would rise by 33 percent or forty million jobs.

The ramifications are likewise considerable, and they go well beyond economics. There should be no illusion about who the tourists are. Not everyone in the world can be a tourist; a middle-class American, though believing he or she is of modest means, still has infinitely more money and opportunity for mobility than an average Zimbabwean. Seven countries: Germany, Britain, the United States, Canada, France, Italy, and Japan—the same countries that form the G7 economic block—account for 30 percent of the world's tourists. Of the traveling segment of the world, the Germans lead the way. In 1994, Germans took 65.2 million trips abroad, an increase of 4.2 percent over 1993. Americans were next, with 47.3 million trips, increasing their travel over the previous year by 3.5 percent. Britons made 34.2 million foreign tours, up 5.2 percent. The ability to participate, at least on the visitor side of this phenomenon, is still largely a matter of the luck of birth. Were I born in Bangladesh or Zaire, I would be infinitely less likely to become a tourist than were I born in the United States or Canada. Those citizens of the other hundred and some countries of the world find their lot as "the visited."

What are the implications of so much travel? Which of them are good? Which of them are not so good? In the interaction between visitor and visited, what is exchanged? In places where tourism is encouraged for economic reasons, do people understand what they might have to give up as part of the bargain? David Quammen, writing in *Outside* magazine about the effects of tourism and mass visiting on wildlife and the natural world, enlisted the ground rules of quantum mechanics to make his point. Even when the best intentions and care are in place, "you can't observe an entity without in some sense touching it, and you can't touch it without having an effect. . . . A cheetah stalking wildebeest in Nairobi National Park, suddenly surrounded by Land Rovers and Volkswagen vans full of walleyed humans, their camera shutters crackling like grass fire, behaves differently than an undisturbed cheetah." This is the effect at the high end, the effect of the most cautious, the most responsible, the most politically correct behavior. Most scenarios are much worse, and most prognoses infinitely more unfavorable. Author V. S. Naipaul observed glumly that "Every poor country accepts tourism as an unavoidable degradation." But he was most pessimistic about his native Caribbean, believing "some of these West Indian Islands in the name of tourism are selling themselves into a new slavery."

There are no travelers anymore, lamented Daniel Boorstin, only tourists. "People go to see what they already know is there." If tourists are seeking an antiseptic, comfortable experience, then tourism's ultimate, extreme creations to achieve this must surely be the modern-day theme parks. There is a certain vogue in looking down one's nose at these creations, but they are enormously successful, attracting millions of visitors. Theme parks are remarkable creations of our culture, and remarkable aspects of the travel and tourist industry. From historic villages to exotic animal game parks, people go to see not what would already exist in a particular location, but what, in fact, has been built, created, specifically and for no other reason than to attract their visit. The crown of all such theme parks is, of course, Walt Disney World. Constructed at Orlando, Florida, in the 1960s and 1970s on top of a marsh and reclaimed ever-glade swamp where alligators waded, birds congregated, and Seminole Indians used to roam, Walt Disney World is now a shopping center of theme parks. The Magic Kingdom, Epcot Center, and Disney-MGM Studios cover forty-three square miles. The whole business contains all the needs of life for the thousands of families who temporarily transport themselves into this travel experience: 19,000 hotel rooms, twenty-seven tennis courts, and five eighteen-hole golf courses designed by top architects. Everything is put together for the indulgence, pleasure, and security of the guests, whose constant arrival through the turnstiles is demanded to justify the place and keep it operating. In the middle of an alligator swamp Disney produced the prototype theme park and, in so doing, the Number One tourist attraction in the world. Several million tourists a year come to see Mickey Mouse and Goofy, jump aboard the amusement park rides, gaze at old models of the space shuttle, and obtain insights into how the special effects worked for such movies as *Indiana Jones* or *Honey, I Shrunk the Kids*.

The handiness of the MGM museum is somehow appropriate because the essential experience of the whole visit is closer to an extended time at the movies than to any kind of travel in a conventional or classic sense. But Walt Disney World's enormous popularity presents its own conclusions. Offer such dazzle, market it cleverly, make it safe, predictable within bounds, and affordable, and your audience will show up in droves. Though Disney offers the biggest theme parks in Florida, California, and now in France, there are hundreds of others from Tammy Fay and Jim Bakker's famous, ill-starred Heritage USA to innumerable historical villages, big and small, local or national in their subject matter. Each in its own way is a rather bizarre concoction. Connections—historical, social, or environmental—to the host community or landscape are incidental, usually irrelevant. Upper Michigan has a full-fledged Bavarian Village; in southern Ontario you can drive the family through an African Lion Safari park.

Theme parks are awesomely successful and integral to tourism as it is understood today. They make piles of money and seem to satisfy and attract people. But what theme parks really do is further separate the "tourist" from what used to be the "traveler." The people of Orlando probably spend little time touring Disney World. But it is not there for them; it was not meant for the enjoyment of Orlando or the citizens of north central Florida. It was built for and is meant for the outsiders. This, however, by no means renders it meaningless to Orlando. Far from it. Like tourist attractions worldwide it has multiple purposes, and one of those purposes has to do with Orlando and north central Florida, which is one of the reasons it was built there in the first place. Other than to make a lot of money for and promote the various entertainment connections of the Disney empire, a specific purpose of Walt Disney World is to draw outsiders to Orlando. Like tourist attractions everywhere, the Disney World theme parks create jobs for the people of Orlando and central Florida so that Orlando and Central Florida can have an economy. Theme parks and tourist attractions fill the same role a giant factory might have filled in the past or in some other place, except instead of working on assembly lines, the local people get their jobs in the hospitality and entertainment fields. They are waitresses, ticket takers, hotel clerks, ride operators, janitors, engineers, actors in Donald Duck costumes, administrative clerks, and accountants. The tourists are consumers, treated as such from the very beginning, through the advertising and social pressures that draw them there, to the processing they are put through when they line up at the entry gate or for the rides, restaurants, and exhibits. They are consumers in every bit the same way that they would be were the Orlando enterprise an automobile factory and the tourists buyers of cars, except that what they are now buying are experiences (and food, hotel rooms, and Kodak film).

The turning of travel into a commodity and travelers or tourists into consumers does strange things to human interaction. It warps and categorizes the relationship between the visitor and those who ought to be the hosts. In a situation such as that of Disney World or any of its copies, the relationship between host community and visitors is defined by a wall of distance and commerce. The roles are defined, the relationships defined. Some would argue that this is a good thing: the tourists are getting what they expect, what they can digest, what they already believe to be familiar; and the host community, while receiving an injection into its economy, is able to maintain its privacy. A good example of this is, say, a place that has a Club Med, a tourist resort that is usually presented as a walled off, self-contained "village." Here the tourists are secure, in both their persons and in their expectations, from the vagaries of the "foreign" culture beyond the site and outside the wall. But the local people are also secure from the invasion of the tourists. The North American and European tourists at a Caribbean or South Seas Club Med will not be wandering late at night through the back streets of the real town, poking their noses into the lives and homes, restaurants, and stores of the local people. The local people will have contained and controlled the tourists to their all-needs-met "village," just as the Club Med administration will have controlled the tourist's holiday experience. The locals will have protected their own privacy, both personal and cultural, and will have restricted their contact with the tourists to the commercial interactions of the jobs they have as cooks, chambermaids, guides, etcetera at the resort. They go in for their shifts, and come out after the shifts end, changing into and later out of the uniforms their service or hospitality jobs require. The relationship between tourist and local is proscribed by rigid tradition that can't be broken down even by those who might wish to do so. Mere friendliness and cheerfulness are certainly not enough to break it down. No relationships other than commercial ones are possible, because the only circumstances under which tourists have anything to do with the local people are the commercial ones, when they are selling to, serving, or guiding the tourists.

Even in the instances where the visitor thinks he or she is encountering a reality, it will likely turn out to have a certain phoniness. Mark Kurlansky in *A Continent of Islands* tells how in Curacao a Chamber of Commerce style committee called the Foundation for the Conservation of Monuments decided to broaden its terms of reference beyond old churches and the mansions of the wealthy planter aristocracy to include peasant and slave huts when it appeared that those too were of interest to tourists. To add some color, an eighty-year-old son of a slave, John Scoop, was paid a subsidy to maintain his corn-thatched slave house as a sort of living museum. "Scoop would show people around his one-room house with traditional tools and a copy of the emancipation decree from 1868, thirty-nine years before he was born. His subsidy was a good deal, since he was just living the way he had always lived. His father had died of a fever cutting cane in Cuba, and John had lived in this house with his mother. He had wanted to modernize but his mother wouldn't let him. Now he was being paid to keep things the way they were." Scoop's reaction was a kind of good-natured puzzlement that nonetheless underlined the unreality of the situation. "Americans are very strange people," he observed. "They always want to make a photo of me wearing my straw hat."

Something very similar happened in Canada at Manitoba's Hecla Island. In the 1970s the government of the province of Manitoba expropriated land, including an entire village, on this lonely and picturesque island close to the shores of Lake Winnipeg, in order to create a provincial park. The action provoked a great deal of angry resistance from the couple of dozen Icelandic fisher-people who had lived there for generations and now were being asked to move. Yet they had no choice but to comply, so they left. Within a year, however, things had turned about. The bureaucrats found themselves sheepishly returning to the locals who had resisted their plans so fiercely—people like Helgi Tommason who told me this story—and asking if they could hire them back. An empty village was too eerie to interest visitors; it needed people who would provide backdrop and local color for the tourists the park officials wished to attract. The government in the interests of tourism had decided to pay the people to live their former lives.

Interesting though they are as stories, in reality these charades probably change little. John Scoop and Helgi Tommason remain part of an "act"; the worlds remain separate, and the visitor remains within his or her "tourist bubble," physically in a place but socially outside the culture. This isn't restricted only to Club Med or the world of theme parks. The same result is achieved everywhere that enough travelers go to merit a response by the multi-national service industry. When you find a Holiday Inn in Belize, or a McDonalds in Istanbul, or a Hertz Rent-a-Car service in northern Portugal, or a Wimpy's restaurant in Zimbabwe you are in the same boat. Whenever and wherever those services and franchises are available, the tourist has great difficulty escaping or avoiding the web of what is becoming the universally familiar. Perhaps the tourist doesn't want to escape, perhaps convenience and predictable familiarity are too strong a draw. But when you go half way around the world only to be enveloped by the same institutions, logos, and services that you have just left behind both at home and in the last place you just visited, you might not be able to resist screaming out your frustration: "Where can real life be found?" Is not the whole point of going on a pilgrimage to pick up a little of *other* people's experiences?

Before a trip to Germany, I spent several hundred dollars on grammar and conversational German lessons. I purchased the requisite phrase books and dictionaries. Though German is the language of my grand-parents, I had never mastered it. But now, as a matter of pride, I was de-termined to develop sufficient ability to get along. I wanted to be able to offer at least common courtesies. I wanted to be poised to learn, to read rudimentary signs and newspaper headlines so I could, even in the midst of another culture, satisfy myself that I could know what was going on. Most of all I wanted to feel I was doing some work, I was ful-filling at least the elementary requirement of a traveler getting ready to acknowledge the culture he was entering, and doing his bit to equip himself to survive within it. I had some things down pat; greetings, menu items, body parts, basic requests for help, and numbers from one to a hundred. However, upon arriving at our hotel in the middle of Heidelberg, I was rudely disappointed. The first person we encountered was a young desk clerk, a student at the university who was working in the hotel part time to pay for her studies. She stepped forward to greet and direct us in English that was infinitely superior to my meager command of German. My phrase book seemed superfluous. The young woman asked where we had come from in Canada, and, showing an understanding that our city was in the middle of the continent, specu-lated on the ways we would find this part of Germany infinitely differ-ent from what we had left at home. Betraying a common German awe about the vastness of the great Canadian plains with all their nature, buffalo herds, and Indian tribes, she allowed a concern lest we find this rather staid and historic part of her country a bit tame and boring. She suggested some things we ought to do to make our stay interesting and wished us well. Then she turned her attention to a group of Japanese arrivals and accomplished the same feat with them.

This scene repeated itself throughout Germany and Austria with all manner of service personnel. It is repeated in different countries all over the world. It used to be that the sophisticated, worldly, and knowledge-able people were the travelers. The panache of the world traveler was a cosmopolitan ease of manner obtained through treks into innumerable back corners of the globe and learned through the necessities of survival and interaction with local natives. Now a tourist can go virtually any-where without so much as a "how do you do" in the local language, and he or she can manage to survive just fine. Even more unfortunate is that a vast number seem to take a perverse pride in this very ability—or lack thereof. The true sophisticates now are not the travelers, who tend to remain overwhelmingly unilingual, but the staff, personnel, and workers who populate the travel industry. They, like our student desk clerk in Heidelberg, are adept in half-a-dozen languages and conversationally knowledgeable about all the cultures and geographies of origin of the visitors. They are the worldly ones.

2

A Trip to Germany

In 1888, my seventeen-year-old grandfather, his parents, brothers and sisters, and assorted cousins, aunts, and uncles left southern Germany to emigrate to America. Their journey was part of an epic migration; millions were leaving Europe to re-settle in then under-populated parts of the world such as America and Australia. Being small figures in a great number, drops in a flood, did not make the journey any less substantial or traumatic for them as individuals. The uprooting of a whole family to move to a new land was a massive act of faith, and their expedition was a strenuous one, both physically and psychologically.

Today I know only scattered bits about that journey—much less, certainly, than I would like to know. The best parts of the story of the trek that took the family up from their rural village in Baden to the port at Bremen and then on the trans-Atlantic voyage to New York disappeared, regrettably, with their deaths and I have missed forever the chance to hear the information first-hand. I find myself now longing to know in minute detail everything that transpired for them, what they saw and what they thought; what everything smelled like and felt like as well as the whole compendium of emotions as they were shuttled along their way. But the anecdotes that would have filled the gaps, details that would have brought color, memories of observations and emotions that would have surrounded such a final departure from home are gone like the wisp of smoke from a fire. Family lore has it that the trip took nine weeks from village door to New York harbor, and then to southern Ontario where my branch of the large family finally ended up. Lore has it also, that it was not an easy journey; it was fraught with seemingly endless waiting, repeated rearrangings of baggage and belongings, storms at sea, illnesses, and discomfort. It was also loaded with a profound finality for almost everyone who embarked; the trip changed the family's life and firmly closed a door. A combination of the toughness of the sea voyage and the circumstances of lives and families, finances, and occupations, not to mention the confusions of ensuing world events, meant that only one person from the group of twenty ever ventured back.

In 1992, a little more than a century later, my fifteen-year-old daughter and I made the trip, in the other direction. This time it did not require nine weeks; to get from Toronto to Frankfurt took a mere nine hours.

In our minds we may have been retracing an ancestral journey, making an important pilgrimage; but we were really doing something quite different. We may have been covering the same ground our grandparents had covered, but beyond that thin parallel, all similarity ended. We were indulging in travel of an entirely different variety. Our trip, all aspects of it, reflected a time and circumstances so different from those of our forebears as to be unimaginable to them. Every assumption, all our preoccupations, were timed to a different age; they were modern, current ones in every way, probably best demonstrated by the ways in which we organized ourselves.

Travel has always been about organization; you can't travel if you're not organized. Even when people just wander, when they muddle along hoping to have spontaneous accidents, a certain organization has to be central to their enterprise; a packing and ordering of essentials, a focus to point them in a direction. But a hallmark of contemporary travel is its peculiar system of organization and the tightness of that organization. The world of airplanes, car rentals, and reservation travel is portioned out not in days, but in minutes, and its bible is the sheet of paper your travel agent gives you: "your schedule," or "your itinerary." Everything is united around and focused on this computer print-out, which becomes your governor, both infinitely valuable and infinitely unforgiving. If you adhere to it, you are secure and well looked after; if you choose to treat it cavalierly, you do so at your peril. I have learned to be exceedingly obedient to these sheets of stray numbers and letters and twenty-four-hour clock readings, the codes for flight numbers, short forms of airline names, departure times and arrival times, gate identifications for transfers, and so on. My deference to these marching orders is great. I understand, wholly, that someone in every party, especially on a day when you are going to be making a serious move, needs to act the part of the commandant, fully cognizant of the itinerary and up to the minute in planning to meet it.

If you happen to make a tactical error, the sense of obedience and need to double check all assumptions carefully gets refreshed and honed anew. As with most learning, the lesson is usually an expensive one; it arrives with an unanticipated high price. Once, in the middle of a lengthy trip that was scheduled through Africa, I, for some reason that I still cannot explain, got into the habit of reading my complicated itinerary backwards. Through some strange dyslexia, I persisted in reading London-Harare numbers in their reverse order. In my mind I identified a return flight and departure time as the one I needed for the outbound leg, and I scheduled myself accordingly. I believed I had lots of time on my hands and was in the midst of wasting a good measure of that time on a leisurely pub lunch in Covent Garden when I realized my error. It was almost too late. In a panic, I raced to get my things from my hotel to Victoria Station and then set off for Gatwick only to find, once safely on the train, that this would also be the day the IRA, which was then randomly busy in London, had selected to issue a bomb threat for unspecified spots along British Rail routes. Train travel was reduced to a crawl. I was crammed, in full panic, in a standing-room-only rail car that tiptoed through south London at a steady ten miles an hour.

Eventually I made it to Gatwick, but I was much too late; I missed the plane, lost a day, my dignity, and a thousand dollars trying to get back on track. And I learned never to take anything for granted, neither my own ability to read nor the whims of any country's domestic revolutionaries. So in Germany, I read our itinerary faithfully, like a gospel, and repeated its messages to my daughter with such regularity that she started to show the kind of exasperation we are all familiar with toward our parents. "You'll be glad somebody's looking after this," I reminded her.

The way I organize in these situations is to count backwards from a zero hour (the time the plane is scheduled to leave the ground) and then I budget accordingly the time I estimate will be required for everything along the way. Then, by following the schedule, everything clicks like clockwork. It's hard to click like clockwork and adhere to such a schedule, though, when the first thing your day brings you to deal with is a humongous German breakfast. We were staying at the Tannhauser, a small hotel in the middle of Heidelberg where, as in every German and Austrian hotel, "breakfast" meant a board groaning with platters of sliced cheese and cold cuts, arrays of breads, jams, fruit, and steaming pitchers of chocolate and coffee. There was no way we could miss this, our last German breakfast. By the time we had packed it away, we were already twenty minutes behind. Then we spent another ten minutes shaking hands, bidding goodbye to the owners, the desk clerk, the waitress, and the cook, all of whom had become like family in only five short days.

Ninety minutes later, however, we were seated in the departure lounge of Terminal B, Frankfurt Main airport. It had taken only fifty minutes to find our way out of the center of Heidelberg and drive eighty-five kilometers up the Autobahn, including a quick stop to gas up and buy a candy bar. A certain good luck was with us, augmenting the extraordinary efficiency of the travel and transportation system we were hooked into. It is a system that increasingly has the capacity to funnel you through as if you are on the conveyer belt of the most modern, spic-and-span plastics industry factory. People have stories about their travel problems, screw-ups, and unpleasantries, but each story is the exception. The very fact that we notice them and take it for granted that such hitches should not exist or be tolerated is itself telling. Our expectations have come to be very high.

Our first task was to return the car we had been using for two weeks, and I worried about the intricacies of that. I needn't have. Immediately after the turn-off to the airport, the "Rent-A-Car Return" signs were everywhere, making our task easy. It took a simple six minutes to find the correct lot and negotiate the disposal of our trusty little Opel. The young woman behind the Budget desk immediately switched to English as soon as it was evident I misunderstood her first question put in German, which was "What is the return mileage on the car?"

We got our things out of the car and wheeled them to an elevator, which carried us up two levels to Departure. There, in short order, we found a cart for our luggage, located the row of Air Canada kiosks, and had Hesse Security X-ray our bags through their Hi Scan 9050 machine. A jiggling, multicolored amoeba appeared on the screen, a representation of the entrails of our luggage. The images made more sense to the two young men in blue sweaters who manned the screener equipment than they did to us, and we were both at their mercy and in their trust. The sturdy young fellows had a repetitive and boring job and tried to disguise their boredom behind a certain joviality. They were ready to joke. "They look all right," said one, practising his English on us. "I guess we won't have to blow them up," offered the other. They tagged our bags fit for travel.

Such repetition and boredom, though, can mask the responsibility and importance of the job. A few weeks later these security screeners would not be having so much fun. This was less than a month before one of their number would fail to catch the starter's pistol hidden under the fedora of a sociopathic young man who was boarding a Cairo-bound flight. Once on the plane, the undetected pistol came out, and the ordinary young man became a hijacker. He moved to the front of the Luftansa plane, entered the cockpit, held the gun to the side of the head of the pilot, and persuaded him to divert the flight to New York. Our friendly security screeners would lose their jobs as, in the ensuing turmoil and recriminations, Frankfurt airport would be taken away from Hesse State Security and given to the charge of the Federal German Border Police, Bundes-grenzshütz. And then a whole new round of debate and analysis of security and risk in the travel industry would be started up all over yet again. These were things they didn't contend with in my grandfather's day.

Two other passengers were ahead of us for check-in, but within minutes we were rid of our heavy luggage and in possession of boarding passes, well in advance of the flight that would not leave for another two hours. This was not going to be complicated at all; our efficiency had over-reached our needs. "We don't have a gate yet," the woman at the counter explained. "Check the screens at twelve o'clock." My daughter, annoyed at having been wakened much too early, gave me a chastizing "so-what-was-the-big-hurry-about" look.

Our personal efficiency, even though I was proud of how we were doing—no losses and not late—played only a small part in it. What is really impressive is the efficiency of the travel industry as a whole and institutions like this airport. Thirty million people a year—as many people as live in California, or more than the population of Canada or five Londons—move through the airport of Frankfurt-Main. Almost all of them catch their planes. Hardly any lose their luggage. The sheer power of this efficiency and the hugeness and potency of the system of which we, our luggage, our next few hours, and our lives and destinies were now inextricably a part, seduced us with its ease. We had virtually nothing to worry about, nothing to occupy us save the anticipation of being met in

Toronto by my brother, Sarah's uncle, in what, ten hours? And though
we were a couple of thousand miles and seven time zones away, we
might as well have been sitting in a hotel lobby or a living room down
the street waiting for him to arrive to fetch us. Try as we might, there
seemed to be nothing to think about, nothing to fret over, nothing to
do. If we had nervous apprehensions, they were only that we might be a
little tired by the time we reached their house in Kitchener (which used
to be called, incidentally, Berlin, in honor of the German immigrants
who, our ancestors among them, were its first settlers). Perhaps our bot-
toms would be sore from sitting so long, or our knees cramped, or our
skin dry from the artificial cabin air. Now that we had time to think
about it, we decided perhaps we weren't looking forward to the airline
meal; after our rich and wonderful diet of Bavarian holiday food we anticipated we might find the airline tray to be less than we had grown to
like. Perhaps we would need a decongestant to ease the sinus pain when
landing, the shock that comes from the decompression accompanying
such a rapid descent from 39,000 feet. For a few minutes I found a diver-
sionary train of thought when I realized that the book I intended to read
on the flight was packed securely away in my now-checked luggage. I
was furious with myself. What would I do for nine hours of air time?
Could I watch the movie, or would it be the one we had already seen on
the way over? These were our pre-travel thoughts and concerns, and
pretty mundane ones at that, in an airport lounge on New Year's Eve day
of 1992 prior to a late twentieth-century trans-Atlantic crossing.

You can be certain these were not the same concerns that would have
preoccupied my grandfather and his sisters and brothers and aunts and
uncles and parents and cousins, 104 years earlier when they made the
same trip. Not exactly the same trip, obviously, which is what this story
is all about. But it was the same trip in that it had a starting location in
Heidelberg, Germany, and a final destination in Kitchener, Ontario,
Canada.

In the preceding days we had used our little rented Opel to find the
village from which they had come in upper Baden. We had visited the
houses and street and store and church that had been part of the family's
life so long ago. We had wandered through the fields and vineyards and
woods and graveyard that had framed their existence. Through it all, we
had been thinking about all the ways their journey would have differed
from ours. They doubtless had more to concern themselves with than
the choices of whether they would read or watch the movie during the

trip. Certainly they had concerns about food. But they were not our petty complaints about Air Canada's caterer. They had had to supply their own food for the sea voyage, and my great-grandmother had carefully planned how she might transport turnips and potatoes, enough for the duration. I tried to imagine her worries: Would her supply be enough? How could she keep them from spoiling before they reached New York? How many ways could she prepare turnips and potatoes day after day to keep her family interested in eating them? In the end, rough weather almost tripled the time it took them to cross the Atlantic from the two to three weeks they had expected, and the supply of food did not last the distance, despite the fact that for much of the journey the travelers were too seasick to eat.

The little village of Eschelbach just south of Heidelberg was, in 1888, typical of southern Germany. The people were leaving. In fact, the 1880s were late in the crest that had been flowing for most of a century; German emigration in the nineteenth century was described as having the proportions of a "floodgate." Richard O'Connor, in *The German Americans,* describes it as driven by both positive and negative factors; equal proportions, no doubt, of fear and hope. In the mid-1800s the German states, pushed by powerful politicians such as Prince Otto Von Bismarck, the Prime Minister of Prussia, were moving toward political union and dreams of becoming an empire. But it was a difficult push, filled with violent skirmishes. Inevitably it involved a backlash; the mid-century erupted into widespread revolt against the authoritarianism and militarism of Prussia, the largest and strongest of the German states, and a reaction against nationalism's excesses. There was also a growing resistance to the yokes placed on the middle classes and the poor, both urban and rural, by the conscriptions of armies, the taxes of princes, and the tithes of churches.

In 1854, 215,000 Germans left for America. "The one great cause of this almost national movement," wrote an editorialist at the time in Chambers's *Edinburgh Journal,*

> is the desire for absolute political and religious freedom; the absence of all restrictions upon the development of society; and the publication of opinions which cannot be realized at home. The great agitation in society, caused first by the French domination, and then by the compulsive rise against it, has never passed away. In that gigantic struggle, when everything rested on the popular soul, the bonds of privilege and class were tacitly abandoned and

could never henceforth be reunited as before. The promises of having constitutional governments, at that time made by the sover-
eigns to their subjects, have been but partially fulfilled . . . there are
many restrictions, and the young, the restless, and the imaginative
thirst for their ideal freedom, and many of them seek for the realization of Utopia in America.

Europe might have been undergoing changes, but for many there was
not nearly enough in what they had or what they could hope for to persuade them to stay. It was one thing to hope for the triumph of national
pride and liberal reforms, but if they could cross the ocean, what was
available for them on the other side was the looming, growing specter of
America. America already had everything Europe's dispossessed might
have wanted: freedom of religion, belief, and expression; political democracy; and, most important, abundant land. America was a bright
Utopia beyond all European possibilities.

Despite agitation and despite hope for liberal reforms at home, thousands, or millions, believed the New World looked infinitely better than
the Old. In particular, peasants were frustrated, believing that not much
would happen to change their circumstances, for the reform movements
had been quickly taken over by urban middle-class professionals. When
the ad hoc Frankfurt Parliament was set up in 1848 to implement social
and economic reforms in German life, there were but four artisans and
only one peasant among its representatives. Being shut out of the
process, these people chose to vote instead with their feet; they emi-
grated at the first opportunity. People were driven to escape. They escaped, hoping to secure a different future for their children; some escaped
to secure mere survival. In 1846, the strange blight that affected the
potato crop of Ireland also hit the mid-continent, causing millions to
starve or go hungry.

The German provincial princes, an incredibly dense lot whose time
was in fact fast hurtling toward its denouement, seemed to learn nothing from the era's revolutions and reform agitation. In Mannheim, a city
near Eschelbach, during the middle decade of the 1800s the local prince
decided to use his tax and feudal-duties money to replicate the palace of
Versailles. It was an astonishingly brazen undertaking (though doubtless
not in his mind). He and aristocratic pals needed a place for the lavish
balls and parties and the extensive hunts that were their pleasures. What
could better meet the need than something as big and as stylish as King

Louis had built for himself next door in France? For the princes, Europe was still the kind of place where this would no sooner be said than it was done. Further down, in Bavaria, Ludwig II—sometimes called "Mad King Ludwig"—expended the state treasury between 1869 and 1880 to build three castles, including the now-famous and fabulous mountaintop Neuschwanstein, or Swan Castle. A century later, Neuschwanstein has proven to be a powerful magnet for tourists from Japan and America (not to mention Walt Disney, who used it as the model for Fantasyland); but in 1880, it was an expensive public work built on the shoulders of Ludwig's grumbling peasantry. Such blatant excesses were repeated everywhere.

The armies and the military adventures of the princes became increasingly expensive to support, both in money and in bodies. During these decades the armies of the German princes were constantly either engaged in battle or preparing for it. They warred with France and Austria and Denmark. They fought with their own citizens when they confronted the liberal rebellions of 1848, and with one another as Bismarck and von Moltke, between 1865 and 1871, led the charge to unify the German states by subjugating them militarily. Wars, alliances, military commitments, and conscriptions preoccupied almost all public activity. All politics played itself out through vast standing and reserve armies.

The armies were staffed by the nobility and soldiered by conscripts. Terms of the military draft varied from state to state, but the usual was to require between two and three years of a man's life, with a further commitment to remain available to the reserve army until he reached the age of thirty-nine or forty. After 1866, the southern states of Baden, Wurttemberg, and Bavaria were forced to agree to place their soldiers under the command of Prussia. Morale plummeted and the conscripts lost what little will they might have had to serve and to fight. Increasingly they dodged the draft and deserted the armies. My great-great-uncle John (1847–1893) served in the Gross Herpztum 3rd Dragoons, but in the late 1870s, sick of it all, he skipped the country to come to America. Part of the decision of his sons and nephews to follow him was their desire to avoid their own conscription, their conviction that they had better things to do than continue to staff Europe's wars. In 1849, according to the local history, after the Prussian and Bundestruppen, or national armies, defeated the regional armies of southern Germany, droves of soldiers, including an astonishing forty-three from the little village of Eschelbach alone, deserted Baden's armies.

Another hugely influential factor in the mass migration was technological advancement. The perfecting of steam technology dramatically
changed both land and sea travel. Railways gridded the continent, and
steamships replaced sailing vessels crossing the Atlantic. After 1855, these
methods of transportation revolutionized traffic and had an incredible
impact on demand. To put it into perspective, one must understand that
the new steamships could cut by half or three quarters the time for a
trans-Atlantic crossing. The length of the average journey from Bremen
or Le Havre to New York, under good conditions, could be shortened to
two to three weeks from the six to fourteen weeks taken up until then by
the sailing ships. This made a fantastic difference not just physically, but
psychologically as well; it was the nineteenth century's equivalent of the
Concorde taking over from old propeller-driven Viscounts. Fares dropped
correspondingly with growing demand and popularity, and by 1875 they
were low enough to accommodate even the poorer emigrants.

My grandfather, Nicholas, was a youth of seventeen in 1888 when he,
his father Friedrich, then thirty-five, and his new stepmother, two brothers, and two sisters embarked on the long journey to America. At home
the family had been farmers; they lived in the middle of their small
village and, along with the other farmers and herdsmen, drove their cattle and sheep daily to pastures in the surrounding hills. At an earlier
time they would have been classified as rural peasants, stuck in their social and economic spot, saddled with duties to the feudal lord, tithes,
taxes, and, like Great Uncle John, soldiering obligations. By the late
nineteenth century their status and that of other village-based farming
peasants was inching toward more comforts and privileges. The children
of my grandfather's family, for example, attended school for a half day
in the mornings. Their house was sturdy and spacious, a duplex style,
two-apartment dwelling of five floors including a street-level shop and a
tiny garret tucked under the eaves. It stood—barn and shed attached at
the back—in the center of the village, just down a steep incline from the
seventeenth-century village church. This was not enough to keep them,
however, and they left. My knowledge of why they left or, more importantly for this story, how they left and what must have been going
through their minds has had to be gathered through numerous round-
about routes. I riffled through the work of other relatives who, like many
other New World families trying vainly to put some history into who
they are in this fast-changing world, have cobbled together a family tree;
I sifted through nineteenth-century histories, trying to piece together

the events and moods and motivations of those times for people like my own ancestors. And, finally, I indulged in some speculation.

Eschelbacher Heimatbuch, the local history of the village written in 1964 by Ludwig Vogely, describes 1850 as a difficult time. Revolutions, hunger, and misery drove people out. Between 1840 and 1870, 150 people left the village for America; between 1870 and 1892, another 277 made their getaway. In fifty years almost a third of the population, 427 people from this one small village, left for America, "das Land der Freiheit und das Land der unbegrentzen Moglichkeiten" (land of the free and land of unlimited opportunities).

Nearly every Krotz left Eschelbach between 1868 and 1890. Friedrich had five sisters and three brothers. The first to emigrate was Katherine, the eldest sister, who with her husband traveled in 1868 to the town of Warsaw in New York State, and from there moved to Canada. All but one of the other brothers and sisters followed, bringing with them spouses and children and settling either in Canada, in southern Ontario, or in the United States, in New York and California. Even their elderly mother, Helena, eventually made the journey sometime around her seventieth birthday.

Within forty hours of leaving Winnipeg, Sarah and I were standing in front of the house we knew from an old photograph to have been that of our family. Our ancestral village was not on our grand Deutsche Zentrale Für Tourismus highway map even though Eschelbach dates from the fifteenth century. In North America you feel it would be a major historic site; in Germany it is merely one more of the hundreds of villages you encounter every four kilometers, no matter which highway you turn down: church and *rathaus*, bakery, houses, school, and store dotting every well-groomed road throughout the meticulously kept countryside. A North American, particularly a Canadian, understands a road map as something stringing together points of settlement in what is still a basically unfathomably vast landscape. Every gas station and two houses becomes a beacon of civilization blinking up out of the forested wilderness or the empty prairie, a welcome spot rendered larger than life on a map that can be ratioed a hundred miles to the inch and can still get pretty much everything in. Not so in the dense settlement of Europe where civilization and human activity has occupied and groomed every square inch. The grand overview maps open up like stacking Russian dolls to reveal, in sequence, ever more intricate regional and area and local maps, where the detail seems never to end.

We negotiated our way from Heidelberg south to Sinsheim using the Deutsche Zentrale map, and then turned to a little photocopied local map that transformed what was just an empty space on the larger map into a new spider's web of little capillaries—roads, railway tracks, and villages—and a whole vocabulary of places: Eichtersheim, Dühren, Immelhauserhof, Bukenauerhof. If you wanted to get it all on one map and do it right, you'd need a map half as big as the country itself.

German drivers are lucky maniacs. I felt forced, as a survival ploy, to try to emulate them. On open stretches of highway I sped up frantically, and then slammed on the brakes whenever a village appeared. However, though my foot was to the floor, slick Mercedes with flashing headlights were constantly on my tail, even on the smallest roads. And then, of course, despite our hurry, every four kilometers we were obliged to slow down abruptly for another farm village. After rounding innumerable bends in the road, from the mid-sized market town of Sinsheim to the village of Duhren, we suddenly were confronted with the two church steeples of Eschelbach.

The village is not much bigger than it was in 1888; it now has 1,800 people and a single street of new subdivision. The surrounding hills—an equal mix of vineyards, woods, and open fields—constantly comfort the spirit wherever you may be in the village. We left our car in a small parking lot by the bus stop at the highway and walked up a main street, tidy as a pin, called Hirschornstrasse, after the Baden king's huntsman and gamekeeper who lived there in the eighth century. We passed a couple of stores, the village kindergarten, and the *rathaus*. Posters on light poles advertised that a serious looking heavy metal group would come to the community hall in February. On a sharp rise appeared the Evangelical (Lutheran) church where my great-grandmother took her daughters while the males in the family walked five minutes in the other direction to the Catholic Church. Two buildings away stood the same house shown in our ancient photograph.

Remarkably, hardly a thing seemed changed. Two world wars have been fought, and civilization has endured the cold war; the world's population has quadrupled; airplanes, computers, television, satellites, and microchips have been invented. The population of the United States has grown by almost two hundred million, from sixty-two million to two hundred and forty million, a fourfold increase; the prairie plains have been broken for agriculture, cities have been constructed, transcontinental railways and highways have been laid down, airports have been built. But on Hirschornstrasse, all the buildings from 1880 still stand in place. The half dozen people on the street in our yellowed photograph are buried either behind the church or in graveyards in America or beneath battlefields; and the chicken in the foreground of the picture has been replaced by a blue Audi. Otherwise it was the same picture. On the buildings barely a brick or a board had been altered. Our family house looked not a jot different.

Suddenly we were trembling with excitement. I almost expected a hundred-year-old version of my grandfather to step out of the house. We needed time to think. Entering a store directly across the street, we searched vigorously for an excuse to be there and decided to purchase a piece of gingerbread. Then we told the woman behind the counter who we were. I wanted to shout at people: "This is my village! I've come home!" Instead we pulled out the ancient photo and explained it to the half dozen people who gathered around us. I tried my language-class German: "Das ist das Haus meines Grossvaters." They looked at me funny, and then at one another. "It can't be," they said. "An old woman lives there." I quickly explained, no, our grandfather left in 1888. "Achtzehn hundert, acht und achtzig." They all began to laugh. An older woman grabbed the photograph and ran around showing it to other customers in the store. My daughter and I were lifted momentarily to the status of minor celebrities.

A woman named Emelia Bender, we were told, lived in the house now. We were urged to go and ring the bell. Buoyed with this encouragement, we marched across the street and pressed the buzzer. There was no answer. We stepped back and gazed up the steep facade of the house to sills of windows on the second, third, and fourth levels. We rang again. After a bit, we turned and moved up the street to the church. The feeling of being connected to some hazy past was overwhelming. We climbed a rise of steep, worn, stone steps, slippery with frost. When we first arrived in the town, the bells of this church had been ringing furiously. Now people were spilling out its doors. It was three o'clock in the afternoon. We encountered a friendly looking couple who, after we explained our desire to find Emelia Bender, insisted we come with them and try her doorbell once again. This time we were lucky. A motherly looking sixty-year-old woman greeted us, and, after some confused introductions and yet another showing of the century-old photo, she invited us in.

The moment was awkward but lovely, complicated by the fact that Emelia was in command of even less English than we were of German. But hospitality won the day; she disappeared for a minute, bringing back coffee, a plateful of cakes, and her supply of old pictures in albums. We consumed the goodies with a lot of energetic nodding and grinning and saying things in our various languages, just to keep some noise and friendliness going. Every time I wanted to pose something really important, I had to take time out to find the appropriate statement in my Berlitz phrase book. Usually by the time I found it the moment had passed. No matter. Emelia got up and beckoned to us. She steered us into various cozy rooms, cluttered with furniture, in order to show us, in turn, the views from each of their windows. From the bedrooms of the third and fourth floors we could look in one direction past the streets of the village to the surrounding vineyards, resting in winter; in another direction to fields fallow and muddy. From windows on another side of the house we could look to the *Wald* (forest) that crowned the distant hills. The emotion of the moment made it impossible to speak, only to look. I couldn't find anything to say, even to my daughter. These were the same vistas that for generations had been part of our ancestors' lives, and the same views gazed at for the last time with we can only imagine what mix of emotions, that day of departure so many years ago. Today it was Christmas Eve. The sky hung gray and sullen against the landscape. It was not yet cold enough to snow; a drizzle kept wanting to envelop us. It felt wonderfully warm.

To get to Bremen in 1888, one would have had to leave this house and village by horse-drawn cart or wagon and travel to the train at either Sinsheim or Horrenberg, two sleepy towns that still have charming, spotless train stations. By the 1880s railways were virtually everywhere in Germany, built during the preceding decade at the rate of 1,000 new miles a year. German iron and steel production in the 1870s was booming, moving quickly toward surpassing that of Britain. In 1888 there were more than 25,000 miles of railroad track in Germany compared to 3,600 miles thirty-five years earlier, in 1850. Still, it would have been tedious and slow traveling. To cover the six miles from Eschelbach to, say, the station at Horrenberg by horse-drawn wagon loaded with luggage, trunks, and children would itself have taken easily half a day. One hundred and four years later, four hours would be about the same amount of time it took us to go by taxi from our front door to Winnipeg's International Airport, board the domestic leg of our flight, make our preliminary trip of 1,200 miles to Toronto (during which we ate lunch and watched a movie), disembark and move to the international check-in to await boarding to Frankfurt. For the trans-Atlantic crossing, our Boeing 767 had a cruising speed of 530 miles per hour and a range of 3,100 miles. After an additional eight hours, when we would be standing at the luggage carrousel in Frankfurt-Main waiting for our bags, grandfather and his family would still have been chugging along on their train journey, perhaps somewhere around Dortmund. Three hundred and sixty miles to Bremen at an average train speed then of twenty miles per hour would have meant a trip of sixteen hours, without accounting for any stops or delays or transfers. By all current-day standards, they would have put in an exceedingly strenuous journey before they even saw the harbor or the boat.

Reaching the port of departure was only the first step. The emigrants then would still face the ordeal of obtaining passage and putting in time until their ship was ready to sail. This might take days or even weeks. If you have ever tried to manage children and luggage and keep things together for a few days when in transit, you can begin to imagine what this must have entailed. Particularly if you were not rich, you would have to look after all exigencies yourself: find a place to stay, feed yourself and your family, and purchase last-minute supplies, all the while trying to make your little bit of savings stretch. You had no idea what unforseen things you might need your money for before all was said and done, for the credit card, the rock and ballast of all modern day travel, was still almost a century away from its invention. All that time, in the backs of their minds, they would be looking forward to enduring the hazards and hardships of the voyage and pondering the wondrous frightening uncertainties of their future.

The business of trans-Atlantic shipping out of northern European ports in the late nineteenth century was ordered in a straightforward way. Bremen ships, up until the mid-1800s, had a standard transfer for their trans-Atlantic turnarounds: from America they brought in cargoes largely of tobacco and cotton; to America they took people, human cargoes, cargoes of emigrees. The tobacco agents did double duty as immigration agents. They accepted the tobacco from America, supervised the quick hammering together of bunks in the holds of the newly unloaded ships, and dispatched the emigrants. They were not universally lauded for their services: a Baden newspaper of the day complained about the fees and price-gouging of the "net of Bremen agents" who received a fee of 25 percent for every migrant forwarded to the shipowners. The travelers, especially the poor emigrants, were mere fodder, grist for this mill. They were treated as such. "Bremen," writes Richard O'Connor in *The German-Americans*, "had been making a living off the sea and its commerce for a thousand years; and cities which live by the sea are not notable for a humanitarian outlook. The inscription carved on the lintel of a fifteenth-century sailor's home expressed the city's tough-mindedness: Navigare necesse est, vivere non est necesse" [Navigation is necessary, life is not].

If you were rich, you could certainly, by 1880, achieve a journey in considerable comfort, a comfort that bordered on the sublime. Richard O'Connor describes a first-class cabin on an American vessel of the day, the *Victoria*. Such a cabin for well-heeled persons taking their leave of Germany would be "lined with satin wood, in panels, banded with rose and zebra woods and American bird's-eye maple, and the ceiling white and gold. There is a center table of choice white marble. The apartment is lit through ground glass; and one of the large panes bears a picturesque view of Windsor Castle, and at the opposite end is Buckingham Palace, surrounded by the rose, shamrock, and thistle. The decorator has not, however, lavished all his taste upon this apartment, for the berths are fitted en suite; the ceiling is in white and gold and the handles of the doors are glass."

State-of-the-art vessels such as the *Victoria*, O'Connor notes, "carried cows for fresh milk, chickens for eggs and meat, pigs for fresh meat." A standard menu indicated that scurvy was not to be feared by anyone with sufficient money for a first-class passage. For breakfast there were ham and eggs, cold mutton, bread, hot rolls, black or green tea, coffee or hot chocolate. At noon one could satisfy the appetite with bread, cold tongue, cheese, port, and liqueurs. Dinner included soup, beef, pork, veal, fowl, fresh milk, plum pudding, preserves, oranges, raisins, almonds, figs, and prunes. Wine was served with lunch and dinner, champagne every other day, and there was an orchestra for concerts and dancing. One first-class passenger reported that throughout day and night he heard "the noise of calling the steward and drawing the corks."

But in the holds of the *Victoria* or dozens of lesser ships, the story for the steerage passengers was quite different. Conditions could be barely short of hell—the crowding caused discomfort, enormous pressures on people's social and psychological well-being, and rapid spread of disease. Eventually, general concern reached such a pitch that Congress felt compelled to make some rules. In 1847, it enacted legislation setting minimum standards for Atlantic crossings. Those standards remained in effect for decades. For every passenger there was to be a minimum of fourteen square feet of horizontal space. Each berth had to be six feet long and eighteen inches wide. On the orlop (bottom) deck each passenger was supposed to be given thirty square feet of space. Families were to be separated by latticework partitions that could be opened and closed. Children under eight counted as half an adult (for space), and infants were not counted at all.

But in an 1853 editorial, the *New York Journal of Commerce* still condemned some of the ships arriving at Ellis Island as "damned plague ships and swimming coffins." "Passengers in [the] cheaper classes were obliged to provide their own bedding, and still the ships were frequently so crowded they were forced to sleep in the gangways or in wooden shacks erected on the top deck. These shacks were so flimsy they often were totally open to the North Atlantic gales."

The class system in travel and accomodation fit neatly and precisely with the strict class system of the time in society as a whole. Those who were noble or wealthy commanded the most lavish and opulent of comforts; those at the other end of the social and financial tally board were considered barely human, and were treated, housed, and fed accordingly. The juxtaposition, side by side, of such extreme levels of comfort with such privation is almost ludicrous to us in the late twentieth century. Despite whatever problems and troubles the world still has, the public view of individual human rights and dignity and levels of acceptable comfort has truly changed over a century. Yet, oddly, we hold on to the principle of the class system in travel. The class system that was identified with train and sea journeys a century ago still persists through the different classes of seat and service available on an aircraft. When we flew from Canada to Germany, our Air Canada Boeing 767 carried 161 passengers in three classes: 10 in first; 30 in business; and 121 in economy, which included us.

This fact is intriguing. Although the difference in the fare between a first-class and a coach or economy airline ticket can be as extraordinary as the differences in boat passage were a century ago, differences in the actual qualitative travel experience, mainly due to the relatively short period of time required now to make the trip, actually seem quite minimal. In 1993, *Condé Nast Traveler* magazine examined thirteen trans-Atlantic carriers and found that all shared a vast disparity between prices in the three classes; the average ticket price for flights between New York and London for the thirteen carriers was $442 in economy, $3,367 in business, and $5,709 in first class. This is a difference from top to bottom of $5,267 or about 1,200 percent. The difference between the $900 seats we had, purchased actually at half that price because one was free through the redeeming of frequent-flyer credits, and the $2,500 or $3,000 seats further forward in our plane amounted only to an additional few inches in seat and arm-rest width and a slightly better quality meal with more attentive wine service.

When *Traveler* evaluated service on the thirteen carriers, they found that, though the meals given to business passengers cost the airlines between $40 and $60 as opposed to $25 for coach (can even that be so, ask we who have consumed those meals?), even the food at the front of the plane was evaluated as only "adequate." Even the snob appeal seems a bit fleeting (though, despite the general democracy of the age, there are still people who consider a stigma to be attached to getting off the back of a plane). And you would have to be very sensitive to be outraged by the distinctions in treatment, what frequently gets described as the differences between deference in first class and indifference in coach. The only really persuasive argument, the only argument that makes any sense for the class differences are those of convenience: the privileges of purchasing your ticket later, canceling without penalty, and altering your plans or stopovers right up to the last minute. By any other standard, $2,000 or $5,000 or ten times the rate of another fare is an extraordinary price to pay for a superior vintage of wine and a slightly better nap.

Yet when the airlines market their seats, these differences are made to sound extreme. A British Airways advertisement for business class aimed at hotshot trans-Atlantic executives suggests that an actual transformation takes place whereby an executive arrives in London in better shape than he left New York. "You'll arrive Tom Cruise in Armani," quipped one observer of the ad, "even if you left Danny DeVito in a sweat suit." But anybody who's traveled on an overnight flight to anywhere recognizes the hyperbole in this. Everybody looks and feels like Danny DeVito in a sweat suit when they get off a plane at 7 A.M., whether they have been in the back of the plane or the front. What is important, however, is the role of the different fares in the economics of the industry. First- and business-class fares are meant to pay the freight; the economy, tourist, and excursion fares are meant to fill the seats and, increasingly in times of slimmer margins, provide what small profit is possible or, if not that, at least cut losses. The passengers back in the cheap seats have to understand (and never forget) how much they owe to those paying for the three additional inches or the extra status or the convenience of buying a ticket on the way to the airport. They are the lions, the scraps from whose kill are left for the scavenging jackals. If you are at the back of the plane, you need them. Were it not for them and the expensive seats they purchase, there would be no cheap seats for you. In the 1980s, admittedly flush years for travel, the front-end passengers in first and business classes brought in two thirds of airline revenue although they made up only one fifth of the passengers carried. Those revenues were absolutely critical to the entire system working; all the deals at the back of the plane were built on the well-tailored shoulders of first class. All the hunkering down that came in the 1990s with the Gulf War and the recession changed the percentage ratios and the numbers, but the fact still remains: the front end subsidizes the back of the airplane, as the upper decks of the ship did for steerage a century ago. We can urge travelers to study the economics and cost benefits of their selections and tell them to get their priorities straight, but then we have to realize that if everybody wanted the least expensive deal, there could be no such thing as a least expensive deal.

At some point we must confront the question: why were we there? What made us become tourists and undertake this trip? This question, I believe, is integral to all travel, whether we're travelers or tourists. Not to ask it, even if an answer is not readily forthcoming, is somehow culturally irresponsible. When travel was arduous and difficult, people had to have good reasons for undertaking it, and so they knew their answers. Now that traveling is relatively easy we risk undertaking it cavalierly, without thought, without a reason that is even good enough to meet our own satisfaction. To grapple with the question of "why," then, it seems is part of the relationship the traveler establishes with the territory and the people he or she moves through and encounters. If the unexamined life, as Socrates said, is not worth living, is the unexamined trip worth taking?

On this trip for Sarah and me, the pat explanation would be to call it a journey of self-discovery, or a recovering of roots. But that opens up a whole next round of questions. What does that mean? Why would it be important? One thing recovering our roots meant was that we would look at the things that tourists normally see in a wholly different light. Everything we witnessed in the country, all its attractions, would be filtered through what knowledge we had of our roots, and what we were finding out about our roots and the place of our own family within a larger history. What was our personal historic connection to the tourist draws we were celebrating?

Neuschwanstein castle in southern Bavaria, possibly the most famous castle in middle Europe, attracts a million and a half tourists a year. It is said that almost as many more would-be visitors turn around and leave once they get a look at the queues and reckon on a wait of as long as two hours before they will even get to the front door. This "Disneyland" palace, with its soaring turrets and graceful perch on the steepest and most craggy of precipices, is not actually a medieval castle but a replica. It was dreamed up by the master of romantic notion, King Ludwig II, in the third quarter of the nineteenth century. We dutifully followed our guidebook there too. We were lucky; it was the day after Christmas and the crowds were small. The wait for a tour after we made the twenty-minute climb from the parking lot up the steep pine and fog-shrouded path was brief. Around us, a tour group of Japanese young people busily snapped photographs of one another.

Possibly the most extraordinary change over a century is the way in which this part of Europe, with its castles, palaces, churches, and cathedrals, is viewed, and the way these great buildings attract hordes of foreign visitors. Many parts of Europe, especially places such as southern Germany, are almost theme parks of their own pasts. Yet there is an oddly sanitized notion about the realities of that history. All the churches, cathedrals, and castles that were the vivid symbols of the oppression and the indentureship of our peasant ancestors are now the places we as tourists most want to visit, and for which we queue up the longest. No one is more eager for this than we who are the descendants of the very people who were most beaten down by the systems they represented. However, we do not go as Jews, for example, make pilgrimages to the sites and memorials of the Holocaust; we go for the most part with bland, romantic notions of art, architecture, and high culture. We are oblivious to and free from history. We look at the structures uncritically, impressed and inspired by architecture that is opulent and lofty. In one sense it is proper to do that, for these are constructions of monumental grandeur and impressiveness by any standard; graceful, enduring, and full of story. But our romanticism seduces us into thinking that perhaps our ancestors themselves lived in such places, and why would they leave such a fairyland, why would they move away from such a life condemning us to live in the uninteresting subdivisions of North America? It is a constant struggle to get it into our heads that they lived not in the castles, but in the hovels at the bottom of the hill, the hovels long disappeared into damp and rot and fire. Their sole connection to the castle on the hill was to work, perhaps, to build it, pay the taxes to support it, and join the army to defend it. And to keep going the genetic line that three or four generations later can return as tourists to revel in and be bowled over by the romantic splendor.

In 1869 King Ludwig told his friend, composer Richard Wagner, that he intended to rebuild ancient castle ruins in the true style of the historic German knights. The result, achieved while his money, his political currency, and his life lasted, produced exactly that. It also produced a grand homage to Wagner, after whose operatic themes the various rooms of Neuschwanstein castle were decorated.

Tourists were definitely not part of the plan of construction; they came later. Ludwig would never have built for the tourists; he hated the mob. Ludwig's castles were built for his very private pleasures, and so he could fulfill personal romantic fantastical dreams nurtured since childhood and pay homage to Wagner and Wagner's operas and to the knights of the age of German chivalry. Neuschwanstein was built on the ruins of a medieval castle, Hohenschwangau. Its site, on the mountain precipice, makes it astonishingly beautiful and spectacular. But this site also made its construction extraordinarily difficult and expensive. More than twenty feet of the rocky summit of the mountain had to be blasted away in order to achieve a level platform upon which the masons and builders could set to work. Water had to be brought up from the valley far below. A road had to be constructed. Then, once the castle structure was completed, no expense was spared in its interior decoration and furnishing.

Yet I could no more picture some fellow named Ludwig actually eating and sleeping and going for a walk or reading a book, or even accepting visitors—sitting down with his pal Richard Wagner at the piano—in such surroundings than I could grasp the theory of the Black Hole. It was far easier to accept this monumental place as a kind of waterslide park built expressly for the purpose of drawing us—Sarah and me and the busloads of Japanese students. So intentionally unreal are they in their

size, their situation, their very improbability, you need to keep reminding yourself that castles such as Neuschwanstein were built for purposes
other than attracting tourists. From the parking lot that has been bulldozed into the base of the mountain, to the vast courtyards and halls, to
the site itself—a cloud-enveloped jut of rock hundreds of astonishing
feet above a swirling river and a deep forest—you wonder how and why
would anyone put anything like this together. I don't know what the
Japanese students were thinking, but the questions running through my
mind were not even about nineteenth-century politics, they were simply
ones of engineering and motivation: How did they build this place?
Why did they build this place? We would be absolutely incapable of
such construction these days, our advanced technological methods
notwithstanding. What would motivate anyone to go to the enormous
risk and trouble to weld this vast castle so precariously to its jut of soaring rock? We could look at it only as a gimmick to attract hordes of paying visitors and so, I realized, we had made the great leap of our time
and generation: History had ended; tourism had begun. Neuschwanstein, and other constructions like it, lured us to Germany, gave us something to do, helped the foreign exchange balance, provided us with the
opportunity to drop some money in the town of Fussen, gave jobs to
the guide and the ticket takers, employed the men who drove the horses
and wagons up and down the steep road between the castle and the
parking lot, brought business to the souvenir sellers whose kiosks lined
the pathway, gave us a chance to give some foreign exchange even to the
teenaged girl who sold us chocolate in the village. It was one of the tickets to economic revitalization in southern Bavaria. I suppose one of the
differences between Europe and America is that Europe's "Disneylands"
already existed, ready for the tourist's use.

   I doubt that's how my great-grandparents would have viewed
Neuschwanstein and its hundreds of companion princely and ecclesias-
tical excesses as they were leaving the country and saw them receding
behind them. They didn't marvel at these castles and palaces; I suspect
they hated them because they had to pay for them. They were headed
for a new land and a new home precisely because it would be empty of
such preposterous presumptions. For them, such castles as this one represented chains that they were throwing off.

   A day after our visit to Neuschwanstein we found ourselves in the
mountains along the German-Austrian-Swiss border, consuming pastries
and enjoying the view in the lovely little town of Berchtesgaden, Adolf

Hitler's holiday home. I made a conscious decision to keep reality intact by not trying to find the Hitler–Eva Braun cottage, just in case it had been turned into an interpretive center and museum. Instead I inflicted on my daughter stories about how the Second World War unfolded, while we strolled through the streets and gazed at the pristine snow-capped mountains that were the same as "they" would have seen. We wondered about the effect such lovely surroundings may or may not have had on the course of history. Did Adolf plan his malevolences here, or just come to unwind?

We wandered up hilly streets and bought postcards; we visited a flea market set up in a vacant parking lot, where among the sale items was a whole table laden with war medals, helmets, insignia displayed unself-consciously and without irony. We parked ourselves for an hour in a sun-filled café, a converted railway station, and were served chocolate and strudel by an aging-Heidi waitress, who had probably lived here as a young child when the war was on. Through it all, it was hard to conjure up the emotions that I felt were due: the knot in the stomach, the angst, the horror or whatever feeling should have been evoked by the knowl-edge of actually being "here." Instead it was all rather benign. Tourism does that to history: a plexiglass shield goes up. You check it off in the guidebook and move on.

People give all kinds of reasons for their travel. Many have been used so often they have become clichés. To have "adventure" or "to get per-spective" is a standard. For some of us, our justification is an internal matter. Travel takes us out of the routine of our life and thereby gives us perspective on that routine and on that life. A time of traveling is usually a whittled-down time, you go with and make do with the most basic of your life's essentials: only the luggage you can carry. You live with your-self and perhaps whichever companions you have chosen to travel with more intensely, with fewer diversions and escapes (despite the contradic-tion that much of travel is a quest for diversion) than is possible in "real" life at home. Elementary undertakings such as eating, sleeping, having a bath, and moving, require enormous amounts of time and attention and energy and wit; you are put back in closer touch with the part of you that attends to simple survival. You learn that you either can do it, or you can't. Or you learn how to do it.

Travel offers perspectives on both the world and on the past. A friend tells me she needs to see the places she studied in history because seeing gives them meaning. She understands Marco Polo's Silk Road by retracing it when visiting the East. She understands her Irish history when she goes there on a tour. "Cromwell's efforts to obliterate Catholicism," she claims, "were much more devastating to Ireland than I had ever imagined from the history books, which, no doubt, were written from an English perspective. This so-called Catholic country even today has no Roman Catholic cathedrals, only (Protestant) Church of Ireland cathedrals." But she had to go to see it to understand that, to realize it, just as she had to see the Roman aqueducts or other castles and churches first-hand to understand the incredible skill and design inherent in ancient workmanship. Travel is a process of checking things out for ourselves. Locations of monumental or catastrophic historical occurrences have always been popular with travelers and tourists; people still tour American Civil War battle sites in states of respectful awe, as if they were religious shrines. Popular tours given immediately at the end of both world wars went to European battle sites even though hostilities had barely ended.

Writer Russell Banks claims that much of what we choose to do is, in fact, "time travel." "We go to Paris, tour Venice, visit Athens and the Holy Land, mainly to glimpse the past and walk about the cobbled streets with a guidebook and a furled umbrella emulating as best we can Henry James in Rome, Flaubert in Cairo. Or we fly to Tokyo, Beijing, Brasilia, perhaps, for a safe, cautious peek into the future. Sometimes, for both the past and the future at once, we make our way to cities such as Lagos, Mexico City, Lima." There is also a preoccupation with exploration. Note the relentless emphasis in travel articles and tour brochures on the "undiscovered places." Never mind that an "undiscovered place" is a contradiction in terms if you find it in a travel article or tourist brochure; the notion is powerfully seductive nonetheless. We are readily seduced by any belief that we might be able to do something original, something unique that millions of other humans are not doing. One friend of mine takes this as a personal challenge, and regards his travel as some kind of test, to see if he can get beyond the brochures to, as he says, "see what the guidebooks left out."

For us to go to Germany had more the element of pilgrimage. Someone, when I was describing our forthcoming plans, called it our "mission." In a way that's exactly what it was; we wanted a connection to our ancestral past that is achievable through visiting landscape and place perhaps more than through connecting with people at a family gathering. I wasn't interested in who we were now, or who my family might be now. I wished to know who we were then, to know where and from whom we came.

Our travel to an ancestral village in southern Germany, I realized, was a connection. It was a connection that turned out to be much more moving and much more powerful than I would ever have dreamed in advance it might be. In the final analysis, it is virtually impossible to imagine the trip of my great-grandparents as they left that village and that land and that continent. In the pages of the history of the village I found their names, coldly listed among the 237 "Auswanderer nach Amerika von 1871–1892"; a fact, a sepia-toned image of bags and trunks packed, children dressed and waiting on doorstoops, an exodus, a trail, a stream of bodies and carts and train carriages converging into a river of émigrés that was soon joined by enough from other villages, from other provinces, so that by the time it peaked at Bremen or Le Havre, it would have been like the tide of a flood. Yet even had I more of their letters and diaries and words, it still would not be possible to grasp fully what it meant to make such a journey. Could I ever know what it might feel like to cut off what they were cutting off, or to hope for and plan for what might be possible ahead? Even though we know the technical details of how a journey by cart and rail and steamer progressed in 1888, we cannot, I realized, truly project the combined feelings of boredom and wonder, fear and excitement, anticipation and panic central to such a journey—not to mention the emotions that would intrude into later life, after arrival and settlement in the new world and the new society. A friend who came to Canada from Poland nearly a century later, in the early 1980s, tried to explain the psychological battle he has had to engage within himself: "If I was to survive and live here, I had to put a deliberate end to the emotional connection I had with people and places and life there, back in Poland. Otherwise I would not have been able to make any transition," he acknowledged. His letters to family who are still in Warsaw are sent infrequently, and he has never been back to Poland to visit, even now when it would be relatively easy to do so, though his family has made visits to him in America. He is ambivalent about the mail and the news he receives even today. He places the political news on one level, dealing intellectually and rationally and critically with that. But the news of a personal or family nature is another matter. His psyche will perhaps never be at rest. "When I sleep, most of my dreams are still set there," he says. "I still have dreams about the landscape."

So was it for us to go back on their behalf, in place of those from two
and three and four generations ago? Is that the emotional task of our
tourism, what we must do now that we can, now that it has become not
the journey of a lifetime but a simple nine-hour hop? What is our oblig-
ation, what happens to us? I had uncles who went to Europe in different
ways, as soldiers to the wars. None of them ever made it to the village,
though they very possibly encountered their own relatives on the battlefields. Sixty-nine Eschelbach men, including twenty-five with my name
or names of my relatives, died as soldiers in World War I; sixty-five died
in World War II. But it was for us to feel the powerful pull of familiarity,
of recognition, of an awesome sensation of completeness as we topped
the hill and rounded the bend in the road between the wall of forest and
the naked winter vineyard slopes, after which the village burst into sight.
I had never been there before; yet I struggled to stem the rush of tears
and the constriction of my heart, for I knew instantly where I was, and
knew instantly that I was home.

Yet how easily it was we came, and how easily we left again.

3

Thomas Cook to Club Med: Seeing What We're Told We Want to See

It starts immediately when you enter a travel agent's office. This is the moment when travel moves abruptly from the fantasy that has been dancing in your mind to a commodity on the table. Here, encountering the marketers and the marketplace, the realization dawns that the exotic adventure of which you have been so fervently dreaming is, to someone else, but a package on a shelf, no different than a box of cornflakes. When I stand in front of my travel agent's desk, I encounter the (to me) always unsettling reminder that, like so much else in our consumer society, my travel or holiday desires have been anticipated and defined, and what I am going to be offered is, in every sense, a product. I am handed the brochures; I am offered the options. This is much the same as when ordering a new car: I can accept or refuse air conditioning, I can choose from a prescribed selection of colors. But I am definitely purchasing a product—the box of cornflakes. Yet this is only the first impression, the first stage; by the time I move on to any of the continent's or the world's large airports—with reservations on a major airline and rooms booked later with a global chain hotel and perhaps a car waiting through an international car-rental franchise—the real truth emerges. It then dawns, even more depressingly, that I am not buying the box of cornflakes—I AM the box of cornflakes.

It is very difficult to maintain a sense of specialness or originality or uniqueness in this world of six billion people. But if you really want to be a nameless face in the herd, book a trip, especially a package trip to a mass tourism destination. The very act throws you immediately onto a conveyer belt that by no means runs especially for you—certainly not you in the singular. You enter a system maze that feels not unlike the forest of moving belts and tables of a wholly automated assembly line— something post-Charlie Chaplin's *Modern Times* but with a momentum that is automatic and prescribed. What is required is that the little packages of whatever is being manufactured drop with regularity through the sequential steps of their processing, and you and your trip are one of these packages.

On his children's television program, Mr. Rogers once took his little audience to a crayon factory. We followed him as he observed the sequence of processes where the machines melted the colored wax, poured it into molds, removed the crayons, and then shunted them along on conveyers through processes of wrapping, labeling, sorting, counting, and packaging. Eventually they bumped out the other end with a satisfying plunk, ready for the stores and kindergartens. The travel industry is now something very much like that; we customers are the crayons. The customer both drives this system and is driven by it, making it an oddly chicken-and-egg situation. The airlines, bus lines, rail lines, cruise ships, rental cars, hotels, taxis, shuttle services, and all the booking agents and tour companies that coordinate them are there in response to demands—they are there because people want to go somewhere. But somewhere, sometime, imperceptibly (perhaps in the middle of the night when none of us were paying attention), everything shifted from a system set up to cater to or respond to the needs and desires of folks who wanted to go places to a system that existed as if entirely on its own, independent and equipped with a great maw needing constantly to be fed. This system and its needs now has become the driving, governing force. Travelers are not so much customers or even consumers anymore as they are fuel. The traveling public has become the fodder without whose continuous feed the huge engine would surely break down.

You need only spend half an hour in any great airport to realize this. Look at the endless lines of gates, the interminable banks of check-in counters, the warehouse-size rooms of ceaselessly chugging luggage delivery carousels. Look outside and take note of the jumbo jets, each with the capacity to strap an entire village's worth of humans into its seats, lifting and descending. Every few seconds one lands, every few seconds another takes off; traffic crisscrosses in the air. Idling airliners queue up like shoppers at the supermarket check-out, waiting their turn on the ramp. The fuel that keeps this gigantic enterprise and all its attendant enterprises of shuttle services and hotel chains humming is not petroleum; it is the bodies of the travelers (and the welcome click click of their credit cards) who must be kept shunting through, and shunted through with predictable regularity, in constant numbers every day, every week, every month.

Imagine for a moment what would happen if no one showed up, if the fuel feed stopped, even if only for a day. The huge conveyer belt cannot run on empty. It needs volume and it needs consistency. Most of all, it needs predictability. The momentary shivers that run through the industry, particularly the airline industry, and across the business pages already tell us what a tight margin this is on. So great and tightly wound is this system that a little blip in the numbers causes a huge shudder in the organism. Margins for error or miscalculation appear to be miniscule. You'll note with astonishment, if you follow the business pages, how airlines and hotel chains with hundreds of millions of dollars in profits one year are suddenly hurled into bankruptcy or desperate salvaging mergers the next. So do not delude yourself, gentle tourist, with Adam Smith's quaint notion that the customer is always right and that you are in any way the boss; you have become but the logs to stoke the fire, the grease to keep a huge system moving.

It's true that it has, for a long time, been in some sense this way. Nineteenth-century ships plying the Atlantic anticipated New World cargo in one direction, immigrants in the other, and quickly renovated their tobacco and sugar holds into bunks and berths and passenger decks, or vice versa, at every turnaround. The great North American transcontinental railways were built on the premise that they would fill up with westward-bound settlers and haul the produce of their new farms back in the other direction. Heavy advertising campaigns were undertaken to induce both immigrants to America and settlers to the West in order to fill these boats and these trains. But such closely managed vertical integration as we find today—hotel chains, car renters, airlines cooperating to offer the customer one another's frequent-user points—is brand new. The system is huge, delicately tuned in its humming, but teetering on a precarious balance, many parts of it swaying between the possibility of grand success and the equal risk of collapse. It is a wonderful system in one regard, breathtaking in its size and organization. It is also dismaying. The sheer, desperate energy required to keep it going can be exhausting just to think about.

When we look at mass tourism today, at how it is organized and its underlying ethic, we have largely to thank an earnest, teetotaling, English temperance fanatic named Thomas Cook. In 1841, Thomas Cook was a slight, balding man of thirty-three, with a concern that bordered on zealous when it came to the moral and clean-living habits of his fellow working-class folk in the English Midlands. He was the secretary of the Leicester Temperance Society, toward which he put not only his personal energy, but the energy of his profession as well. Cook was a printer, and his printing company made the biggest part of its income turning out temperance pamphlets. But if young Cook was earnest, he was also singularly enterprising. In short order he connected his evangelical passion, his genuine concern for the well-being of working people, his printing business, and his entrepreneurial spirit into the most enduring travel business ever founded. Thomas Cook virtually invented mass, packaged, cheap travel, and to this day the term "excursion" harkens back almost solely to him.

Cook possessed a genius for bringing a variety of interests together. That is the trademark of package travel still, 150 years later. In his very first venture he got the bright idea that he could persuade the Temperance Society to permit him organize the promotion and transportation of folks from throughout the Midlands to a mass rally in Leicester. Immediately upon getting their agreement, Cook sped off to convince the Midland Counties Railway Company, one of hundreds of companies trying to find their spot in the new world of rail in England, to participate in the scheme. Learning the ropes quickly, he scrambled between the parties to secure all tickets, fees, and arrangements, calculating a modest profit for himself as part of it. If the Midland Railway, which had not yet figured out how to enlist passengers in advantageous ways for itself, chartered him a train at a reasonable price, he would guarantee to fill it. The first expedition crammed 600 people from the surrounding towns of Derby and Nottingham into the open trucks of the Midland train and sent them off to a weekend of fervent temperance rallying in Leicester. As part of the deal, Cook provided all his traveler customers with tea and ham sandwiches.

Six hundred people bought tickets for the trip, but four hundred had to be turned away. Through this Cook, on the spot, learned a valuable lesson about demand and potential demand. He set himself and his wife and young son, John Mason Cook, up immediately in the business to undertake more promotions for more trips for more people. Before long, a huge opportunity presented itself; the one-of-a-kind Great Exhibition in London in 1851, the hottest ticket of the decade.

Thomas Cook's revolutionary and lasting legacy to travel is seen not only in his marketing, promotional, and business genius, but also in his democratic spirit about the act of travel. The abiding belief that informed Cook's business was that it was the right of the common people from the middle of England to visit such a pivotal event as the Great Exhibition. His job of organizing the railway charters to get them there took on the flavor of a mission. In the process, his fledgling company pioneered ventures—indeed, it invented the systems that would set the tone for package excursion travel still in place a century and a half later. He went ahead and found not only his tourists' transportation, but he scouted the hotels (or in this case the boarding houses and hostels) where his people could stay. He made the same kinds of deals with them for room and board that he had made with the railway companies for transportation. He lobbied for and negotiated reduced-rate entrance tickets to the exhibition for his clients, even writing to Queen Victoria's husband, Prince Albert, to argue that his subjects who had come all that distance should be entitled to a reward, a discount of four days' entry for the price of one.

Cook provided the tour guides: himself, his wife, Marianne, and young John Mason Cook, then only sixteen. Finally, he used his printing press both to promote the tour through turning out the billboards and advertisements and to print the tickets and agreements. He then commenced to publish probably the world's first travel magazine: *The Excursionist and Exhibition Advertiser.* Through it, Cook not only promoted the idea of mass travel to the masses themselves, but pushed it as a value to their employers and their bosses, and all those who felt themselves superior. "Why should the working man not go to the Great Exhibition?" one of his articles demanded. The articles of his magazine drummed away at reassuring working people who might have doubts about their right to enjoy leisure, and especially travel, while pitching their masters on its educational value, twin themes that still govern mass package tourism today.

Soon the popular travel enterprise took on a regular rhythm that became known as Cook's Tours. Thomas Cook's trains took working people on never-before-dreamed-of journeys to the seaside resorts, to Scotland, and eventually, by the 1860s, to the Continent. People who had never dared imagine leaving England found themselves off to Paris, Switzerland, and Italy. Cook, all the while, continued to refine his systems, controlling every aspect of every package: conceiving, promoting, advertising, ticketing, escorting, and guiding. Sometimes he even became the financier. He explored the possibilities of travel on credit, engaging a pawn broker to advance the price of a ticket; for foreign tours he handled exchange and provided vouchers that ultimately turned into the first travelers' checks.

Thomas Cook singled out a particular type of customer. His tourists of the mid-1800s, according to Edmund Swinglehurst, author of *Cook's Tours: The Story of Popular Travel*, were not "the hedonists of later years," in search of beach, sand, sun, and fun. They were serious-minded, earnest seekers (like Cook himself) of self-improvement through travel and the broadening of education it might provide. They were sincere people in search of cultural upgrading: "therefore, they visited those towns and cities which had marked the peregrination of that class of person whose education was not complete until he had done the Grand Tour of Europe. By visiting those places, the tourists felt that something of the gloss of their social superiors descended on their shoulders; and, as many of them were the teachers, doctors, clergy who served the upper classes, they reasonably hoped that in the course of time the closing of the cultural gap would lead to the bridging of the social gap as well."

Even with this careful-minded clientele, Cook's ventures were considered revolutionary. Needless to say, the new phenomenon of mass travel, and the parvenus escorted by this most middle class of entrepreneurs, were hardly embraced with open arms by their upper-class countrymen who for generations had been the habitués of the seaside resorts, the French and Swiss towns, the Italian museums. The arrival of the masses was resented and heartily detested. James Lever, the British consul at La Spezia in Italy, writing under the pen name "Cornelius O'Dowd," griped, "These devil's dust tourists have spread over Europe, injuring our credit and damaging our character. Their gross ignorance is the very smallest of their sins. It is their overbearing insolence, their purse strong insistence, their absurd pretensions to be in a place abroad that they have never dreamed of aspiring at home."

It all sounds strikingly familiar to the rap laid today at the feet of the Hawaiian-shirted American or the video-camera-toting Japanese tourist. This was the clash of the snob and the plebian. Those who believe they are first to discover a place feel they hold a proprietary interest. They become smug and snug in the belief that their motives are more pure, on a higher plane, more legitimate, and they are affronted by the appearance of ordinary people arriving into "their domain," into "their territories."

Cook let none of this bother or deter him. He stuck up for his clients, defending vigorously and publicly their right to travel—much to their enthusiastic response. He plowed ahead into a new, lucrative market, the professional people whose status hovered between the working and the leisured classes. In the 1850s he began to woo teachers, clergy, lawyers, and accountants for jaunts into continental Europe, just as a decade earlier he had wooed the British workers for the excursions within England. "Deacons and wealthy members of churches and congregations," he appealed, selecting one likely target group, "do what is necessary to liberate your pastors from study and the increasing and onerous labour; provide them, if they are in circumstances not to provide for themselves, with the means of a trip, and you will have a reward in their lengthened lives and pulpit and pastoral efficiency."

As soon as people responded to this pitch, Cook's expanding business was right there ready to accept them, backed up of course by the expanding world travel infrastructure. The Swiss and the Italians were overjoyed at the prospects that were opening before them for making money by hosting tourists; there was enormous activity in the building of hotels and the construction of railways in the countries visited by British tourists. The expansion of Cook's travel ventures was phenomenal. The first round-the-world Cook's Tour in 1872 took eleven people on an Atlantic crossing on the *Oceanic,* the most modern boat then afloat, by rail across the United States, and then from San Francisco by ship to Japan—then just newly open to Westerners. From Japan they returned home to London via China, India, the Red Sea, and Cairo. In 1880, by which time Cook's three sons were running the business, they had 60 offices and agencies around the world, and 500 hotels accepted Cook coupons. By 1885, a short forty years after his beginnings with the Midlands teetotalers, these numbers had doubled. *The Excursionist* was published in French, German, Indian, Australian, and Oriental editions.

Thomas Cook made three monumental and lasting contributions to our culture. He understood, crudely at first but refining it all through his career, that he could package travel as a commodity. An experience such as a trip was not something separate from commerce; it in fact could be exactly like a box of soap. He was among the first to define everything that went along with travel as a comprehensive industry; the vehicle of transport, the hotel, the guide, and the financing were all part of a con-

nected service, increasing the convenience of the travelers, but also increasing the control of those who ran the businesses. But probably his
most important and lasting breakthrough was his identification of the
mass of working and lower-level professional people, the 50 or 60 percent
of society who live unheralded between the very rich and the very poor,
as a market or an audience. Cook, for them, created trips as a legitimate
and realizable form of holiday. Because of this, the world since has never
been the same.

Cook understood that a vital part of the industry would be advertising and promotion, powerful and indispensible tools in opening up and
offering travel to ordinary people. He promoted and marketed tirelessly,
constantly developing new angles. Again, he was the pioneer, and seeds
he planted have grown astonishingly. The system of advertising and
marketing and agency work now in place is the grease that makes the
whole travel business turn. It is infinitely more sophisticated and integrated than at any other time in history. It works very effectively for the
travel industry, but it has sometimes powerful, unsettling results and implications for the travel consumer.

The major implication is that hardly anybody, were he or she to examine it carefully, ever goes where he wants to go. Rather, the place and
power of marketing and advertising makes sure we go where we are told
to go. If it is done well, as it usually is, we respond without realizing we
have been manipulated, or at least we do it without thinking about it
very much and without complaining. Some may protest it is paranoiac
to claim we are told where to go or what to do. But the same result is
there because we are, if we examine matters carefully, told what we want.
Then, like Pavlovian dogs, we choose accordingly where we will go.

Travel industry advertising is a mammoth business, and easily the
biggest advertisers in the travel and tourism field are governments promoting their countries as destinations. The advertising dollars spent by
governments—national, state, and sometimes municipal—are huge. I
have just put aside a random copy of *Travel & Leisure* magazine (itself a
publication of American Express, a company that is increasingly expanding its integrated array of travel services) in which are featured elaborate
color ads placed by the governments of Bermuda, a consortium of Caribbean islands (the Caribbean Coalition for Tourism), Singapore, Spain,
Ireland, Greece, Austria, and a whopping 24-page section from Canada.
There are also ads placed by the state governments of Texas, California,

Hawaii, New Mexico, Indiana, Oklahoma, and Kentucky. The city of Nashville bought two pages, and Palm Springs also put in an ad.

All this advertising is coupled informally with a vast system of travel magazines, travel-book publishing, and travel video and television enterprises, all of which quiver in sympathetic harmony with one another and with the travel industry as a whole. Thumb through one of the literally dozens of travel magazines staring out at you from a newsstand and see if you can find some good, objective, no-bias journalism. Not likely. The relationship between publications and their advertisers—whether they are carriers, hospitality services, or governments and destinations—is one of mutual need and support.

As a magazine writer, I once contacted a prominent travel publication with a story about what you do when you get into trouble when traveling. A friend and I had our car broken into in Portugal and we were relieved of just about everything of value: passports, money, return airplane tickets. After going through the standard bouts of despair, anger, and blame (including wishing for an opportunity to personally execute the thieves), I brightened. "Okay," I thought, "at least there is a magazine story here." Later I contacted a magazine, believing I had a useful article that their readership might find interesting, helpful, possibly even funny—at my expense of course. After all, this sort of thing happens to people, so how do you prevent it from happening to you? And what do you do if it does happen? How do you marshal your resources when you are stranded, alone and penniless, in a strange place? What steps do you take to do things like replace airplane tickets or get a new passport?

The publication was a prominent national one and should, I thought, have been amply big enough to exercise lots of journalistic independence. But the editor hesitated. "You can't mention that it happened in Portugal," she said. "Why not?" I asked. "*Where* is one of the five *W*s of journalism." She seemed uncomfortable. "I realize that," she said, "but it's a little tricky. Last year we ran a piece that mentioned the heavy traffic and air pollution in Athens. It was not even a direct criticism, but the Greek Tourist Board pulled its advertising. Thousands of dollars."

This is how sensitive things are; and this is the kind of protective power that can be arrayed. The entire system responds in sympathy to guarantee the survival of any of its parts. Everything in mass tourism is built on image and public relations; the governing principles of image and public relations are: there is no room for negatives, there is no room for error, there is no room for anything that is beyond damage control.

(You might add that there is precious little room for truth.) Remember what happened to tourism in southern Florida in 1993 and 1994 after news spread of a handful of drive-by shootings and tourist robberies? Or what happened to Kenya when a British tourist was killed? In both cases the tourism industry would have been happy for a news blackout. In Kenya, it was one murder in a world where there are hundreds of people murdered each day. But the reaction was a tidal wave running in the opposite direction. Flocks of potential visitors were now not going to go to Kenya not so much in response to an act of violence, because violence is a daily occurrence there, but it was the news of an act of violence. One news flash had turned an entire country into a pariah destination.

The good image/bad image balance is so precarious that it is not just violence or unpleasantness toward tourists themselves that can have a negative effect. Sometimes it is simply the creation or altering of a general image. In the winter of 1993 media attention was turned for a few days on the northern Canadian mining town of Flin Flon, Manitoba. The reason was a horrific one: a teenaged boy had abducted his girlfriend and had shot and killed two other members of her family. It was a grim story, but it was the kind of passion-filled escapade that seems to fascinate everybody. Soon the American tabloid television show, "A Current Affair," arrived with its cameras. What upset the good folks of Flin Flon, however, according to reports, was not the terrible tragedy of the murders of their neighbors and townspeople. But "A Current Affair," seen by millions of Americans had, within the context of telling the story, described Flin Flon in unflattering terms. "Flin Flon was a tough town to live in," the televison reporter announced, "and its people are couch potatoes." Flin Flon's Chamber of Commerce was livid. Why? Because this town had carefully cultivated an image of rugged outdoorsy nature, with jeweled lakes, pristine forests, and fish of record size, and now that was spoiled. The people of Flin Flon wished to be thought of as Paul Bunyon types in a fresh, log-cabin sort of wilderness; not as couch potatoes in a tough town. The implications behind the irritation were intoned pompously by the Chamber of Commerce. It was fear—fear, of course, that such a negative portrayal on continentwide television might "adversely affect tourism."

When information becomes a commodity, divergent interests are able to use it for their own purposes. In 1992 Alaskan natural resources officials decided to kill, or "cull," as they put it, 400 wolves. They made the decision, they claimed, to protect moose and caribou herds. Unwittingly they stepped into a quagmire. Animal-rights activists as far away as San Francisco were upset and decided to respond. Their strategy was to mount a campaign they believed would hit the Alaskans where it hurts; they would aggressively push a boycott of Alaska tourism. To the state of Alaska, tourism is worth a billion dollars a year, and negative publicity is not something an industry of that size can afford. So the strategy worked; the Alaskan officials had to re-think their wolf culling project. Because tourism is an industry, a big, integrated, susceptible industry dependent on public opinion, it can easily be held hostage to public opinion and be badly assaulted by anyone who can successfully manage public opinion against it. Travel is commerce and commerce is run by marketers. In such a world everyone becomes hostage to the requirements of happy public relations and public opinion.

In such an amosphere the public and the traveler-consumer can become the fool. What are the ramifications, over the long term, of such attitudes and such a system? What are the results of manipulated public opinion and managed news? Stop for a minute to think about how it works. The glossy, corporate in-flight magazine you pull out of the seat pocket in front of you during an airplane trip, for example, is not offered simply so you will have something entertaining with which to while away the hours of your flight. Every aspect of the editorial content is carefully designed to support destinations, opportunities, possibilities, and services that are part of where the airline is taking you. The advertising is intricately linked to and smoothly becomes part of the whole package. For the traveler-consumer it is part of a slick bamboozlement. We are totally managed; we are offered choice, it is true, but only the illusion of freedom. It's possible that that is how we've come to want it.

It was a humid night, one of those nights when the hot wind disturbs dreams and brings on concerns about sanity. I was in a little beach town on the Pacific coast of Mexico. The whole evening had been covered, like a mosquito net, by a prevailing sense of something eerie. Earlier, just off the town square, I'd watched two policemen put three bullets into a dog. They'd fired at close range; bam, bam, bam. The dog somersaulted on the dusty street. It was a sleek, ostensibly well cared for Doberman, but it had been running erratically through the streets. "It had hydrophobia," the policeman explained, pushing his pistol back into his belt. Rabies. The word is the same in Spanish, the cops pronouncing it "heedrowphobeea."

The wind had been blowing off the ocean all day and I was tired and sunburned. I wanted to seclude myself in a darkened bar I knew at an isolated end of the beach facing the thundering Pacific. I found a stool and ordered a Carta Blanca beer. I was feeling a bit weird, especially after the dog. The bar was almost empty: there were only three or four other men, local fishermen, and one American who spent every winter in this town. The expansive, parquet dance floor, which took up more than half of the room, was totally deserted and dark. There was no music playing. Presently the two policemen also arrived, as did a young man smartly turned out in a uniform of the Mexican army, a lieutenant.

Suddenly there was a flurry of commotion and another large group of people pushed their way in all at once; breathless and laughing. They were young—or early middle age still trying to fancy themselves young. All were foreigners, North Americans or gringos, an almost equal representation of women and men. Their arrival changed the atmosphere completely. In short order, I learned that they were holidayers from a Club Med resort just up the beach. Immediately I was intrigued; this was my first close contact with people from the famous organization that has, in my time, revolutionized tourism and holiday travel the world over. This was my first personal experience with Club Med.

If Thomas Cook was the most successful manifestation of the travel industry in the nineteenth century, its most aggressive, compelling face in the second half of the twentieth is Club Méditerranée. In 1950, two young men who found themselves at loose ends in the aftermath of the war in Europe serendipitously also found each other. Gerard Blitz was a diamond cutter and Belgian Resistance hero; Gilbert Trigano was a young businessman working for his father's company, selling and leasing surplus army tents. They got together, and their collaboration changed the world of tourism. Blitz and Trigano's concept—and it remains Club Med's guiding principle—was that they would not sell travel, they would sell "fun." The war, doubtless, had something to do with it; people were fatigued with sacrifice and duty, deprivation and rationing. The world had been opened up; old boundaries were gone, old patterns broken. Into the breach stepped Blitz who wanted to take war-weary people, who feared their youth had been stolen from them, on carefree camping junkets. They would live in tents rented from Trigano. The venture of the two young visionaries would fly directly in the face of stuffiness and formality. In their first "village," in Alcudia on the Spanish island of Majorca, the guests pitched in to help cook the meals and wash the dishes.

It all went from there; Club Med developed a reputation for raucous, carefree, good times with sexy libertarian overtones, and this reputation preceded it, serving as its calling card through the 1960s, 1970s, and 1980s. It was a decidedly different image from Thomas Cook's day-trippers heading off to a temperance meeting. "Happiness is our business," was the signature title and is the motto still used in annual promotional reports forty years later.

The travel infrastructure that had been serving the Cooks so well was expanding; by 1950 it included highly reliable air travel to almost anywhere. Blitz and Trigano took this and added a notion of fun that was liberated and free of care. The club concept, with its corny little designations—*gentils membres* for the tourists, and *gentils organisateurs* for the workers—might have made everybody seem like Mouseketeers, but it stuck and it worked. The quirky insider sense of belonging appealed, the silly traditions took root, and people signed up. At first it was pretty rugged: camping, backpack style treks to tent villages with cold-water showers and outdoor privies. But over forty years, with popularity and expansion, the style was honed and made more permanent and sophisticated. By 1990, Club Med owned or leased ninety-eight resort villages from Malaysia to Brazil, with accomodations and amenities decidedly more permanent and luxurious than their earlier tents and latrines.

Club Med redeveloped for the twentieth century the approaches Cook had pioneered in the nineteenth. Part of this was its efficent, businesslike approach, with full computerization and listings on the Paris Bourse and later the New York Stock Exchange. Club Med also perfected a philosophy, both for the tourist and for the host. The first thing was to take the daily concern about money out of the minds of its guests. As in Cook's system, the price for a holiday was all inclusive; with Club Med this meant it took in your tennis lessons and your horseback rides. You paid, and then you could forget about it. The notion of the cashless trip extended to the famous beads guests use to pay for drinks while in the Club village.

Club Med went beyond Thomas Cook when they decided that not only would they take charge of their guests' trips, they would also take charge of the destination—they offered a controlled environment. "Specially designed" was a prominent term in their promotional brochures. They promoted their locations as "authentic"; the Playa Blanca resort on the Pacific coast of Mexico was billed as an "authentic Mexican village." But it was far from that: few authentic Mexican villages offer air-conditioned rooms, tall drinks by the pool, and free scuba certification. In contrast to Barre de Navidad, the tough neighboring fishing village of weather-beaten locals with its handful of hotels and small family restaurants where I was staying, Playa Blanca had pink adobe haciendas, a glistening swimming pool, and horseriding trails. "Authentic" was an attractive word that meant nothing. But the control would prevent nasty surprises. At Playa Blanca no dogs would be shot in the street. There woudn't even be any children under the age of twelve.

When they ventured away from their safe village that black March night to "slum it" in Barre de Navidad, what the *gentils membres* from Boston and Calgary and Kansas City were celebrating was the end of a week-long holiday. But it was no ordinary holiday. Rather it had been an experience in which, through the constant contact of eating together, drinking together, swimming, volleyball, aerobics classes, dancing, horseback riding, and partying, they had become very close, a family of pals. They were probably much closer and more superficially intimate with one another than they would have the opportunity to be with anyone else during any other comparable time period in any other circumstance of their adult lives. It was like the instant emotional closeness we remember from a term at summer camp as kids when, while waving tearful good-byes, we scramble to exchange addresses and swear to meet again. The *gentils membres* had been living in the rarified atmosphere of an isolated village where their camaraderie had been carefully choreographed. Shared practical jokes, dress-up and skit nights, a common unique currency of beads that could be used to buy anything that still needs buying in the all-expenses, all-needs-covered society had all worked together marvelously to achieve a sentimental intensity. Now, on the last night, this mood was being transported to the tables and the dance floor of the Bar Playa. Those of us—the fishermen, the army lieutenant, the policemen, and me—who were there first to nurse our moody, quiet drinks were first dumbfounded, and then fascinated. We couldn't ignore them; this was like an invasion of fraternity members. We had no choice but to turn on our stools to watch.

Felipé, the bar tender, hustled out trays of margueritas, piña coladas, and other pastel drinks. The sound system jumped to life and music started to boom. The energy level intensified. Pretty soon the group, who were feeling pretty good even on arrival, were ready to break into the party games Club Med is so famous for. I looked on, half bemused, half astonished, and, I confess, perhaps a sliver envious as teams were drawn loosely dividing men and women equally on each. When they turned up short one man, their female leader, a deeply tanned *gentille organisatrice* with a no-nonsense "let's get the party moving" manner, marched over and conscripted the Mexican lieutenant. The abashed young man seemed now suddenly less the military officer than the shy boy from chemistry class who has just been flirted with by the cheerleader who has lifted his glasses off. He was inserted to make the teams equal, and the first contest began. This was a simple, adolescent tease of a game; the men (including the hapless lieutenant) were required to strip to their shorts and throw their clothing into a great mixed pile in the middle of the dance floor. Then, at the sound of a shrill whistle the women, shrieking wildly, scrambled to be the first to get their team's men back into some semblance of clothing. The wild melee was unmistakably a North American rec room party game; I'm certain its equivalent doesn't exist in Mexican culture. But no matter; everyone had a whoop of a time, including the weathered bar-side fishermen who, grinning with anticipation, waited for the next round when the tables would be turned and the pile of clothing in the middle of the floor would belong to the women. Outside the open-walled bar, the night was black as pitch. I walked out just beyond the immediate noise of the party to where the surf was rolling against the beach and then stepped back quickly. A heavy, dark form was being pushed back and forth by the water against the edge of the sand; it was the lolling body of the bullet-riddled hydrophobic dog.

"Club Med," wrote Patrick Blednick quoting a former *gentil organisateur* in his book, *Another Day in Paradise*, "is for people who like to be very lazy, and have everything scheduled. They don't want freedom. They wouldn't know what to do with it." This is an intriguing commentary both on the Club and on our society. It is also an intriguing testimonial to the successful ability of the Club Med entrepreneurs to read the mood and appetite of society. Other lines used with great effect in Club Med corporate reports are: "We invented the club. Magic followed." Or: "Magic was there, the club captured it." These are the kinds of advertising statements that can't really bear much scrutiny, and yet they are very telling. Club Med is not about anything objectively real. It is very deliberately the opposite of real.

Its numbers are *very* real. In 1995 1.4 million people traveled, some of them halfway around the world, in search of these magical holiday experiences at Club Med resorts. Almost a million and a half men and women (and increasing numbers of their children) boarded airplanes in western Europe and middle America and jetted off to China, Spain, Senegal, the Maldives, Turks and Caicos Islands, Martinique, and twenty-seven other countries to Club Med villages. Except one must assume that they were not really searching for China, Spain, Senegal, the Maldives, Turks and Caicos Islands, or Martinique. These people, who we are told in the Club Med corporate fact sheet have a median age of thirty-seven and a median household income of $50,000, were searching for Club Med. When they got there, when they stepped off the plane, though they may have been hit with alien sounds and smells, a different level of humidity, a different temperature, they had arrived, again, not in any of these places, but into some local variation of Club Med–land. In the same way that Club Med played with the word "authentic," it tinkered with the traditional notion of travel. Though Club Med destinations by 1990 were everywhere on the globe: Japan, Rumania, Tunisia, the Ivory Coast, Mauritius, Indonesia, the Bahamas, Mexico, Polynesia, New Caledonia, on every continent but Antarctica, Club Med wasn't really about travel, it was about holidays. In fact it did everything to ease its guests out of the notion that they had really gone anywhere, certainly not anywhere foreign, frightening, or strange. The *gentil membres* have little reason and usually little inclination to venture beyond their secure, pleasant compound. On the rare occasions when they wander even so far as the local real town, they might elicit a mixture of curiosity, amusement and disdain from the cynical, world-weary locals.

The travel component of all this is a strange one. You could, one would think, build a Club Med that would achieve everything the villages provide right down the street from the Londoners or New Yorkers or Torontonians who want it. If sand and a change in humidity is required, surely that could be artificially engineered. For the Club Med villages (even the staff of *gentils organisateurs* are largely transported in from somewhere else) have almost nothing to do with the host country or people. They are deliberately isolated in geography, economy, and culture, and their holiday experience is designed to stand alone. The Club's literature states that "extraordinary natural beauty is Club Med's primary criteria" when selecting locations, and that "great care is taken to ensure that the Club fits in with each country's indigenous atmosphere." But the villages are self-contained and even when the Club Med world ventures beyond the confines of its village, as when the group arrived in the Barre de Navidad bar for their last-night party, it is to carry on with the energy of their world, not to absorb or confront the energies of the outside world. So, one must ask, is the airplane trip really necessary?

It seems, thus far, that the airplane trips *are* necessary. Even if we might not wish to confront the dirt and dangers and strangeness of a foreign place, people, or culture, it seems nonetheless to be important to "go somewhere." Even if there were sun and sand down the street from where we live, we have come to believe, through some awesomely powerful cultural stimulus (that no doubt has only partly to do with the advertising onslaught of the travel industry), that it is important to go somewhere. We are urged by primal, primeval, notions of quest and movement to get up and travel to some place. The odd thing is the degree to which it seems to matter very little *where.*

On the balcony of a resort hotel in Belize I fell into conversation with a Canadian who turned out to be a travel agent from a small town in Manitoba. It was early April and she was enjoying an Easter break with her husband and three children and another family of relatives. Travel agents, I have found, tend by nature to be travelers of more the traditional sort; that generally low-paying business attracts the kind of vagabond souls who by and large remain interested in exploration, both of the world's geography and their own restless spirit. Kathy (maybe it had something to do with the fact that her Icelandic ancestors had been Vikings) was not an exception. She listed the places she'd been able to travel to because of her work and waxed enthusiastic about the things she'd been able to do with her children during this brief week in Belize. She had wanted to come here for a long time, had studied and read up about the country, and was transporting husband and children off daily on expeditions reminiscent of Ponce de León; one day they were off to the reef, the next inland to a jungle lagoon, then to tour a Mayan ruin, a visit to the Baboon Sanctuary, and so on. But when she started to talk about her job and her work and her clients, a pall of resignation clouded her face.

The urge to go somewhere is a powerful one in our society, Kathy said. But there, she feared, any sense of discrimination often ended. The basis on which many of her clients seemed to make their travel decisions were, in her opinion, incredibly narrow; they considered mainly safety and cost. "During the Gulf War in 1991, a great fear of flying across the Atlantic took hold and nobody went to Europe. People worry incredibly about their personal safety and the political situation in the location they are heading to," she observed. Apparently this doesn't mean they want to study the political and social history of the place, but they are obsessed with the surface and the immediate implications. "People worry about being taken hostage, or about bizarre things happening to them. So a story in the newspaper or on television about the misadventure of one little tourist in some place can devastate the whole business as the word spreads along the grapevine and the horror story grows to take on mythological proportions. One IRA bomb can kill tourism in Britain for a season. Do you know where the future lies?" Kathy asked. "Cruises. Cruises are growing in popularity. They are safe, controlled experiences with no surprises."

It is astonishing to think back to the legacy of great traveling and see safety and no surprises as the most desirable component of modern travel. Can we imagine Livingstone and Stanley, or Burton and Speke arriving in Africa, hoping for "no surprises"? Can we think of Marco Polo heading off for the Orient only after being assured it would be safe? Yet safety and no surprises has become the major selling point in one huge part of the industry. We all know people whose attitudes have been bred somehow to want travel to be nothing more than "home with sunshine." Or home with heat, or home with water, or home with sex. But no other surprises, and definitely nothing bothersome.

Another offense that would make Christopher Columbus roll over in his grave is the degree to which cost rather than location has become primary in determining people's travels. Kathy described her typical offender, a young couple who appeared in her office a month before their wedding seeking ideas for a honeymoon. Responding to their request, she prepared five options: Mexico, Barbados, Hawaii, Jamaica, Cuba. In cost, all were within $200 of each other. The betrothed youngsters perused the possibilities she presented and, in the end, "they didn't even book with me," she says, "they saved a further $50 somewhere else."

Possibly we can understand a couple on their honeymoon wanting to save a few bucks and not caring where they are going to spend their two weeks. We can presumably also become arrogant in our judgments of public taste. But if destinations have all become so interchangeable in people's minds that they are different only as two brands of bathmats at K Mart are different, one a little cheaper, what does that say? A friend shocked me when I ran into him in a late-night drugstore one cold winter evening. He was buying a few last-minute supplies because he and his wife had tickets the next morning for Ixtapa, a resort north of Acapulco next to the long-standing Mexican town of Zihuatanejo. He is an educated man, but he admitted that he wasn't sure if Ixtapa was on the Pacific or the Caribbean coast. All he cared was that this was January and he was headed somewhere in much-warmer Mexico. If our decisions come down to the equivalent of whether we will go to the earlier or the later movie, where does that mean we are going? How has such an attitude been formed?

I suspect that a great deal of this attitude and mind set can be traced to the Cook system and the Club Med system, where travel is packaged and presented as commodity. With commodities, price comparison is valid and important; that is how we are used to dealing with them. The presentation of travel as a package has, without doubt, been influential in cementing the notions of safety, security, and no surprises. For people like my newfound friend, Kathy, this is an irksome world. But sad as it is for her and some of her colleagues in the travel industry, it is also a world they have played their part in creating. Packages are the easiest things for them to sell, and the travel agent is the indispensible cog in the wheel that sells package travel. Points out Edmund Swinglehurst, "The travel agent, formerly a leader of public taste, has become the provider for its satisfaction. Sun, Sand, Sea and Sex, the brochures announce in all their more colourful than life photographs, and those who think nostalgically of the Mediterranean of Durrell, Douglas, and Lawrence sigh with despair."

In such a scheme of things, what is the price that we pay? Are people who are happily laying down their credit cards to purchase travel as a commodity being shortchanged on anything? Are they shortchanging themselves on life? The airplane that brought me back to Canada from a trip to Belize stopped to pick up additional passengers in the Mexican resort city of Cancun. I know I'll risk accusations of trading on stereotypes if I describe the preponderance of those who boarded at that Cancun stop sporting golden suntans, wearing monkey-ball bedangled souvenir sombreros, and carrying packages of duty-free tequila (so that the party could continue). But the picture is nonetheless true; Cancun, after all, is the epitome of fun-in-the-sun spots, the Disneyworld of beach towns. The stereotype of the tourists, though, disappeared quickly when things hit the personal level. The fellow who took the seat next to me, needing the requisite three feet of extra room to accomodate his sombrero and possibly his sunburn and lingering hangover, turned out to be a wheat farmer, about thirty years old, from the great plains of Manitoba. During four and a half hours of airplane ride we were able to exchange our stories.

Bruce went to Cancun with his girlfriend. It was the end of a hard winter, they had some extra money, and they wanted a break. They asked a travel agent what was possible; she pulled out brochures of Cancun. They looked at the photos of the beaches, the ruins, and the sparkling nightlife, then looked at each other and plunked down their deposits. They were being offered what they had come to expect a winter vacation should be.

"So how did you enjoy it?" I asked. "Hardly anybody spoke English," complained Bruce. "It was too hot most of the time to go on the beach so we stayed by the pool at the hotel. Everything was way too expensive."

Bruce didn't seem very happy. One day they had rented a Suzuki four-wheel-drive vehicle and headed off in the direction of the famous Mayan ruins at Chichen Itza. But they left late in the day and it was almost dark when they got there. So they had turned around after a very brief stop, having seen hardly anything of the ruins. Much of Bruce's time, about three days out of his week, had been spent entangled in negotiations, horrendous in retrospect, first getting into and then getting out of a deal to buy a time-share condominium. An itinerant hustler had snagged them, guards fully down, with his promotional offer of a free breakfast. All in all, Bruce was glum about his Mexican experience.

He asked me where I'd been. I'd had a different kind of trip and I wasn't sure whether an accounting of it would make any sense or interest to him. I'd traveled alone in Belize and parts of eastern Guatemala. Inland, I had moved around with no advance reservations, often on public transportation. I told him about some of the countryside, the towns, the hotels I'd stayed at, and the people I'd encountered. I didn't always have reservations or plans, and one night it had been midnight before the small group of Americans I'd taken up with and I found a place in a Guatamalan village that had room. Another night I slept in a hammock out under the stars. But I'd seen an ocelot and howler monkeys in Guatemala, and chicken farms in central Belize owned by Mennonites who fifty years ago had run away from Canada. Another day, we'd made the acquaintance of the man who had designed the Belize Zoo. Bruce looked at me with astonishment and new-found interest. "You're kidding," he said. "I didn't realize trips like that were even possible. Why didn't they tell me, instead of sending me to Cancun?"

4

Belize:
Life as Flavor of the Month

Wednesday is the day everything changes over. On Wednesday the big chartered airliners from North America, from places like Houston and Toronto and Minneapolis and Winnipeg, make their turnarounds at Phillip Goldston International Airport, where they pick up the seasoned veterans, holidayed-out, and leave behind new groups of fresh, pale, eager new faces. At the coastal and off-shore resorts, the tourists who are completing their one- or two- or three-week packages (which means most of them) look around their hotel rooms one last time, have a final breakfast under a thatched cabana looking at the sea, and murmur a sigh. They are like summer campers who have to go home to their families, back to school. They dress once again in city clothes, or at least traveling clothes. They will have to return to the strange sensation of wearing socks with their shoes. They lug their bags and their sunburns over to the little air strip and climb on the waiting commuter plane that will ferry them to the international airport in Belize City.

Given a few hours of breathing time, the hotels have a chance to administer a thorough cleaning to their rooms, sweeping out all reminders of tenants just left; the better-known restaurants let their staff take the day off. Everyone involved in Belize's tourist industry tries to relax, catch up, and replenish energies they will need for the onslaught of the next group, the next week.

Belize is a tiny country the size of Vermont on Central America's Caribbean coast. In 1993, when I went there, it was that season's tourist world hot spot. This bizarre, flavor-of-the-month phenomenon happens regularly in tourism; countries, like restaurants in your home town, are "hot" or they're not. They are "in," or they're out. As you might expect, however, almost by definition, the phenomenon of their being hot doesn't last. They get chewed up quickly, and then, when that word gets out, the tourist droves move on and the country is discarded, passé. But for the brief moment that a place is "hot," or "in," it is king of the roost. It is known throughout the industry, in every travel agency office from Seattle to Liverpool, as a "Destination." For a couple of years in the early 1990s, Belize was a Destination. This was its time, its turn, as previously it had been the turn of Costa Rica, and Barbados, and Jamaica to be top choice in the long and changing list of tourism's wet-dream locations; it was the flavor of the month, the most recent attraction whose brochures over generously use terms such as "unspoiled," and "be among the first to discover." I went to Belize for this reason. I did not go to be the first in line; I knew it was much too late for that, like a hit play or movie, by the time you're aware it's a hit it's also too late. You are not the discoverer or the explorer, you are part only of the herd. But I wanted to see what happens to a place that is flavor of the month. I also wanted to find out what people—both locals and outsiders—expected would come after that: when Belize was no longer flavor of the month, what did they expect would be left behind?

If you go to a "hot spot," you must also check out the "hottest spot of the hot spot": the epicenter. In the case of Belize, this is Ambergris Cay and its main settlement, the village of San Pedro. Instead of leaving from the international airport, my friend and I went first into Belize City to have a look around, and then we went to the smaller municipal airport where we boarded a Tropic Air six-seater for a fifteen-minute flight to the island. It was a pleasant hop; we moved along at about 5,000 feet above the reef and the cays, (pronounced, as in Florida, "keys"). Identified from the air by its white wall of breaker foam, the reef, second in size and magnificence only to Australia's Great Barrier Reef, divides the deep blue of the Caribbean from the shimmering, unexpectedly bright tourmaline green of the protected lagoons. The 200-mile-long outriders of coral island cays are the crown of the reef, and in the seventeenth and eighteenth centuries they were the havens behind which pirates like Captain Peter Wallace went to hide between raids on the Spanish fleet. The lagoons back of the reef are the great drawing card of the Belize coast. Like a continuous 200-mile-long aquarium, they provide placid sanctuary to a fragile world of coral, plants, rock, and a thousand varieties of shallow sea life. For the Mayans, who were the first human inhabitants of the Belize and Yucatan coasts, these lagoons were aquatic larders. For the divers and fishermen who flock to Belize now as tourists and visitors, they are Heaven.

In order to do the full tourist thing, I had selected a hotel in San Pedro from a fat booklet called *Adventure Vacation Packages*. There, in my travel agent's office, while a January blizzard howled outside, I thumbed through this directory trying to let my imagination and flight of fantasy fill in where the initial tease of photographs and brief, over-written public relations descriptions (the kind where most sentences were terminated with an exclamation point, such as, "Sunset may be just the start of the action on your holiday in Nassau!") ended. The catalog offered everything from Antigua to Venezuela, with Costa Rica, Cuba, and the Florida Gulf Coast caught in between. On the basis of its name, and a tiny photograph of what appeared to be a courtyard filled with red tile and coconut palms, I chose a place called The Sunbreeze. I also made a quick judgment that I could afford it. Some fifty hotels, most of them only a couple of years old, overwhelmed little San Pedro, all of them competing to have us stay in their beds and lounge by their pools. After arrival, I tried without success to find the spot on the balcony from which the brochure photograph might have been taken. The Sunbreeze was clean enough, but it was really a big, rambling, two-story concrete horseshoe without much intimate charm. The brochure didn't mention that we would be right across from the airstrip; but there definitely was sun, and a steady breeze rattled the palms in the courtyard.

When we checked in, the desk clerk handed my friend and me tickets for a complimentary rum punch. The waiter at the outdoor bar rewarded us with plastic cups filled with a strong, sweet concoction. We then headed for the beach. Immediately we were assaulted by loud—much too loud—music throbbing through gigantic outdoor speakers. This was somebody else's idea of a holiday; reggae tunes alternated with Gloria Estefan songs. That blast of sound was supposed to set the tone for our stay. Those of us who had chosen to stay here were to be happy, carefree. We should forget ourselves and perhaps do things we might not want to be reminded of after our week was over. We were perfectly free to go crazy if we wished.

There was no way to fight against it—this too was part of the package. Even if it was not your nature, it was what would be required of you here. Again, it was like arriving at camp; for the people whose soft, pink bodies dotted the beach chairs and lounges in front of the wind-thundering surf and sizzled in the relentless 98° sun like fresh meat on the barbeque, much would be proscribed. Intellectual repartee or education of any kind would be frowned upon. Everyone was here simply to soak up a sun-saltwater-eat-drink-rum-tonic experience that would beat, pummel, and massage middle-management stress and mid-winter worries into submission. The overbearing, relentless mantra of the music was the signal, the way of insisting on that.

Under a cluster of palms, we found beach chairs and sat back to watch a newly arrived tour group. The tour members were like adolescent schoolchildren as they gathered at the outdoor, bandstand-style bar. Their leader, a tour-company representative, might have been a waiter, so crisply pressed was his white, short-sleeved tropics uniform, so neatly trimmed his moustache. Actually he could have been a waiter anywhere else but in San Pedro; waiters here were much more casual, their tone set through blue tee shirts with the motto: "No shirt, no shoes, no problem." So the young man who was busily explaining the intricacies of Belizian currency to his new charges was definitely a tour-company representative. Tour operators, with their all-inclusive, minimum-decision trips, consider beach destinations the best pickings for their packages. Once the tourist's finger has settled on a picture in the travel brochure, and you have written the check or given your credit card, all your responsibilities have ended. "Two to one for a U.S. dollar," the guide explained as he held up a Belizian dollar bearing a picture of Queen Elizabeth. It should have been simple enough, but the new arrivals were still confused, bewildered by their first hour in the sun.

In a week they wouldn't be. In a week these pallid North Americans still squinting in the bright sun would be veterans, familiar with the intricacies of money exchange and local purchasing power (and possibly comparing it with values on their trips to Mexico the year before, or to Barbados the year before that). They would be browned, if not broiled, by the sun; weathered and turned into old hands by their dives and chartered boat trips. They would consider themselves experts at picking the best places for breakfast coffee, fruit, a dinner of broiled fish, the biggest, sweetest piña coladas; and the best late night spots for music. They would have earned their tourist stripes for another winter.

Aldous Huxley declared that if the world had any ends, British Honduras—which is what Belize was called until 1981—would certainly be one of them. "It is not on the way from anywhere to anywhere else. It has no strategic value. It is all but uninhabited," he wrote. So it is interesting that it should have its moment, its turn in the spotlight. This seems to mean that everything is fair, that everybody, if they wait long enough, gets a chance. To past observers, Belize was an unlikely place. Even the ancient Mayans, with their civilization founded on highly developed forms of mathematics and astronomy, inexplicably abandoned it. For several hundred years the little sliver of Central America below Mexico, if it was thought about at all, was considered a pestilential swamp, home to mosquitoes and pirates.

After 120 years as a British colony, British Honduras gained its independence and became Belize on September 21, 1981. Within half a decade it had also found a home on the map of popular imagination. This happened suddenly, in 1986, when actor Harrison Ford walked out of its jungles and onto American movie screens in the film of Paul Theroux's story, *The Mosquito Coast*. It seemed not to matter that the real Mosquito Coast is a couple of hundred miles further south, along the mangrove swamps of Nicaragua and the other Honduras: for the movie location scouts, Belize worked just fine. For the little country, newly independent and struggling to find its place, the attention and publicity carried it into a new incarnation, defined it and changed its life. Movie-aficionados and Harrison Ford fans still search out, like a shrine, the corner table at the Holiday Inn's restaurant in Belize City where Harrison Ford took his meals during the filming of *The Mosquito Coast*.

In order to find out more about the country, I turned to my tourist guidebook to find some reference points, things I could look for and then check what I encountered against the guidebook ideal. The *Belize Guide*, by Paul Glassman, describes San Pedro as "a little town of colorfully painted, mostly wooden, tin-roofed houses criss-crossed by a half dozen sandy streets." "The adjectives usually attached to San Pedro," Glassman goes on, "are 'delightful' and 'charming.' The houses are huddled close one upon another, and much of the foot traffic of the place moves through narrow alleys. The same houses in Belize City would constitute just another shanty town, but in San Pedro, they are well-maintained, the streets are fairly clean, and a refreshing breeze usually blows through."

This, I decided, was all basically true, and basically as I found it too. Ambergris Cay is the biggest of the islands that constitute the Belize Cays. Much of twenty-five-mile-long Ambergris is a low, soggy tangle of mangrove swamp, with human settlement restricted to the narrow southern tip. There, along the sandy streets of San Pedro, is more than a hint of the old fishing village: all the trappings of Caribbean island village life—school; church with the obligatory statue of St. Peter, patron saint of fishermen; and little hole-in-the-wall stores—remain. A good number of the local population of 1,500 Spanish-speaking, Mexican-descended island folk still go out to the sea to fish, still mend their nets in the evenings on the flimsy docks that run the stretch of the village, still tinker at their boats or tend the village stores and market stands. They seem to try to ignore the fact that their island and their country is a "Destination." But here also are all the myriad trappings of the burgeoning tourism industry, which all but overwhelm the quaint village painted in the guidebook. The balance is precarious, giving the impression it is about to be tipped at any minute. The San Pedro airstrip, for example, built in 1984, is capable of handling only smaller planes—up to twenty-four-seater size. During the tourist season, twenty flights a day, operated by three separate airline companies, arrive and depart; the buzz of their engines is a constant moan over the village. Side by side with its fish markets and vegetable stands, San Pedro is crammed with the kinds of establishments that have nothing to do with the needs of the local people—restaurants and dive shops and charter boat operators. Then there are the things that the tourists require when they take a rest from strolling about looking at the obligatory charm; the mangrove swamp at the edge of the town is being pushed back daily by bulldozers, and San Pedro is bustling with hotels. For half a decade the number of hotels grew at the rate of six a year. In 1992, there were 1,300 beds in 719 rooms, a hotel bed for every local San Pedro resident.

How, I wondered, did this come to happen? What sequence of events, what cause and effect, what unfolding of growth and development and demand had carried things and brought them to this point? For a start in the story, I was advised to go to one of the older hotels in the center of town and find Celi McCorkle. A handsome, formidable woman in her fifties with sparkling, dark eyes, Celi McCorkle is the mother of tourism in San Pedro. She hauls two chairs together on the back patio of her hotel, so we can talk. Celi's ancestors were Mexicans and Mayans and her father, Lebanese, arrived on a cargo ship. She has always possessed a restless spirit. One day she met an American, got married, and before she knew it she found herself living in the United States, in Kentucky. But the marriage ended, and in 1964 Celi McCorkle came back to Ambergris Cay and San Pedro where she had grown up. But, as she explains it, the absence and the experience of living in America had armed her with a new perspective. She missed her home village, but she had started thinking about it differently. While living away, she had gone on vacations throughout the United States. She had started to make comparisons in her own mind between the places she was seeing and her home back in San Pedro. She started to think about San Pedro, tried to see it as an outsider might. She tried to think of it in terms of its "attractions." As she did this, she became excited; she came to believe in its possibilities. "Our water was cleaner, our seafood tasted better, our sun was brighter. Why wouldn't people want to come here?" she asked herself. Eventually she devised a plan and decided to see if it would work. When she came back home to San Pedro, she hired some local carpenters, and in the very middle of the town's main street she had them nail together a little five-room building that she christened the Holiday Hotel.

Our eyes linger on the cool aquamarine of the late afternoon Caribbean. "In those days you could walk into the shallow waters and pick up lobster and conch by hand," Celi tells me, as if a part of her regrets what she got started. Such an idyllic site, though, didn't make for the speedy, automatic success of her tourist venture. There were many doubters. "An American said to me: Celi, nobody's going to come all the way here to eat seafood. They want to eat steak." Yet by instinct more than by plan, she persisted, not responding to a demand but anticipating one. She got lucky; among her guests during her second year in business was an American freelance writer named Jim Woodman. Woodman had heard about Ambergris Cay, and had decided to visit. He flew from Miami to Belize City and then caught a ride on the supply boat to San Pedro, "where he stayed in the one and only hotel that had no guests not to mention no electricity, no phone, a gas stove and fridge, and a pot of beans constantly cooking." Woodman wrote an article that appeared in 1966 in the *Chicago Tribune*. It was picked up by the *Los Angeles Times,* and the letters of enquiry started to pour in to the Holiday Hotel. Thirty years later, tourism is virtually the only game in town, and fifty more hotels have joined the one owned by McCorkle.

If you've ever spent much time in a town that is really just a beach, full of tourists and loaded with tourist traps, you might understand the kind of desultory pall that can settle quickly, enveloping your mind and psyche. The symptoms should be noticeable quickly: you probably drink too much and get too much sun, or you indulge in the kinds of activities that, rather than making you feel enlightened and fulfilled, turn you a little despondent. On my third night in San Pedro, I went to the "Chicken Drop." Signs that were posted all over town, from the airport to the front desk billboards at all the hotels, and the bait shop on the pier, advertised this as a weekly event not to be missed. So I followed the directions and found, at a little before eight o'clock, a sizable crowd already gathered outdoors, on a kind of concrete-pad patio, behind a restaurant called "Little Italy." It didn't take long to figure out what the whole business was about. A sort of crap table (literally, I'm afraid) had been drawn on the patio floor with numbered squares running from one to one hundred. This patio floor checkerboard was encircled by a one-foot-high wire-mesh fence. For a Belize dollar, each bettor got to pick a number, as many dollars and as many numbers as you wished. A fat man with a bullhorn cajoled everybody to gather round and give him their money. Then his assistant, a pretty young woman of about twenty, brought out a lumpy sack from which she withdrew a bewildered-looking mature, live, hen. I probably don't have to tell you much more. When all the bets were in, the young woman tossed the chicken onto the make-shift crap table and then everyone waited for it to shit. The owner of the square that got dropped on collected the money, a hundred dollars. But none of this happened quietly. The fat man with the bull-horn continued to urge the crowd to move in and make lots of noise. Perhaps a terrified chicken defecates more readily. Whatever, a forced sense of frenzy and fun became a large part of the group psychology that then took over at least most of the people assembled. Maybe I wasn't yet quite adequately holiday-ized. My main emotion at the moment, I recall, was embarrassment. But I was almost alone. Around me, orthodontists from Wisconsin, shirtless in the early evening heat, jumped up and down and screamed loudly at the confused-looking pullet. People who might have been day-care workers back home in Cincinnati bellowed obscenities at the helpless hen. Stock analysts from Toronto dropped to their hands and knees to beg the chicken to move three steps to the right. It was amazing and, I have to admit, a bit disturbing to see. I felt a witness to a ritual that I wasn't certain I wanted in my repertoire. I watched both the chicken and the crowd. For the hen (which eventually laid a big poop on square number 23) this was, no doubt, the defining event of its life. For the tourists, it was a license. After the chicken drop they were sent off in a herd, or a series of herds, up the beach to see what larger havoc they might wreak, now that they were liberated from the normal discretions of their urban northern lives, and now that they were so far from home. Who knew what might be possible next?

Watching people relax in a strange environment is instructive. Personality alterations are common. But a lot of compulsive behavior persists as well, certainly among the kind of people who like to collect things, people who want to take things home. For many people a suntan is still a good trophy, despite the cancer warnings, despite these times of supposedly heightened health awareness and sensitivity about ultraviolet radiation. In many quarters, trophy-level sunburns are still prized; people still defy common sense and broadly based general advisories. In San Pedro good trophy tans were gleaned by people who burned themselves to a crisp on the beach at midday or who lingered too long in the snorkeling shallows. Belize didn't seem yet to have beaches where the visiting North Americans and Europeans could go nude or topless, as I'd seen on the other side of the border, on the Cancun coast of Mexico. But there were plenty of people eager to go out in the blistering noonday sun with only the minimum little strings. As much skin as possible exposed to as much sun as possible still seemed the rule. Not among the Belizians, of course, who were either too modest or too busy (or too smart) to indulge. But plenty of foreign visitors were baking like clams, turning themselves red like lobsters, with the goal of returning to their northern homes at the end of two weeks well seared, their darkened skin a wordless advertisement that they had been away, somewhere hot and exotic and probably full of fun and adventure. In the meantime, you'd see people every evening in the restaurants who had had too much sun that afternoon, squirming painfully as their clothing touched tender shoulders, their faces glowing like tomatoes threatening to heat the room by pure radiation.

Another popular trophy are photographs; both the standard ones and the more unusual. Though we were perfect strangers, a young man from Houston pulled me aside in a bar and regaled me in explicit detail with the tale of how a grouper fish had made off with his underwater Kodak and more astonishingly, how he had got it back. He had been snorkeling and momentarily lost control of the camera. As he watched it float toward the surface, just out of his reach, the fish, "no word a lie," swooped in and gobbled it up. But that was only the beginning of the story. This action, according to the man from Houston, caused the snapping of a picture inside the fish's mouth before it then coughed the little camera back up. My new friend then hauled out a blurred, dark photograph, supposedly a view into the esophagus of the fish.

Nothing goes hand in hand like tourists and their cameras or camcorders. Some of these people belong to the odd but growing slice of humanity who only take pictures. I befriended a couple from Ohio for a few days. They were making an extensive journey through Central America but, while his wife pointed him in the right directions to get the scene or the view or the moment that would make the perfect picture, the husband experienced their trip only through the viewfinder of his Minolta. A trip to the ruins of a Mayan pyramid was treated like a location scouting for a Hollywood movie; we spent the last hour of the afternoon searching not for the best spot to watch the sunset, but the best vantage point from which to photograph it. The spectacular red drop of the sun into the dense jungle foliage would happen for them later, when they got home and got their projector and screen set up, the popcorn popped, and perhaps the friends and neighbors comfortably settled.

For some people, their sun-provoked craziness takes the form of a quest for romance. Romance is a highly legitimate article in the currency of sun and sand tourism, extravagantly suggested on almost every page of the magazines, the brochures, and deeply embedded in the holiday travel mythlogy. My first evening in San Pedro, the entertainers at the beachfront restaurant where I had dinner were three sad-faced local guitar players who opined musically their version of the romance message. "Come to San Pedro," they sang, "fall in love . . . fall in love with the Caribbean, fall in love with me!" So people do. Sex is the fourth S completing the sun, sand, and surf quartet; and it can be seen either as the product of an impossible romantic longing or as a collector's item. An airline pilot from Philadelphia named Philip—handsome, dark haired, well tanned, lithe, thirty-five years old, and single—told me matter-of-factly that he'd had five conquests during six days in San Pedro. It's probably no trouble for a dashing pilot to find a short-term girlfriend anywhere. So Philip takes advantage of it. What he did on his frequent trips to beach locations was screw madly between diving and snorkeling excursions. Part of the thrill, for Philip, was possibly the trouble he constantly risked. While we talked, a bikini-clad blonde gave him an over-friendly wave only a few seconds before a dark young local woman, who worked as a desk clerk at our hotel, walked by murmuring a shy hello. Philip sighed. He had them both on the line and understood well the jealousy, anger, and recriminations that lay in store just around the corner. It was inevitable; he would have to pack and move on. Nevertheless, nothing stopped him; this is how he spent his trips. He let loose this side of his personality and passed his holiday time; it was his adventure, his trophy hunt, his gathering of memories. It was his form of collecting.

At the bottom of it all, you realize that a large part of what everyone is doing is avoiding boredom. Each person must do something to deal with the inevitable bubble of fear that rises during that dreadful moment shortly after arriving at a resort: somewhere between the evaporation of the fantasy promised in the full-color brochure back in cold wherever and the ultimate full adoption of the ritual—simple or manic—that will sustain you for your time. You have to face that awful existential question: "What the hell am I going to do here for seven days?" Each needs to find his own method. Two thoroughly sunburnt young Texans, probation officers from Austin, explained to me that they had been drunk for six days on a diet of beer in the afternoon and rum at night. Their eyes, behind their shiny red noses and the cracking red skin of their faces, were glazed with weariness. "But," they insisted, "it's really been a lot of fun."

If you mix license for compulsive, almost maniacal behavior, with a place's picture-postcard charm, you get what San Pedro has achieved and hundreds of other places hope for. When Belize's popularity skyrocketed in the early 1990s, hotel revenues jumped by 29 percent, from $17,302,804 in 1990 to $22, 314,979 in 1991. Hotel capacity increased from 210 hotels with 2,115 rooms in 1990 to 271 hotels with 2,913 rooms two years later. The increase in each category approached 30 percent. The dramatic nature of the growth and its impact was most vividly shown through the increase in numbers of foreign visitors: 215,442 in 1991, a 116 percent increase in four years. Everywhere the tourist numbers were hopping, and nowhere more than in San Pedro. Tiny San Pedro, in 1991, led all of Belize in tourism income as measured by hotel accomodation revenue. It was a full million Belize dollars ahead of Belize City (66,000 population), and the increase in 1990–92 was 29 percent, a greater increase by 11 percent than that of the city.

"Tourism is going to be the best performing sector of the economy," Belize boasted to *Fortune* magazine in 1993. By then it was already the country's second largest industry, behind citrus, and it was growing rapidly. Tourism's main problem, in the opinion of some, was that growth was too rapid. As a young man Paul Hunt came to Belize from England, married a Belizian, and worked his way up through the hotel industry until he owned the local Radisson franchise and was elected president of the 350-member Belize Tourism Industry Association. At first he was for rapid growth, but has reconsidered. "In 1988," explained Hunt, "we had none of the major car rental outlets. Now look at them." He counted on his fingers: National, Hertz, Avis, Budget. "All in five years." In 1990, Hunt's Radisson-Fort George Hotel was the first Belize hotel to connect with a worldwide franchise operation. Three years later, a plethora of international chain and franchise hotels had arrived on the scene: Holiday Inn, Ramada, Westin, Biltmore. One of the first big billboards confronting a visitor leaving the airport heading toward Belize City is the familiar green-and-white logo of the Holiday Inn, which instructs: "Stay With Someone You Know." The chains are part and parcel of an official tourism industry. "The chain hotels are important," insisted Michelle Gabourel at the government-run Belize Tourist Board, "because they give name recognition to the American visitors." But their presence also signals a monumental change in the personality of the country. They are international; they are homogeneous.

The Gulf War and the global recession caused a brief dip in the tourist economy in 1991, because for a few months a lot of Americans chose to stay home. In a country where the tourism industry was fledgling, this dip did some damage. Some operators who had been optimistic and had over-extended and over-borrowed found they couldn't weather the lull. One of the casualties was Paul Hunt, who lost control of the Radisson— no doubt inspiring his later opinion that slow growth is better. But the lull didn't de-rail the industry as a whole or discourage the head-long trend toward globalization.

As appears to be the case everywhere, globalization seems inevitable. Yet it is also regretted. It is a two-edged sword, embraced and lamented in the same breath. Celi McCorkle, her Holiday Hotel in San Pedro grown now to a prosperous sixteen rooms, grumbled like bosses everywhere about the headaches of owning an expanding enterprise. "When I had one man working for me," she complained, "everything got done; now that I have a bunch of them working for me I have to do it myself." But more than that, she has watched changes that have altered the country she once knew. Celi wanted tourism, but tourism is taking Belize away from her and her people. Of the fifty-one hotels in San Pedro on Ambergris Cay, Celi told me, only eight are owned by local people. Celi's Holiday Hotel is the largest of these; most of the rest are small eight- to ten-room places facing the sandy street in the middle of town and carrying their owner's names, Tomas' or Ruby's. The bigger, newer, sprawling hotels with poolside or beachside bars and promotional entertainment packages are owned by outsiders. Sometimes the foreigners have Belizian partners; mostly they do not. Of the dozens of restaurants in San Pedro, only five are owned by locals.

Celi, even though she had her time out in the big world, is vintage San Pedrano. Her grandfather was a conch fisherman and coconut gatherer; her father was the island's barber and tailor. Her ninety-four-year-old grandmother still lives a few houses away from the Holiday Hotel, in the cottage where she was born. But Celi can look around her town and itemize the changes tourism has brought. From the outset, it meant money; jobs in guiding, transporting, and in operating the small stores and curio shops all brought prosperity. But even more money came from the sale of land as more and more hotels and restaurants and condos and marinas went up, and more and more money and investment came in.

This prosperity, however, offered a bargain of Faustian dimensions. "One morning the San Pedranos woke up and realized they had sold their birthright," declared Celi. "On one level you can't blame them; pieces of land that were worth one thousand dollars were suddenly worth fifty thousand dollars. But they only saw the fifty thousand dollars, not what it all meant." Quick money changed the people. Prosperity became so great that San Pedranos developed a snobbish view of themselves. They felt, according to McCorkle, that they shouldn't have to perform the mundane chambermaid, busboy, and waiter jobs in their town's hotels and restaurants. Instead, other Belizians from other parts of the country have arrived to take on those jobs. The San Pedro people, with new prosperity, send their children to school on the mainland, or even out of the country. They want their children to have professional, not menial, jobs. Celi listed the employees at her hotel; when she was done we realized that less than half were San Pedro people. "So the culture has been changed, not only by the tourists, but by all these people from other parts of Belize who have come here to live and work."

The role of the foreign owners in this is significant, whether the big corporate chains or the small, individual entrepreneurs. For the restless adventurer or the enterprising risk-taker, Belize, along with other places like it, holds out the same "land of opportunity" flavor it had three hundred years ago when pirates chose it as a base for operations. A hunger for investment and entrepreneurship that is believed can only come from outside, combined with few prohibitive restrictions and an attractive tax situation, has hauled in lots of foreign owners to Belize.

One of these is a fit-looking, sunburned man in his middle forties named Jerry Gilbreath. On a Sunday morning we stood on the patio of his restaurant and bar, the Purple Parrot, surveying the morning-after effects of the previous night's party, which celebrated his bar's sixth anniversary. Gilbreath plays the part of the "Good Ol' Southern Boy," complete with an Atlanta Braves baseball cap on his head and a glistening gold chain around his neck. Back home in Laurel, Mississippi, he is a lawyer and also a Republican Party stalwart (he was once the youngest member of the Mississippi legislature). Gilbreath looked for and found Belize specifically to indulge a lust for adventure and a hunger to be an entrepreneur. He wanted to have interests in an exotic place and make some money. He made his first scouting trip in 1986, admitting, "I was looking for opportunities, perhaps for a small cay." He bought the Purple Parrot a year later and has been part of the San Pedro action ever since. Now he flies down to Belize to look after business for one long weekend each month. As well as the Purple Parrot, he holds part interests in a variety of other ventures—another hotel and restaurant up the beach, the Belize Yacht Club, and the Shell Oil distributorship. He handed me a tee shirt emblazoned with his restaurant's logo.

The Purple Parrot's birthday party, which included a transvestite fashion show, was a grand success in Jerry Gilbreath's opinion. It not only celebrated an anniversary, but also acknowledged the foothold, if not yet the triumph, of a lifestyle and a business style Jerry Gilbreath believed in. As we talked, he spun out New Orleans or Key West–style fantasies: "we want San Pedro to be the French Quarter of Ambergris Cay." Who "we" might be was not immediately clear. Perhaps he meant the couple of dozen American college kids and the British Royal Air Force flyers on leave from their base at Belize City. The Brits, in a holdover post-colonial deal, still defend this country that was not big enough to have its own air force. Wearing short pants and flying Harriar jets, they aren't quite certain who they are keeping at bay—possibly the ever-unpredictable Guatemala. Underneath the rustling palm fronds and in full view of the shimmering ocean, a representation of these two groups were desultorily nursing weekend hangovers and teasing their breakfast eggs. One would question whether "we" meant the native San Pedranos. Most of them, the night before, were not celebrating Gilbreath's bar's anniversary but were, rather, up the beach at the outdoor basketball court where they

formed a lusty audience for the local team that was shellacking the visitors from Cozumel. Gilbreath's "we" certainly didn't mean the ghost of
nor the descendants of Fido Nuñez. Fido Nuñez used to live in the house
that became the Purple Parrot. Gilbreath bowed in his direction briefly
when he named the patio bar "Fido's Courtyard," but that looked like a
marketing strategy more than anything. The San Pedranos, past and present, represent something different in the equation. More like extras in a
movie, they form a kind of set, the colorful atmospheric backdrop
against which business is done. "What we want," Jerry Gilbreath explained, "is steady, controlled, growth. We want to work with the Belize
government to keep the same atmosphere, to bring in paying jobs for
Belizian people, and to give them the chance to get businesses going."

The position of the foreign entrepreneur is delicate, and Jerry Gilbreath acknowledged this. Even in this country founded by marauding
buccaneers and in an industry in which national boundaries are only
things you fly over, "there is resentment that will be there unless you become part of the community." At all costs, Gilbreath wanted to avoid
being resented. He listed some of the things he had done to prevent that.
He sponsored a local soccer team. Part of the profits from his anniversary
party would go as a donation to the Belize Zoo. "There will be resentment
if I take profits out and don't put money back in," he told me.

No one should blame Jerry Gilbreath and people like him for grabbing an opportunity when it presented itself. He is possibly among the
more responsible of the host of visiting businesspeople; Gilbreath emphasized that his eighteen employees were all Belizians. When I was
there, a storm of contention was brewing around a proposed development by another Mississippian, a shopping mall developer who wanted
to redo 22,000 acres at the north end of the island. These 22,000 acres represented three-quarters of the cay. At the time of my visit, no plans were
firm—in fact the biggest commodities were speculation and gossip. But
the development was said to involve two major hotel chains (Hilton and
Hyatt) and some figures within the Belize government.

The proposed development would be a test of Belize's will and in-
tegrity. Belize claimed it wanted to institute regulations around development to protect the environment and look after local needs. Such regulations had already gone some distance; when Jerry Gilbreath arrived in
the mid-1980s, it was almost a free-for-all. A person with enough money
could do what he wished: "there was not much regulation of any kind."
Now there have been changes. He listed off a string of newly imposed

stipulations: set-back laws for buildings; permits required to build a pier; water and sewer regulations; three-story height regulations. Foreigners needed permits to work in Belize; there was a more stringent enforcement of work laws. But the trade-off between money, politics, and the public and environmental good is a treacherous one. In the proposed Ambergris Cay development, for instance, local people, including Celi McCorkle, were very bothered by the involvement of people connected to the government. They feared corruption. "There was a process of environmental review about the development," McCorkle explained, shaking her finger. But she accused the government of abruptly cutting that off when too many San Pedro people became critical. "Figure that out," she said.

Tourism workers get on and off airplanes as often as tourists. The industry attracts restless, unsettled souls, hungry for experience or adventure or things that are different. In the hotels and restaurants, dive shops and outfitter agencies, executive suites and front desks of Belize I encountered Americans, British expatriots, Jamaicans, and Mexicans. I was also not surprised to find a couple of Canadians working away happily. Hugh Penwarden is the kind of footloose nomad who would hate an office job; a friendly, knowledgeable fellow in his mid-forties, he spends his summers in beautiful, pristine corners of the Canadian wilderness employed as a gardener for the Canadian National Parks service. But he has been lucky enough to have organized his life to avoid the fate of an indoor job during the cold Canadian winters as well. Since the late 1980s he has balanced his summer of gardening with a winter occupation that is the envy of every romantic wanderer; he is an ecotour guide. He gets paid to conduct tours deep into the jungles and rainforests of Belize: ten- to fourteen-person groups of birdwatchers from Britain or environmentalists from Switzerland.

Another Canadian, Shelley Derksen, also found herself in a tourism job in Belize, though hers was more mainstream than Penwarden's. Twenty-six years old, with a degree in history, Derksen still believed she had the perfect job for someone of her disposition. She was bar manager and activities director for Captain Morgan's Retreat, an American-owned resort in an isolated cove on the east side of Ambergris Cay. Tanned and fit, her blonde hair cropped short and bleached by the sun, she stood barefoot and in shorts at the edge of the deep end of the swimming pool kibbitzing with her guests. She was three countries, two thousand miles, and ninety degrees removed from winter in her native Canada.

For both Penwarden and Derksen, their jobs and the connections those jobs gave them to Belize were a personal thing. But both, likewise, fit a slot in the infrastructure of tourism; their expertise and willingness to work know no boundaries—they could work in tourism anywhere in the world. Both had worked out philosophical justifications that were personal but also went beyond personal. Hugh Penwarden's philosophical motivator was his belief in ecology. Shelley Derksen's motivations beyond a job, exotica, her own brand of travel, included the opportunity to learn about this place in a different way than was presented to her by her family and church (she is a Mennonite, a group which has serious missionary intentions in Central America). Hers was the adventure of a young woman who was liberated, liberal, free, and wanted a career and life to suit those inclinations.

But what about other people? What about the Belizian natives for whom tourism is a more and more likely occupation? Two young women serving drinks at the bar by the pool at Captain Morgan's Retreat are Belizian. Esther comes from San Ignacio, a town of about 7,000 up in the far corner of the Cayo District close by the Guatemala border; Elena is from Punta Gorda on the tropical jungle coast in the far south. What were they doing here? How did they get from the far corners of their country onto this island and into this exclusive hotel with its clientele of well-heeled Americans, Canadians, Germans, Englishmen, and Spaniards?

Esther, jolly and outgoing, roared at a joke made by a visiting Costa Rican and brought everybody another round of fruity drinks. She explained that she started out working in restaurants back home in San Ignacio. But she soon decided to move to San Pedro because it was a much busier place and she anticipated better opportunities. She met Elena and persuaded her friend to join her in trying for the job at Captain Morgan's. Captain Morgan's consumes their lives. Esther could barely remember the last time she went back to San Ignacio to visit her family, even though she said she missed them greatly, especially her child who was being cared for by her parents. "There is never enough time. It takes a full day by bus to get there, and if I have only a couple of days I have to turn right around and come back. It's not worth it." Her time off was spent in San Pedro. She described a party she went to the night before in town, and said she figured life was pretty good.

In a restaurant in town I had a conversation with another Belizian, Rojelio Cana. His home, Corozal, is a small city in the extreme north of Belize, on the Caribbean coast and just across the border from Chetumal, Mexico. Rojelio came from there to San Pedro, sight unseen, with his brother. They had heard there were jobs and good money. Rojelio was the second eldest of a sugarcane farmer's seven children. In school he had studied drafting, but he didn't finish. "Everything in Corozal is political," he explained. "So if you are not with the ruling party there are no jobs for you." A shy, good-looking, quiet young man, at nineteen Rojelio got a job as a waiter in the restaurant of the Sunbreeze Hotel. When I spoke to him, he was brand new on the job, wearing a bright blue shirt with "STAFF" printed prominently on its front. After four days he still struggled to get the hang of things. For example, I first paid notice to him when a woman at the next table to mine, a stern, middle-aged woman, summoned Rojelio to her table. He had brought her white instead of brown toast. Rojelio looked confused and fearful, shifting from one foot to the other, not comprehending. He kept pointing to the toast insisting that it was indeed brown, white bread toasted brown. This made the woman even more annoyed. She appealed to me, hoping for sympathy; she had paid for service and felt she wasn't getting it. "The help here . . ." she snorted. Suddenly aware of Rojelio's perplexity, she had trouble finding the words to finish her exasperated diatribe.

In contrast to jobs in Corozal, jobs in San Pedro, Rojelio told me, were easy to get. One didn't need political connections. His brother was already on his second job. His first had been with the local branch of the Atlantic Bank, but he had left that, moving on to become the office manager for a dive shop. The brothers were making enough money, Rojelio confirmed, both to send some home and to save some for an eventual return to their studies. Rojelio was careful; he insisted he wouldn't drink his money or party it away, or spend it on women. "I don't have a girlfriend; they give you too much of a headache,"—he pointed to his head—"and I am not yet old enough or ready to settle for one and only one." But he was far from his close-knit family, with only his brother for company, and he admitted that he was lonely. He had two shifts a day, 6–10 A.M. and 6–10 P.M., six days a week. After a year, he expected he could get some holidays, but until then there would not be much opportunity or time to visit his family up in Corozal. The money sent home in the mail would have to suffice.

The promise of jobs and employment drew the young and the ambitious, like metal filings to a magnet, from the far corners of the hinterland to the centers of tourist action. They were coming in waves, seeking opportunity and the chance to modernize their lives. Providing those jobs, in a modern, up-to-date industry, is one of the powerful arguments behind tourism in developing countries. It is the compelling argument behind a small country's decision to spend public money building the infrastructures, the airports and service systems tourism requires. It is the justification for their allowing foreign owners to operate unhindered. These things they will do if jobs can be provided for their people. Analyst Kreg Lindberg developed an economic input-output model for Belize that demonstrated the impact of tourism on the economy. An average tourist expenditure of 100 million U.S. dollars per year led to an estimate that tourism generated 211 million U.S. dollars in sales throughout the Belizian economy. Out of this came 41 million U.S. dollars in direct payments to households, mostly in the form of wages.

This sort of economic multiplication is what the strategy is intended to achieve. But it often seems less than fully thought out. For example, there seemed to be little or no specific training for personnel in the tourism industry in Belize. Neither Esther nor Elena nor Rojelio went through anything other than haphazard on-the-job introductions and orientations. A woman at the Belize Tourist Board told me that tourism is on the curriculum of the public school system, introduced to little children at the elementary school level and then part of the social studies curriculum in high school. But when I asked Shawn Colton, a thirteen-year-old boy whose family owned the guest house where I was staying in Belize City, he said he'd never heard of it. "It's a plan," explained his mother, Ondina, "but it's not yet a fact." Ondina employed help at her small guesthouse, but she was not sure what training opportunities might be available to them, either in hospitality arts or in management, finance, or planning.

Belize is a small country of only 180,000 people. There is no university. Paul Hunt, former head of the Belize Tourism Industry Association, claimed the industry and the government wanted to get foreign aid dollars from the European Community and from Canada to pay for ongoing training for young Belizians. Courses he said he wanted offered included everything from cooking to tour-guide training. But at the moment, the country's education system and its ability to train and prepare people lagged pathetically behind the pace of its fastest-growing industry.

Hunt said it's urgent that something be done. He estimated 8,000 Belizians to be employed in the tourist industry, from chambermaids to boat drivers, ecotour guides to accountants. With growth bringing thirty or forty new hotels each year, you can imagine the demand for competent help in all areas. The challenges of anticipating, meeting, and keeping up with demand preoccupies everyone's attention. But without proper training and preparation, the question arises not only of how to provide good service to the visitor, but also of how to serve your own people, your own communities, your own economy, and your own objectives. How can tourism benefit Belize and Belizians if not enough of them have the training to take on not just its key roles, but all its mundane and day-to-day tasks as well? How can Belize and Belizians grasp and maintain control of the rapidly growing behemoth? Can they get control of enough of the money it generates to pay for it?

A criticism of globalization is that profits are taken out of a developing country, or that the money doesn't come in at all. In some economic jargons this is called "leakage," which makes it sound more gentle and benign than it turns out to be. If you are going to stay in one of the chain hotels in Belize, for example, you book in the United States, you pay in the United States, the hotels operate on an overdraft, and the money never sees Belize, and Belize never sees the money. The same is true for the airline fares that tourists pay for their trips. If you subtract air fares and hotel fees from a traveler's budget, what is left is only small change. Only the small margin items remain for the host country, or the host community; the minimum-wage jobs, the handicraft and curio sales, local guiding and transportation, food and beverages. It's hardly leakage—it's more like a drought. On top of this, the developing country has to bear the cost of the social consequences.

Celi McCorkle, the pioneer of tourism in Belize, is now one of its critics. Life in her home town of San Pedro, now that her dream of tourism's arrival has come true, is full of ironic twists. San Pedranos barely own what's left of their town. As pointed out earlier, only eight of the fifty-one hotels (and they are the smaller, middle-of-town hotels) and five of the restaurants remain owned by local people. The beachfront was sold for quick money to developers, operators, and speculators. One can no longer walk from the sand into the water off San Pedro and scoop up conch or lobster by hand. In fact, there are few spots along the three miles of beach that fronts the town where you can step into the water at all. Boat docks, marinas, yacht clubs, breakwaters, boardwalks, and waterfront cafés are crammed side by side for pretty much the full distance of the waterfront. The fish and sea creatures, once so close and so plentiful, now are scarce from overfishing and must be retrieved from greater distances. Quick money came to the townspeople from selling out to tourism developers. But the money had two effects—selling out removed individual San Pedranos from the game, and it placed the industry of the town into the hands of outside conglomerates and foreigners. The immediate prosperity changed the attitudes and the social status of San Pedro's families. Many considered themselves and their children to be a cut above the kinds of jobs available in the tourist industries. So the jobs in restaurants, hotels, marinas, and bars went to Belizians from elsewhere in the country who migrated to San Pedro and Ambergris Cay for work and money.

For those who remained, San Pedro became a round-the-clock party town. Every morning, children in crisply turned out blue uniforms march in file into their classrooms in the San Pedro Roman Catholic Elementary School, a narrow building sandwiched up against the concrete wall of a big hotel compound. But across the yard from the school's two tiers of wooden verandahs, other children their age from North America, on holidays with their families, frolic on the hotel's beach. The San Pedro children must try to concentrate on arithmetic while the other kids lie in the sand or get ready to go swimming or out in a boat. "It is hard to work," Celi McCorkle told me, "when there is a constant party going on around you. It is hard when you live side by side with people who are on vacation and you are working." The group for whom this is most difficult are the youth and young adults who find themselves swept forcefully into the vortex of partying. "The Americans have money, and it is impossible for the local young people to match them," complained Celi. But they try. The young Belizians burn the candle at both ends, working or studying by day and partying by night. They make new, temporary friends among the visiting holidayers and they try to keep up with their social life. "More and more of our young women are drinking," Celi pointed out. "There is a breakdown of family values, a breakdown of family life, of respect for elders. I don't blame the kids; they can't separate reality from what they are looking at."

In Belize City, Ondina Colton lamented the changes that she had witnessed around her. Ondina is a little like Celi McCorkle: a year after she lost her job at a bank, she and her husband Alan turned four bedrooms of their graceful sixty-year-old home on Cork Street into an appealing bed-and-breakfast. So she is, on the one hand, one of the Belizians who has been cashing in on tourism. But she had yet to evaluate what the trade-off was worth. "I'm afraid now to walk into town," she told me, describing the trip from her house to shops a ten-minute walk away in the center of town. Hustlers and beggars operate aggressively along the route, hustlers and beggars who had never been there before. Mainly, they try to extort donations from tourists. I had been marked my first day in town by a young woman who greeted me enthusiastically on a street corner as I was still orienting myself (I guess too obviously). Our exchange went like this:

"Hello! Don't you remember me?"

I seemed puzzled, and she continued: "I saw you at the hotel where you are staying."

At that point, I walked straight into it, a lobster into the trap: "At the Colton Guest House?"

She was well rehearsed, and didn't miss her cue. "Yes! I was working there." I could not remember her and didn't know her from Eve.

"But alas, I can't go to work there tomorrow because my poor baby is sick. I am on my way to see him in the hospital, but need to get diapers to take to him. Though unfortunately I haven't got my pay. Could you help me out if I paid you back?"

The hustlers love the tourists, but they don't discriminate against the locals, so Ondina was nervous. "There's one big fellow who always bothers me, and I'm afraid of him," she told me. I remembered him too, a much more menacing character than the diaper woman. On one of my first days in Belize City he had stopped me as I rounded a corner on my walk into town: a big, wild-eyed fellow with an explosion of dreadlocks. I learned later he was considered mentally deranged and had spent long periods in prison. He fell in step, matching my pace, and struck up a conversation. After only a few seconds, he got to the point, offering to be my personal guide. This would have been in exchange, of course, for money. I declined the offer, telling him I didn't think I needed a guide. He became angry. He was no longer my good friend; he switched quickly from being my potential guide and protector to my potential nemesis. "The foreigner in Belize who has no personal guide," he hissed, "is going to feel pain!"

Although his threat did not come true, our exchange remained like a cloud over me for days, ugly and unsettling. I thought of him and watched for him every time I walked to the shops. The threat was unsettling in as much as it was personal to me. But more than that, it was a foreboding promise for a society where things were happening too fast, where money and strangers and new rules were injected without a blueprint, or with only a minimum of thought, or planning, or taking care of all the other ends of how people function side by side one another. The tourist droves had arrived, the culture wasn't ready for them.

The ironies of all this run deep. It is tourism that supposedly causes the social change that makes Belize City a more menacing place. Ondina Colton, who lamented the changes and drew them to my attention, was making her living from that same tourism; the tourist business had more than made up for her lost salary from the bank. Yet tourism gets only mixed reviews from Ondina. She still had family on Cay Caulker, one of the smaller islands. She lamented the change in the people she had grown up with, change that had come about, she believed, because of tourism. When she returned for visits, she found the prevailing attitudes and the psychology all changed. "You go back there now and the things that you used to get through hospitality, people now want you to pay for. A drink is not offered for free when you arrive like it used to be. Tourism has changed people, now it's all money, money, money. People get some, they want more. It's all greed."

If there is an ideal for a place like Belize, it is that progress will come slowly, and people, like Ondina Colton and Celi McCorkle, will be part of defining it and will grow with it. But Ondina worried that that wouldn't happen. "The government talks a good line, but it is all words; 'eco-tourism' is probably just another word. They have no controls to make sure tourism stays for the benefit of the people. In a few years Belize will be just like Cancun." She pointed to the new addition to the Radisson Hotel that dominates the street across from her house. Its ten-story glass tower fully blocked her view of the sea. "That's not Belize," she explained. "That's just money, money, money."

5

Unspoiled,
and Hoping To Keep It That Way

The advertising slogan for the tourist industry in Belize is "Undiscovered and Unspoiled." This is an enticing advertisement indeed, and not far off the mark. If anything differentiates Belize from other places in the Caribbean and makes it special on the globe, it is surely the variety of the country's phenomenal natural splendors. Belize is a tiny country; its 8,866 square miles (22,700 square kilometers) make it no bigger than Vermont, or Wales. But the beauty and diversity of the land and water is stunning. One traverses the country pursuing a panorama that moves from the magnificent coastal reef and island cays across to the mainland. There, from a mangrove swamp that is barely at sea level, almost subterranean, the land fans out toward the west ascending to abrupt inland elevations of 3,800 feet in the Maya Mountains. Interior regions are rich and well watered; in the north, pine forests alternate with savannah grasslands; in the south, rainforests are dense and animal filled. Only a fraction of Belize is farmed or otherwise exploited by humans. Though the southern arm of the Mayan civilization inhabited much of the country 4,000 years ago and it has had successive populations in more recent centuries of pirates and slaveholder loggers and timber cutters, Belize now has only 180,000 people, fewer citizens than a small suburb of most Latin American cities. The flora and fauna of this small country dwarf in numbers and variety most other places in the world, its diversity drawing comparisons with the Galapagos Islands. Belize is home to seven hundred species of trees, as many as the entire continental United

States. Animal and bird life abounds in sufficient variety and sufficient numbers to make naturalists drool. There are ninety kinds of bats, fifty-four species of snakes, six kinds of opossoms, and five types of wild cats, including the elusive jaguar.

The Mosquito Coast movie and Harrison Ford may have brought the transcendental beauty of the Belize landscape in front of a wide North American and European audience. But another moment was equally important in focusing intense attention on this hitherto unnoticed country. In 1986, the Coca Cola Company of Atlanta Georgia bought 100,000 acres in the northwest corner of Belize, near Blue Creek Village and the Mexican border. Coca Cola's plan was to clear the jungle and plant orange groves. There had been some risky years for the Florida orange crops that had been damaged by successive midwinter frosts. Belize, however, had no such vulnerability. It had already been determined as an hospitable environment for citrus crops, and a future as a grower of oranges in a climate that was guaranteed to be frost-free was an appealing prospect.

Something happened, though, that Coca Cola hadn't counted on: CBS's *60 Minutes* crew and Morley Safer showed up. Some say a nudge had come from the lobby of the threatened Florida citrus industry, but 1986 was also the apex of the growing world consciousness and a galloping global dismay over the disappearing rainforest. The world public had begun to understand that rainforests grew not only in the Amazon basin of Brazil but in other places, too, and that many of these forests likewise were threatened. So when Morley Safer went on TV and told forty-three million Americans that Coca Cola was going to kill a rainforest in the jungles of Central America in order to produce orange juice, proverbial hell broke loose. Safer stood, backed by a heavy green canopy of jungle screaming with howler monkeys and multicolored birds, and told North Americans: "I think Coca Cola should leave Belize alone; it's far too nice."

Angry calls flooded the switchboards both at CBS and at Coca Cola. The publicity was intense and uniformly negative; the company appeared to have no choice but to back off. Eventually, instead of cutting down the rainforest and getting its citrus groves, the company found it could retrieve its good name only by donating the land to conservation. Ninety-two thousand Coca Cola acres became part of a larger 200,000 acre parcel of what became subsequently one of Belize's premier nature preserves.

The *60 Minutes* item criticized Coca Cola, but it also created intense

interest in Belize. Millions of people who'd never heard of it before suddenly knew where Belize was. Thousands spontaneously put it on the
list of things they cared about. Among the calls of inquiry were many
from people who had decided they wanted to visit this place they had
seen on television. What's more, there was an additional corollary: what
interested the callers was not a traditional tourism destination with
curio shops, casinos, and a beach; these callers were attracted to the idea
of unspoiled wilderness, untouched rainforest and jungle, animals,
birds, and plants still safely in a pristine state.

Belize, some people started to believe, might be the birthplace of a
whole new way of traveling and experiencing and behaving. The possibilities of nature-oriented tourism, or what was then starting to be called
"ecotourism" began to stir. Belize decided to grab the moment. The government of the day took a lead: Glenn Godfrey, who was Minister of
Tourism and the Environment at the time (he held the post until 1993
when the government changed) appealed to conservation-minded people in North America and Europe to make Belize their destination of
choice. "Our commitment to ecotourism is strong and steadfast,"
claimed glossy Belize tourism brochures. "We are unwavering in the protection of our environmental treasures." In 1992, Godfrey told *Fortune*
magazine, "People don't come here to dance in discos or attend the
opera, the unspoiled environment is what attracts people. We want to
develop our tourism resources but also make sure that things stay as they
are. Properly developed, tourism can be an instrument for environmental conservation because people in the business are committed to preserving it."

A government agency, the Belize Tourist Board, was put in charge of
marketing. The Belize government opened tourist sales offices in New
York, Berlin, and Cancun, to deal with the appetites of North America,
Europe, and Mexico respectively. The woman in charge of public relations, Michelle Gabourel, explained the strategy to me. They hoped that
a neatly functioning system would match intelligent customers—who
had been alerted through well-placed advertisements and magazine articles via travel agents, package dealers, and wholesalers—with the pleasures and delights offered in Belize. The visitors would make the trip and
act responsibly toward the natural and historical wonders, the country's
people, and its wildlife. They would leave money and good will behind
and would come away enriched immeasurably in experience and knowledge. Gabourel explained once more the party line: Belize was commit-

ted to achieving this utopia; it would stop short of encouraging mass tourism and would be strict about protecting land, vegetation, and benefits to local people.

The Belize Tourist Board was not a big, formidable machine by any means. When I went to visit them, I found the entire bureau working out of an upstairs office above a law firm. But they were trying their best to look like marketers. The office walls were brightly papered with posters of Belize tourism's mythology: the national animal, the tapir; the national tree, mahogany. Tourism tee shirts, in a glass case, were for sale. The half-dozen front-desk clerks, all young women, were dressed identically in jaguar jungle motif jackets.

Belize recognized that if tourists were going to be drawn by wild fauna and natural wonders, the country would have to take prompt action to protect rare animals and its environment. Through both public and private enterprise a chain of natural, national park–style sanctuaries were built. They depended heavily on the country's handful of well-off individuals and companies to do their part. Barry M. Bowen, whose family company owned both the largest brewery and the Belize Coca Cola franchise, is one of the country's biggest private entrepreneurs. In western Belize it fell to him to pioneer the building of ecological retreats, the most famous of which, the rustic twelve-cabana Chan Chich Lodge compound, sits in a pristine rainforest setting dotted with Mayan ruins. Chan Chich's development was symbolic of Belize' transformation: the area was once controlled by marijuana growers, hunters, and tomb robbers but, boasted Bowen of his intervention, "We make sure wildlife, vegetation, and ruins are protected."

Belize, though, soon realized the ironies involved in using the slogan "Undiscovered and Unspoiled" to lure tourists. How can you remain undiscovered and unspoiled when the purpose of every new visitor is to discover something, and the effect of every footfall in the jungle is to spoil something? Can a busload of people, camera shutters clicking, really file through the preserve of a troop of howler monkeys and spoil nothing, not change the atmosphere? Even if no gum wrappers are dropped, no empty soft drink cans left behind, no trees cut to clear the walking path, can ecotourists from Stuttgart, or Houston, or Edmonton enter and exit a jungle (or a village) and leave no change behind—no change in energy, no change in stress?

In 1986, the year *The Mosquito Coast* came out and the year Coca Cola backed away from its plan for orange plantations, 99,266 foreign visitors came as tourists to Belize. Five years later, by 1991, the number had more than doubled, to 215,442—a number that represented a ratio of 1.2 tourists for every Belizian. That many visitors and all they represented—from their money to their expectations—have to change a place. Belize and its 180,000 people were suddenly put under tremendous pressure; they had to decide what to do about the sudden burst of popularity. Pitted against those who argued that tourism would be the economic savior of Belize was a growing group of voices wanting to add another phrase to the slogan: "Undiscovered and Unspoiled . . . and Hoping To Keep It That Way." Could Belizians control their new tourism, or would it control them?

Tourism infatuates Third World countries. Because it gives a quicker return on hard currency investment than anything else, it is an attractive proposition for a local economy. It is labor intensive and there is a spillover into a myriad of other industries, such as handicrafts or restaurants. Such rosy prospects can deftly seduce a developing country. But once a country has been seduced, the downside quickly follows. Some people looked at Belize and worried about problems tourism would create. Writer Tom Barry, in a 1992 book called *Inside Belize*, argued that the pressures of tourism have a serious negative side. Among the sins are the inevitable ones like an extension of transportation systems into more and more remote corners of the country. If the charm and strength of Belize is that the country still has 90 percent of its original vegetation cover, that surely won't last long under such developmental pressures. Tourism, in Barry's opinion, is central to those pressures. "Tourism leaves in its wake increasing boat pollution, waste-disposal problems, environmental degradation of the cays, and motor traffic. Developers have begun combing every inch of Belize, examining its investment potential for tourism. Previously unvisited forest wilderness and small cays are now being explored by an ever-expanding number of 'eco-tourists.'"

An example for Barry of pressures on the environment was what was happening to the mangrove swamps that line the eastern coast. Mangroves are a low-lying, aquatic, saline plant, which are a vital component of stability in a wetland ecosystem. They also provide the habitat for huge numbers and varieties of wildlife and birds. But "to make room for hotels, industrial development, and beachfront housing, mangroves are being removed," wrote Barry, "resulting in serious beach loss and soil erosion in the developed cays and around Belize City. Developers view mangroves and the sea grasslands that extend from the coast and the cays as useless and unsightly. But these eco-systems anchor sand and provide some protection against hurricane losses."

The advocates of tourism in Belize argued that despite those short-comings, proper conservation over the long haul was not possible without the tourist dollars. Tourism might put some pressure on the environment, but all other forms of economic activity were surely worse. Given the alternatives, tourism was the best bet for the long-term preservation of the wildlife, reefs, rainforests, and ruins in which Belizians took such pride. Public officials started to take this line as a mantra when they traveled around the world to conferences and conclaves to make speeches about the tourist economy and conservation. Belize adopted a circular equation that became: the country's unspoiled nature would attract tourists; tourism, in turn, would justify and pay for the conservation of nature. The equation looked lovely on paper, but could it work?

In Belize, the lion's share of the responsibility for sustaining the precarious equation landed on the slight shoulders of a soft-spoken thirty-five-year-old woman with a pleasant round face. When I visited her, Virginia Vasquez was the executive director of the Belize Audubon Society. Until the 1990s both the promotion of nature conservation and its financing came heavily from outside Belize. American-based Audubon Societies in places such as Massachusetts and Georgia took an intense interest in the country. These outsiders started up important conservation programs, but eventually the need for local control and self-sustaining finances became critical. In Belize, as in all post-colonial countries, fledgling institutions had to move in short order into positions of huge responsibility. The Belize Audubon Society, chartered in 1969, now carries much of the responsibility for conservation, having been given charge of managing and staffing seven of the important protected areas, including the country's two national parks. When we met, Virginia Vasquez had just returned from a ceremony that further extended her responsibilities: she had opened a visitor center at Cockscomb, an increasingly popular nature area in the Maya Mountains of the southern interior. After initial work by Canadian zoologists and with financing by the Jaguar Motor Company, a sanctuary zone for the increasingly endangered jaguar was set up there. From an organizational standpoint, the opening of the visitor center completed a circle; foreign agitation, study, and money were the initiating catalyst, but the Belizians then had to run it. The culmination was a nature preserve supported by the Belize government and under the management of a Belizian conservationist society.

There should be no misapprehension of scale. The Belize Audubon Society is like other things in tiny Belize: it may manage all the country's national parks and sanctuaries, but it does so with a mom-and-pop corner-store-sized staff and budget. Nineteen field personnel and five administrative people—who occupy a steamy, cramped, upstairs office in a tiny house in the middle of Belize City—constitute the entire army. The office of Virginia Vasquez consisted of a cluttered table surrounded by papers and plans and maps and pictures. But Vasquez told me she considered her mandate and the possibilities to be as exciting as they were daunting. The first objective was to work out the connection between conservation and tourism. "There is no question," she declared, "that tourism is and will be important in paying for conservation." Belize is under enormous pressures both from within and from without to get out from under the burden of foreign aid. "We can't," said Vasquez, "continue to rely on foreign aid to pay 90 percent of the costs of conserving sanctuary areas, so we have to learn to manage our areas and make them financially self-sustaining. Tourism is part of doing that."

But is it possible tourism can support and not contradict conservation? The best route for this, insist its promoters, is ecotourism. A precise definition of ecotourism is a bit of a moving target. David Quammen, writing in *Outside* magazine, declared, "At its best, nature-oriented tourism can make a big contribution to preserving landscapes and cultures; at is worst, it's a travesty and a curse." At its weakest, ecotourism is just a word, or possibly a way to dress. But at its best it insists on tourism that does not overtax local resources, it makes sure most money spent by tourists stays in the country they visit, and it includes local people in its benefits. It is not, argues Quammen, "just any hell-bent sortie to the outback that puts wild animals in the cross hairs of a Minolta. Ecotourism is not beer and Pringles in the rainforest."

To its critics, ecotourism's morally superior tone sometimes becomes a tiresome irritation; ecotourists are the spoilsports of the party, like having animal rights activists at your barbeque. But for its true believers, ecotourism represents the only responsible way to act, like being a vegetarian, or composting and recycling one's garbage. For the truly converted, ecotourism is a way of life, with a structured belief system and moral code. Their credo is to travel carefully, "leave only footprints, take only photographs." They believe travelers must be knowledgeable and sensitive. They believe in conservation and that their expenditures as tourists should go toward paying for it. Ecotourism has its own organization, the

Ecotourism Society, which is headquartered in Alexandria, Virginia. They hold conferences and send out newsletters, reading lists, and reports. The phenomenon has grown into an industry; special magazines have ecotourists for their audience; the *EcoTraveler*, published in Beaverton, Oregon, bills itself as "the magazine for people who want to experience adventure, nature, and culture in an exciting and responsible way."

For ecotourists, Belize has become a proving ground. It was an unspoiled place worthy of a fresh start. The government and the powers that be in the country were receptive; they understood ecotourism terminology and used their language when they talked about tourism and the environment. They believed they could create its new tradition. "The true definition of ecotourism should mean several things," Virginia Vasquez suggested. "One thing it should mean is economic benefit to local people. It also means that visitors to a natural area interact with the ecosystem. And it must mean too that it is [an area for] visiting by local people as well as those from abroad."

René Nuñez, senior project coordinator with another conserving organization, Programme for Belize, offered a rationale for how conservation must be made to pay for itself and insisted that tourist dollars are a critical part of that. Programme for Belize is the privately funded manager of the lands Coca Cola was shamed into giving up in the northwest corner of the country. The resulting 200,000 acre Rio Bravo Conservation and Management Area was meant to remain a permanent tropical rainforest habitat. But doing good does not come cheap. To get the project going, six million dollars was required to purchase additional land and develop a research station. And that was just the beginning; the Programme for Belize estimated it would then need $400,000 a year into the foreseeable future to meet ongoing management and program expenses. Though it was remarkably successful in corporate and private fund raising, most of it in the United States (Programme for Belize owned a post office box in Vineyard Haven, Massachusetts, through which it collected American donations), everyone agreed that couldn't go on forever. More of the required money, explained Nuñez, would have to come from "sustainable development,"—which is to say "low-impact ecotourism."

"Tourism is one of the easiest, if not the the only way to make money off land that is in protective status," René Nuñez told me. But that creates its own dilemmas. Nuñez, as coordinator, has a large stake in seeing his program survive. But if tourism is the route to pay for its survival, what would that mean? Would it mean pressure to bring more people than might be wise into a pristine region in order to get more dollars from the volume? In 1993, ten groups came from all over the world for educational tours of the Programme's lands. If they want to realize more money, Nuñez acknowledged that this number would have to be expanded to fifteen or twenty groups per year.

The circle of the dilemma could continue, round and round. Will ecotourism—both in Belize and elsewhere in the world—have to resort to charging fewer people more money? If higher prices must be charged, will those higher prices prove to be exclusionary? The many students and young people who travel to environmentally special places out of a desire to help save the rainforest inevitably have little money. Will that mean they can't take such trips, or will their numbers have to be augmented by groups of, say, birdwatchers who, because they tend to be older, will have and be able to spend more money? Ecologically responsible tourism, by definition, means the availability of fewer of the comforts and amenities travelers have come to expect in their accommodation and transportation, so the planners have to assess whether these new types of tourists might happily agree to pay more to get less. Are older and more affluent tourists going to demand more comfortable accommodations and facilities, thereby throwing the whole principle off its axis? Will ecotourist hosts have to compromise on their ideal? Will they have to alter the rustic nature of facilities that exist in rugged, natural spots by bringing in electricity and modern refrigeration? Will they have to allow more water to be used for hot showers and bring in other conveniences in order to make their destinations more appealing? Or perhaps rich people will have to rough it in ecological preserves, while those with more modest means end up with more creature comforts for much less money, forced, as they will be, to take their holidays elsewhere.

Are any of these gestures compatible with maintaining a pristine, rainforest habitat? Is such an environment possible anymore, anyway? These are all questions for which Programme for Belize and Belize tourism must come up with answers.

Kreg Lindberg, an American researcher who analyzed tourism's impact in Belize for the World Wildlife Fund, cautioned that tourism "can have significant negative impacts on the natural environment, and the benefits of ecotourism do not always lead to more support for conservation." Lindberg warned of pitfalls and disappointed expectations. Ecotourism's economic satisfactions, he determined, were far less predictable than optimists might hope. "A more common concern," he wrote in his 1994 report, "is that relatively few jobs are created through eco-tourism and those jobs tend to be seasonal. One of the critical issues facing ecotourism is the difficulty of merging community job creation with a tourism industry that is often owned and managed by foreigners, or at least people outside the local region. Moreover, the benefits of eco-tourism jobs may be outweighed by the economic and social costs. For example, in some communities, tourist demand for resources can lead to local inflation and/or reduced domestic consumption."

Belize has had to struggle with its commitment to conservation and the problem of paying for that. One strategy it considered was to spread the conservation load around and make everyone, not just the eco-tourists, pay. A surtax of twenty dollars U.S. was proposed as a levy on all visitors to the country, whatever the purpose of their trip. This money would fund a Protected Areas Conservation Trust. But when I asked Virginia Vasquez—whose organization's goals would benefit substantially from the additional money—about it, she said that the proposal was experiencing heavy sledding on its way through government committees. The hotel industry was resisting it, believing, incredibly, that a twenty-dollar surtax would drive people away from Belize. Another fear was that the conservation tax dollars might not end up financing conservation, but would find their way, instead, into the government's general coffers.

Such balancing acts are delicate. Ways to find more money need to be balanced with what should become increasingly vigilant protective measures. But whenever one side of this balance sheet improves, the other side suddenly becomes more difficult. Conservationists who established a 400-square-kilometer jaguar preserve in the south of the country in 1988 were concerned at first about the threat, or at least competition, from loggers and poachers. They geared up for that conflict. After a few years, the conservationists seem to have won the battle with poachers as they persuaded the government to extend the sanctuary portion of the preserve from 3 percent of its area to 100 percent. They also upped the status of wardens, giving them powers of arrest. But this battle against loggers and poachers was no sooner won when the battle over tourists had to be engaged. In 1990, 3,000 visitors came to the jaguar preserve. A year later, that total was passed in only eight months. In the years since then, the numbers have been growing exponentially.

Tourists are not loggers or poachers, but the impact they make on an area, an environment, carries its own stresses and costs. Virginia Vasquez knows that these have to be addressed. An immediate task, she declared, has to be the creation of strict management policies for the parks and sanctuaries. She admitted that this may mean quotas for the numbers of visitors each day, or in a season, and that Belize would have to come up with policies. "Increased traffic will eventually mean too many visitors. Numbers quickly reach critical pressure points, and we have to know in advance what those pressure points will be. We need to identify the capacities of all our different locations and set quotas on the visitation that is allowed." She also talked about a need to do more in the way of planning and design, and about the need to establish admission fees, something that, astonishingly, was still rare in Belize.

When it works well, the partnership between tourism, conservation, and local economies can point the way to what, it is hoped, will be the future. A frequently cited example of this unique partnership in Belize can be found about thirty miles north of Belize City: the Community Baboon Sanctuary. Here in the tangled forests that shroud the banks of the Belize River are some of the best examples of the world's diminishing colonies of black howler monkeys. In the fast-gathering dusk, Fallet Young flagged down our car by stepping into the road square in front of us. We slammed on the brakes in order to avoid flattening the skinny, wiry, forty-year-old man, flapping his arms in his torn shirt like a bird struggling to fly while the dust of the road swirled around him.

Fallet Young exercises his reckless maneuver several times a day for the tourist cars that come more and more regularly to Bermudian Landing, his little village of gray, weathered, doorless houses. The day we chose to visit had been a slow day, he explained; there had been only twenty guests in five cars. Some days Fallet and the other guides share five times that many. Our quarry, black howler monkeys, are like two-year-old children; most noisy and most active just before bed. The forest eventually becomes perfectly still and quiet, but this hour, just prior to that, is like the storm before the calm.

"Do you want to see the monkeys?" Fallet leaned in the car window. A half-smoked cigarette had been snuffed and was parked behind his ear. "We'll have to hurry. It'll soon get dark." All around us we could hear their noises, loud squeals and roars like a fight or an ongoing vicious argument. The name "baboon" settled on the howler monkeys by error; the first Europeans, explained Fallet, mistook them for baboons and out of either deference or carelessness the misnomer was never corrected, either on maps or in Belize guidebooks. And howl they do: their roars rained down all around us from the dense foliage of the riverside jungle like eerie messages from a primordial time.

We scrambled along a path that required a climb through a barbed wire fence and then passed between two small houses. This was a village, but in no way the kind of organized or orderly village North Americans understand. It was more like an extended family's compound. On the road stood the centers of commerce and institution, an open-doored school and a thatch-covered stand selling beer, soft drinks, and other necessities such as bars of hard soap and rusty pocket knives. Should you drive your car off the road, you would end up between people's houses on a track among ragged trees that soon disappeared into littered yards; one person's backyard was also somebody else's front yard. The ground was trampled. Wood piles, little patches of kitchen gardens, heaps of excess furniture or cooking utensils were scattered haphazardly. A family group, which included three young women and an elderly man, was outside the houses. Fallet introduced his son, a boy of thirteen dressed in a starched white shirt and carrying a book bag, who had just returned from school. They exchanged a few words, and then Fallet beckoned us to follow quickly down a path into the forest.

Fallet tilted his ear this way and that, trying to discern the whereabouts of the monkeys. The noises were so much from above that I had no ability whatsoever to determine location or even direction. I deferred to our guide. "They'll soon settle down for the night," he explained, "and then it will all be quiet, silent."

Fallet, for us and everyone else who comes through the hamlet of Bermudian Landing, is much more than a tour guide; he is a walking encyclopedia, a gracious man filled with a complete program of minutiae of horticultural and zoological facts about everything from ants to medicinal plants. Carefully he led us along a trail that was part jungle, part woods, sporadically opening into small pastures replete with drying cowpies, all the while delivering an informal lecture about the natural history of all the new things we were seeing. "When I was young I didn't hang around with kids my own age, I listened to the old guys and that's how I learned all this," he explained. He pointed out a billywebb tree and declared that its bark can be chewed as a form of birth control or boiled into a tonic that you drink to cure a cold. The leaves of the bullhorn acacia are used for relief from snake bites. The gombo limo, or "tourist tree," is useful in treating the effects of poison ivy. He pointed out another small plant whose root he had incorporated into a cure for

his wife's back pains. His dissertation caused my mind to flood with stories about all the herbal and plant remedies that are being lost by the
hour while the world's rainforests disappear.

Lecturing appeared to come naturally. For twelve years, Fallet had
been a school teacher, employed in the local elementary school; now he
addresses groups all over Belize, imparting his knowledge of traditional
remedies and bush lore. There is a large demand for his services; there is,
by all accounts, a re-awakening and expanding of interest and concern
for this knowledge both at home, throughout Belize, and abroad. He
had, he told us, been to conferences in the United States and had even
appeared in a program aired on the Discovery Channel. This afternoon
his task was to take newly arrived North American tourists and show us
how our interest as visitors was connected to his job of preserving endangered habitat for his very special monkeys.

Black howler monkeys live in a unique habitat of riverine and cuhane
palm forests found interspersed through areas of Belize, Mexico, and
Guatemala. They spend their lives entirely in the trees, moving comfortably through an arboral world, sleeping, breeding, and giving birth in
the trees and feeding on a variety of foliage. As for so many species of
Earth's flora and fauna, their world is closing in and getting ever smaller;
their habitat is shrinking, the areas hospitable to them are becoming increasingly limited. In 1980 University of Wisconsin monkey expert, Dr.
Robert H. Horwich, came to Belize and was alarmed by the depletion of
the monkey's habitat. The land they favor along the Belize River, in the
northeastern part of the country, was becoming more heavily populated
by humans; the palm and mahogany forests that line the banks, and in
which the monkeys live and on which they depend for food, were being
cut either for lumber or to open land for cultivation and grazing. The
landowners, however, were small farmers whose cash income from meager crops of corn, rice, beans, a cow, and a pig, was paltry. If they let the
monkeys live, how would they support their families? At Horwich's in-
stigation and with help from the World Wildlife Fund, the landowners
got together and came up with a plan that involved both conservation
and economics.

One hundred and thirty-five landowners from eight villages along
the river signed a pledge that committed them to conserving the monkeys and in which they agreed to farming and land-use practices consistent with this conservation. They would leave the trees along the river-
banks uncut. And they would leave strips of forest untouched along all

their property boundaries as habitat for the howlers. They would also leave enough trees to form aerial pathways across large cleared areas, and "baboon bridges" across roads. When clearing land, they promised to leave specific food trees behind for the monkeys.

The affected territory eventually grew to eighteen square miles and stands as a fine example of local, community committment and small-scale conservation. "Grassroots conservation" is the term used in all the publicity brochures. "The motivation to protect the monkeys was high," explained Fallet. "We have grown up with them and are fond of them. They have always been here. We also have an affinity because they are so much like humans in their actions, in the ways they use their hands, in their behavior. So to agree to protect them was not difficult for the people here."

I asked Fallet about compensation for the farmers who participated in the scheme. He looked as if I had asked a very stupid question, a question whose answer should be obvious. "The compensation is that we are preserving our land, our soil, our riverbank doesn't erode, and our monkeys live in harmony with us." But this was the noble answer. He should also have explained, and later did, that the compensation includes tourism. What has happened because of the conservation program, and because of the way the people are managing it and the way they are distributing publicity about it, is that the local economy of Bermudian Landing is becoming a meld of farming, conservation, and tourism. The three overlap and intertwine. Tourists, whether they be fifteen on an admittedly slow day or the hundred who come through on a busy day, are becoming as much a part of the economy of Bermudian Landing as the rice and the corn and the pigs. And they are starting to be recognized as such. The twenty dollars we left with Fallet for being our guide and the four dollars we paid at the little grocery stand to Helen and her son for beer was all part of the cycle. And we were among the cheap tourists; many others stay over, spending the night and leaving another twenty dollars at one of the half dozen bed-and-breakfasts that the local families have opened up. They might well hire a guide for a longer period, rent a canoe for a drift down the river for a look at the monkeys from that perspective, and thus leave more cash behind. Researchers, or serious enthusiasts, come and stay much longer and leave more money. A young American woman was staying for a month, paying room and board to a family while she trekked out each day to observe and make notes on the monkeys. "Yes, it was the plan that tourists would be part of this," said Fallet. "And they are starting to come as we get more publicity."

"Can there be too many tourists?" I asked. Fallet didn't think so. He paused. "Not yet. If we had too many, we would have to decide how to have controls. For the sake of the monkeys and for the sake of the village. But there are not too many yet."

The sun dropped and it was almost dark. The noise of the monkeys diminished, and the night silence enveloped us, punctuated by the chirp of crickets. The young American researcher we encountered on the road said that a troop of monkeys was settled in a tree in a certain pasture. The tree was bare, an almost dead tree, so they would be easy to see. We proceeded up the road and entered a pasture through a worn gate. On the way, we met an anteater ambling out of a thicket who stopped, surprised to encounter us, and then scrambled away. Fallet picked up a soldier ant the size of his thumbnail with his notebook and watched while it sawed off a piece of a page. Turkey vultures circled in the darkening sky. Up in the leafless tree the monkeys were nothing more than black furry balls—safe in their sanctuary—settled in, getting comfortable so that they could sleep until daybreak.

6

Three Trips into Africa

In January of 1857, Captain (later Sir) Richard Francis Burton, British soldier, explorer, linguist, Arabian scholar, and adventurer, arrived in an Arab dhow on the spice island of Zanzibar, in the Indian Ocean off East Africa. Carefully probing along the coast of what is now Kenya, he and his partner, John Hanning Speke, looked for an appropriate place from which they might marshall an expedition inland, into the continent. They tried without satisfaction as far north as Mombasa, and then finally settled on Bagamoyo in what is now northern Tanzania. In a small boat borrowed from the local sultan, they made the crossing from Zanzibar island and landed on the shore of Africa.

Here their adventures began. Under the coconut palms of Bagamoyo, with all of Africa stretched out in front of them, Burton and Speke set about trying to hire the porters and organize the help and transportation their expedition would require. Their stated objective was to search for the headwaters of the Nile. The mystery of the source of the Nile, the storied river of ancient civilizations—biblical and prebiblical—whose annual floods sustained Egypt, had obsessed dreamers for more than a thousand years. By the nineteenth century, the obsession had settled on the English, who were then at the height of the intrepid restlessness that drove the expansion of their empire. With bases at Khartoum and a small presence now at Zanzibar, the English were circling in ever closer on central Africa. Burton and Speke predicted that they, finally, would strike right to the heart.

But in many ways this search for the Nile's source simply provided a rationale; Burton was an inveterate wanderer and explorer—any excuse for an expedition into territories uncharted by whites or Europeans was good enough for him. He was thirty-five years old; in previous adventures he had wandered from his military posts to explore back villages in India. Disguised as an Arab, he had been the first European successfully, and undetected, in and out of the Moslem holy city of Mecca. "Of the gladdest moments in human life," he wrote, "methinks is the departure upon a distant journey into unknown lands. Shaking off with one mighty effort, the fetters of Habit, the leaden weight of Routine, the cloak of many cares and the slavery of Home, one feels once more happy. The blood flows with the fast circulation of childhood. . . . A journey, in fact, appeals to Imagination, to Memory, to Hope,—the three sister Graces of our moral being." Four years earlier he, then too accompanied by Speke, had made a brief foray into Somaliland. But that had been only a preliminary trip, to get his feet wet; now he returned to make what his biography called "The Great Safari," his real, major trip into the African continent. It was the trip that Alan Moorehead, author of *The White Nile* , declared was the beginning of the great age of Central African exploration.

Fifty years later, the bitter quarrels over whether Burton and Speke had actually found the source of the Nile had barely subsided when, in 1908, Winston Spencer Churchill, a thirty-four-year-old budding politician, undersecretary of state for Britain's colonies, landed on the same coast, at Mombasa. Officially, Churchill, in his role as a colonial master, wanted to make a fact-gathering journey inland. Unofficially he wanted to go big game hunting. The Uganda Railway had, by then, been constructed from Mombasa by British engineers, and Churchill's plan was to take this train up to the village of Nairobi. Later, after trekking around the great Lake Victoria, the lake Speke had first seen fifty years earlier, he would resume his journey, taking a boat all the way down the Nile.

Churchill's "safari" started when he got off the train at the end of the line in Uganda. "To this point," he wrote, "we have proceeded by train and steamer with all the power and swiftness of modern communication. If we have traversed wild and lonely lands, it has been in a railway carriage. We have disturbed the lion with the locomotive, and all our excursions have but led back to the iron road. But at Ripon Falls we are to let go our hold upon machinery. Steam and all it means is to be shut off. We are "to cut the painter," and losing the impulsion of the great ship, are for awhile to paddle about upon a vast expanse in a little cock-boat of our own. Back towards Mombasa, three day's journey will cover nine hundred miles. Forward, you will be lucky to make forty in the same time."

After another half century, in 1958, the well-known British author Evelyn Waugh would cover the same territory once more. He would travel from Zanzibar to Mombasa, then move inland to Nairobi and Kilimanjaro before turning south into Tanganyika (Tanzania) and going as far south as Rhodesia (Zimbabwe). The travels of each of these writer-adventurers were meticulously documented. Burton published several books from his copious travel and field notes: *First Footsteps in East Africa, The Lake Regions of Central Africa, The Nile Basin,* as well as having his travels documented in biographies: first by his widow, Lady Isabel Burton and later by Edward Rice. Churchill, after his trip, published *My African Journey*; Waugh wrote *A Tourist In Africa.*

Three famous travelers took three journeys, spaced fifty years apart over a hundred years, into the same countryside. But they would be incredibly different expeditions. If the same journey were documented again now, almost forty years after Waugh's, how different it would be again.

For westerners, travel into Africa has always been, and still is, the most exotic trip of all. The mere thought takes a stranglehold on our imagination. Nowadays, when thousands of tourists a year go in and out of the one-time "Dark Continent," its images—photographs of lion safaris and the pyramids of Egypt—are still consistently the most popular to grace the covers of travel magazines. No place in the world, however, is a better example of how travel, and everything about it, has changed—both in its techniques and methods, and in the attitudes toward it—than journeys into Africa.

In 1856, writes Alan Moorehead in his epic study of African explorers, central Africa was "almost as remote and strange as outer space is today." In the century between Burton and Waugh, the technological changes brought to travel were so dramatic it would be a gross understatement to label them "remarkable"; such changes would have been unimaginable to those who had traveled but a generation before. Also dramatic were the physical developments that changed the landscape of Africa: with colonization, road, railway, port, and town building had exploded everywhere. It was not in any way the same world.

Burton, on his journey, traveled on foot most of the time. But

Churchill, a mere fifty years later, had the trains of the newly constructed Uganda Railway as well as everything from bicycles to steam
boats. Waugh, another short fifty years later, had access to airplanes,
automobiles, and buses, and the wild countryside had been transformed
into the nations of Kenya, Tanganyika, and Uganda. Were any of them
to go now, their airplane and bus travel could be scheduled—to the
hour—far in advance; their hotel, rental car, and safari camp reservations could be secured instantly on worldwide telephone, computer, and
fax networks. A hundred and fifty years ago, Burton and Speke had to
negotiate everything as they went, hacking their way along jungle paths,
never sure where they were going or what awaited them at the end of a
day. Had they waited a century and a half, their itineraries and every
move could have been planned and plotted from the comforts of home
or from the office of their travel agent. Their task then was not to follow
a plan; rather, with the assistance of their crude instruments, it was to
make an original record, meticulously notated, of flora, fauna, temperature, geography, and peoples. For Burton, points out Alan Moorehead,
"nothing was beyond his observation: the languages and customs of the
tribes, the geography of the land, its botany, geology and meteorology."

It is not enough to say that things such as technological advances
alone were what made the journeys of our three travelers so different
from one another. What had changed dramatically as well was the zeit-
geist, both for the Africans, but more significantly, for the Europeans.
Burton's Africa was the "Dark Continent," a land of mystery and danger.
Maps at the time showed detail only for thin ribbons along the coasts;
the interior was a huge blank space often labeled in large, foreboding
letters, "Unexplored Territory." Only the bravest and most intrepid of
Europeans would venture there, and their exploits immediately became
legend. Burton's famous contemporary, missionary doctor David Livingstone, at this time had been much further south, on the Zambezi in
what is now Zambia and Zimbabwe, where he had been the first white
European to sight Victoria Falls. But no European had ventured where
Burton and Speke wanted to go: to Lakes Tanganyika and Victoria; to
"the mountains of the Moon."

Believing it would ease his journey, Burton fell to an old habit and
disguised himself as an Arab, using the name Haji Mirza Abdullah. In
part, this was a matter of comfort; Burton had spent much of his life in
hot countries and understood that the loose, flowing fabrics used by the
peoples native to those places kept them cool, protected from both the

temperature and the blazing equatorial sun. But he also had a precautionary reason; he didn't want to be recognized too readily as a European. Convinced such recognition could be dangerous, he ordered his companions to follow his example. This, in the end, was all for nought because Burton failed to convince the stubborn Speke who, maintaining his Englishman's stiff upper lip, insisted on suffering in his tweed jacket, hat, tight woolen trousers and knee-high boots (though with the peculiarly Victorian notion to "toughen himself," Speke sometimes went without the boots).

By the time Waugh arrived at Dar-Es-Salaam a century later, things in this regard had changed dramatically. To be white was no longer anything of a compromise; a British person could stride freely into East Africa as if he owned the land (and in many cases he believed he did). With colonial arrogance at its apex, he felt no need for disguise. Correspondingly, Burton's rules for comfort rather than Speke's prissiness had won the day. "During the day," Waugh reported on his observations, "the officials who are the main white population, wear white shorts and open shirts, looking like grotesquely overgrown little boys who have not yet qualified for the first eleven at their private schools." In a throwback to the attitude of Speke and other British officials who had been appalled by Burton showing himself in any way other than as a British colonial officer, Waugh grumps, "I wonder how much the loss of European prestige in hot countries is connected with the craven preference for comfort over dignity."

Evelyn Waugh spent his time calling on an array of Africa-based English friends and officials. He also went "on safari." A "safari," the trek within Africa taken for granted by every visitor nowadays, is a word introduced into English usage by Richard Burton. The word comes from Kiswahili possibly with Arabic roots, and means "to journey." A safari, which today can mean something as simple as a day's jaunt through the country in a Land Rover, for Burton required elaborate preparation. Most caravans in those days still set off in search of slaves, and maybe a bit of ivory. A caravan heading for the interior would expect to be away for at least a year and would have everything required to sustain it for that length of time carried on its porters' heads. Alan Moorehouse observes that a caravan of 100 men plus an armed guard was regarded as quite a modest affair.

Burton proposed to take 170 men with him and Speke. No amount of preparation, of course, could quite ease his mind and expel the fear that,

no matter what he did, he would inevitably face severe hardship and serious danger. But Burton did his best. A well-furnished expedition for
him required, according to his own lists: Arms and ammunition, including 100 pounds of gunpowder and 20,000 copper caps, shields, swords,
daggers, and knives. For comfort at the end of the day, there was camp
furniture—tents and bedding, chairs, tables, mosquito nets, mats, car-
pets, and whatever else was needed for the proper English home in the
field. Mapping and surveying instruments, including several types of
compasses, thermometers, a chronometer, sundial, rain guages, and numerous other pieces of scientific equipment would help him know
where, or at least in what direction, he was going. For his reports, he carried numerous writing materials and blank diary books, packets of paper,
pencils, inks, meteorological tables, maps, star charts, account books,
water colors and other drawing materials, atlases, grammars of African
languages, and manuals of surveying and mapmaking. Burton's medi-
cine chest included quinine, morphia, citric acid, chiretta root, and a
preparation known as "Warburg's drops," a mixture of quinine and
opium flavored with sloe plums that was touted as a cure-all. For personal use there were one dozen bottles of brandy, a box of cigars, five
boxes of tea (each six pounds), and so on, including spices, pickles, soap,
vinegar, and oil. His porters also carried numerous miscellaneous items:
scarlet broadcloth for presents to important chieftains, umbrellas,
knives, penknives, 200 fishing hooks, a sewing kit, toilet articles, nails,
grinders, augers, bits, saws, and chisels for a traveling carpentry shop,
and a Union Jack for flying at any opportune moment or occasion.
When all was elaborately prepared, they set off.

The routine of a day's journey was tedious, disciplined, methodical,
hard work. At 3:00 A.M., the Goan porters would rise and build a fire for
breakfast. Burton and Speke would have tea or coffee, rice-milk gruel,
and yogurt-raised flat cakes or a porridge. In the background the Baluchi
(Arab guards) chanted their morning prayers. Setting out is described in
Rice's biography using Burton's diary notes: By 5:00 A.M. the camp was
"fairly roused." This was a critical moment: "The porters have promised
overnight, to start early, and to make a long, wholesome march." But
then arguments began: the pagazis were cold, still tired, lazy, rebellious;
they importuned for more pay. Burton developed a strategy to deal with
them. "We return to our tents," he wrote, "in this manner ignoring
them and thus implying a loss of pay—for some haggling on his part
seemed to be the only way to force the porters to work. Then, in a rush,

the pagazis would pick up their loads and start the march. My companion and I, when well enough to ride, mounted our asses, led by the gun-bearers . . . when unfit for exercise, we are borne in hammocks, slung on long poles, and carried by two men at a time."

When all was ready, the chief guide, dressed in animal skins, raised a furled blood-red flag, "the sign of a caravan from Zanzibar," and set off followed by a pagazi beating a kettle drum. The pagazis would pour out of the kraal "in a disorderly mob" and wait a few hundred yards away for stragglers; the huts would be fired either by accident or mischievousness, and finally the caravan would be on its way, accompanied by "mindless noise." The normal recreations of a march are whistling, singing, shouting, hooting, drumming, imitating the cries of birds and beasts, repeating words which are never used except on journeys . . . and abundant squabbling."

Trouble was never far from them. Three days into the trip, his Baluchi guards mutinied. Rice wrote, quoting Burton's report:

The Baluchis seemed continually mutinous, taking any forebearance on Burton's part as a sign of weakness, and became daily more insolent and threatening. One day as he was marching along, gun over shoulder and dagger in hand, he became conscious that two of his men were unpleasantly near, and after a while one of them, unaware that Burton understood his language, urged the other to strike. Burton did not hesitate a moment. Without looking around, he thrust his dagger, and stabbed the man dead on the spot. The other, who fell on his knees and begged for mercy, was spared.

Wrote Burton of the journey; "I tasted all the bitterness that can fall to the lot of those who explore regions unvisited by their own colour."

Without doubt, what makes Burton interesting to us and what has turned him and other similar explorers a century and a half later into mythic, fabled characters, were their incredible troubles. They confronted the kinds of difficulties few of us can even imagine enduring, and whether they were undertaken for reasons of altruism or egotism, it still lifts them and their exploits into the super-human realm. Every journey, even though undertaken with military-like planning and organization, faced serious misadventures. Catastrophe was standard for Burton. On his earlier trip into Somaliland he had almost been killed. One night everyone was asleep, but sometime after 2:00 A.M. Burton was awakened by shouts that the camp was under attack. "Hearing a rush of

men like a strong wind, I sprang up, called for my sabres, and sent Lieutenant Herne to ascertain the force of the foray." This Lieut. Herne found
the enemy everywhere and learned that their own guards had run away.
Speke, Burton, and Herne tried to fend off the attackers. The marauders
bore javelins and long heavy daggers. Burton was armed with only a
sabre, but "Speke and Herne had their Colts which they used with
deadly effect. But soon the chambers were emptied, and unable to reload
easily, they had to use the revolvers as clubs." They were against twenty
or forty Somali attackers and, remarkably, lost only one of their own,
Lieut. William Stroyan, who was "cut to pieces by the Somalis." Burton
himself was left with a serious wound to his face, his jaw smashed by a
javelin. "A spearman stepped forward, left his javelin in my mouth, and
retired before he could be punished."

Attacks, mutinies, illnesses; to travel into unknown regions such as East
Africa a century and a half ago implied heavy doses of all three. Burton
had to recover from a case of malaria before even leaving Zanzibar. Rice
recounts, "Continually, both Burton and Speke were ill, pursued by illnesses, as if illness had become a permanent member of the expedition,
an unseen, unfriendly companion who nagged, teased, struck down,
and even paralyzed. When Burton threw off his latest fever, his mouth
became ulcerated, and he was unable to talk. At the same time, he could
not walk. The bad food, the climate, the jungle, and the nagging illnesses turned his mind into two split sections. He experienced insom-
nia, depressions, delirium. . . . The native members of the caravan fared
little better, and they deserted steadily, pilfering what they could. The
very coin—the cloth, wire, and beads—needed to pay daily expenses was
stolen by men eager to make their way back to the coast and better
health. Burton and Speke were now so ill that they could not control
their men. Burton wrote that he and Speke were "physically and morally
incapacitated for any exertion beyond balancing ourselves upon our
donkeys."

A hundred years later, a safari for Evelyn Waugh was a relative piece
of cake. Waugh set off on his long safari pronouncing it "a term now
used to designate a luxurious motor tour." Waugh would travel through
land that had become a colonial nation, Tanganyika, (now Tanzania)
with a friend, a colonial ex-army officer, in his Mercedes Benz. He also
was able to fly when he wished and, most important, had the luxury to
make such choices: "Today I booked to fly to Kilwa. My resolution to es-

chew aeroplanes—like Belloc's to eschew trains on the "Path To Rome"—has had to be broken. The road is impassable at this season; a steamship plies from Mombasa but to take that would have extended the expedition by some three weeks and inflicted a visit of unbearable length on my kind hosts."

A short hundred years earlier Burton and Speke could be bogged down in a camp for three weeks just to recover from their illnesses, get their rain-soaked gear in order, or placate and harmonize their rebellious employees. By the time they reached Lake Tanganyika, available to Waugh in an hour's plane ride, they had been in Africa fourteen months and on the trail seven and a half months.

The personalities of these three individuals may certainly have been very different, but the times that created them, too, were different and were changing with extraordinary speed. The post-war 1950s and Clement Attlee's England could not have turned out a Richard Burton, nor would it have been able to abide him, should he have shown up. When Evelyn Waugh arrived in Tanganyika, he was entering a different Africa than Burton and Speke could have dreamed of a century before; but he had also left a different England than they had. The two wars, industrialism, and modern communications had changed England and Englishmen as much, if not more, than colonialism and road building had changed East Africa. As Alan Moorehead observed, "the doubts and uncertainties that have overtaken life in the twentieth century through two world wars and a plethora of political and scientific inventions were unthinkable then." Africa had moved from the slave trade through colonialism and was about to enter a phase of post-colonialism. The Western empires that had dominated the nineteenth century were shaky, worn-out shadows, increasingly filled with self-doubts. Not only the British Empire as a fact, but also the notion of colonialism as a theory was about to collapse in upon itself everywhere.

The differing personalities of our writers reflects in a larger way the change in attitudes and enlightenment at home in England and in the western world in general. Much of this change came as a result of westerners witnessing the impact of contact and development in the visited lands. Biology, sociology, and anthropology were as important in making the trip of Waugh different from that of Burton as were technology and engineering.

A fascinating case in point is the attitude toward wild animals and how that changed from Burton's time to Waugh's. Burton and Speke were not far into Africa when they had an opportunity to pause from their arduous travels to hunt hippos. The following account is partly in the words of Burton's diaries, partly edited by Edward Rice's biography:

> They set out in a forty-foot canoe with the Baluchis and Sidi Bombay (their main guide) at early dawn, when the wild beasts are hungriest and tamest.
>
> They came to a pool where they found their prey.
>
> The mise en scene is perfect: the bright flush of morning, the cool, clear air, the river with its broad breast swelling between two rows of tall luxuriant trees, and, protruding from the mirrory surface, the black box-heads flanked with small pointed ears, and, not a little resembling the knight in old chessmen . . .
>
> My companion (Speke), a man of speculative turn, experiments upon the nearest optics with buckshot and two barrels of grape. . . . The eyes, however, are obliquely placed: the charge scatters, the brute, unhurt, slips down like a seal.

Finally Speke makes a successful hit.

> There is a splash, a struggle, the surface foams, and Behemoth, with open mouth like a butcher's stall, and bleeding like a gutter-spout, plunges above the surface. . . . At last a coup de grace, speeding through the ear, finds out the small brain; the brute sinks, fresh gore purples the surface, and bright bubbles seeth up from the bottom. Hippo has departed this life: we wait patiently for his reappearance, but he reappears not.

This is killing of a quite wanton nature. It is impossible to recover the carcass of the kill. The dead animals will not provide supper for the troops; Africa is filled with a zillion animals, and for Speke to pot a few is mere recreation. For Speke, like so many explorer-adventurers of his generation, the hunt and the kill were deeply ingrained. It was what he did and wanted to do everywhere, whether in India, Tibet, Africa, or on his father's property in the West Country of England. He lived and traveled to "collect specimens." His objective, he had stated, of a trip through unexplored Africa was to find the Nile and sail down it, gathering specimens of rare birds and animals with which to furnish a natural history museum in his father's country house in England. The slaughter-style hunt, inconceivable today, was undertaken without a second thought by him and so many others in his time.

Winston Churchill, fifty years later, was no slouch either when it came to the enjoyment of a big game hunt. A photograph in *My African Journey* shows the future savior of democracy standing with his rifle in classic trophy pose, his foot perched on the head of a freshly felled elephant. Another photograph has Churchill and three companions riding (by all appearances comfortably) on the cow catcher of a Uganda Railway train engine, the best vantage point, they argue, from which to spot game. Churchill writes:

> One of the best ways of shooting game in this part of the world, and certainly the easiest, is to get a trolley and run up and down the line. The animals are so used to the passage of trains and natives along the one great highway that they do not, as a rule, take much notice, unless the train or trolley stops, when their suspicions are at once aroused. The sportsman should, therefore, slip off without allowing the vehicle or the rest of the party to stop, even for a moment; and in this way he will frequently find himself within two hundred and fifty or three hundred yards of his quarry, when the result will be governed solely by his skill, or want of skill, with the rifle.

For Churchill, a little like for Speke and Burton, Africa was a continent of limitless game; no notion of depletion of species entered his mind. He likened the railway to "one slender thread of scientific civilization, of order, authority, and arrangement drawn across the primeval chaos of the world." Beyond it,

> the plains are crowded with wild animals. From the windows of the carriage the whole zoological garden can be seen disporting itself. Herds of antelope and gazelle, troops of zebras—sometimes four or five hundred together—watch the train pass with placid assurance. . . . With field-glasses one can see that it is the same everywhere, and can distinguish long files of black wildebeeste and herds of red kongoni—the hartebeeste of South Africa—and wild ostriches walking sedately in twos and threes, and every kind of small deer and gazelle.

Although Churchill does his share of shooting and may view the populations of game as limitless, a twinge of conscience, nowhere evident in John Hanning Speke, sneaks in, signal of a small change in attitude. After a day's successful hunt, where he has brought down a rhinoceros in a particularly graphic kill, the future leader of Great Britain allows himself to reflect on the relationship between visitor and prey. He writes moodily, almost regretfully, with a sensibility that, at least in the popular literature, was novel. "There is time to reflect with some detachment that, after all, we were the aggressors; we it is who have forced the conflict by an unprovoked assault with murderous intent upon a peaceful herbivore; that if there is such a thing as right and wrong between man and beast—and who shall say there is not?—right is plainly on his side." Churchill, ever the soldier, couldn't resist an analogy that made him even more apologetic toward his animal prey. "Suffice it to say that, in all the elements of neurotic experience, such an encounter seems to me fully equal to half an hour's brisk skirmish at six or seven hundred yards—and with an important addition. In war there is a cause, there is duty, there is the hope of glory, for who can tell what may not be won before night? But here at the end is only a hide, a horn, and a carcase, over which the vultures have already begun to whirl."

By the time Waugh arrived in East Africa, the hunt and slaughter of animals were the furthest things from his mind or desire. He was not a hunter, and neither, by then, were many in the larger society. Certainly among travelers, there were by then reasons other than an elaborate hunting expedition to lure them into the wilds. Waugh and his host visited a customs shed where he viewed, with some revulsion, great heaps of elephant tusks and rhino horns bound for India. With implicit disdain, he observed that the purpose of this vast pile of horn, from which the Asians ground out a powder to make aphrodisiac elixirs, was "eventually to inflame the passions of the Chinese." And there was a lingering worry. The animal populations by this time were no longer seen as limitless or infinite. Poaching had become a troublesome issue. The relationship between man and beast, in the growing opinion of many who could think, was one to be regulated, one that must be balanced. This implied that what also had to be balanced was the relationship between visitor and host landscape.

If the attitude of the traveler toward the wild fauna of Africa was changing, so most definitely had the traveler's attitude toward the people of the continent. In Burton's time, Africans were reduced to types. First, they were trouble or potential trouble, always to be guarded against. Then they were servants, porters, guards, and cooks. Women, if they weren't doing the labor of oxen, were for sex. Burton categorized the Africans he met in a totally narcissistic or egocentric manner, based completely on their responses to him. He typed Africans according to the looks they gave him. They were types who aproached him either with "the stare furtive," the "open stare," or the "stare curious or intelli-gent." In all, he identified a dozen such types of stares, leading all the way to "the stare greedy," "the stare drunken," "the stare flattering," and "the stare contemptuous." None of this, of course, assumed any possible connections between real, communicating people; the distances were formalized and unbridgeable.

Burton, however, was an exception in one sense among Europeans of his time. He had the reputation of "going native" at every opportunity and was frequently criticized or ridiculed for this propensity. A fanatical linguist, he took every opportunity to get close to tribal and foreign peo-ples so that he could learn their languages and study their practices. Bur-ton developed a system to help him learn the basics of any new language within two weeks, and by the end of his life he claimed mastery of twenty-nine different tongues. Many of the exotic practices he was fasci-nated by were sexual—later in his life he would translate the *Kama Sutra* and other eastern erotica—and he had a reputation for bedding as many women as he could—again, supposedly, in the interest of anthropologi-cal science. Everyone he met—threatening, troublesome, or benign— was to him an interesting specimen.

Because of his peculiar personality and unusual openmindedness, Burton was more likely than his contemporaries to recognize and appreciate in-telligence in an individual and ascribe it to a group. His fascination with people pompted him to grant them at least a bit of humanity. To many of his contemporaries, a native person was totally objectified: either for use, to be put to service; or troublesome, to be avoided or eliminated. Individ-ual natives who were pet favorites among the entourage—such as Speke's guide, Sidi Bombay Mubarak—might be referred to by name in the ac-counts of the trip and might be recognized as possessing human quali-ties, although probably more in keeping with those allowed your favorite labrador retriever. Other natives participating in an expedition were like mules; fed and ignored when doing their job, whipped and complained about when not. All the rest of Africa was not to be trusted, and barely to be known.

In Churchill's time Africans were essentially caricatures in the eyes of whites, wild and pagan beings who were believed to be in need of the gentle though firm hand of civilization. The half century since Burton had seen Europeans not only explore East Africa, but also wage wars with tribes and slavers and carve up the continent into their own

spheres of influence. British expeditionary forces had fought and defeated the Arabs on the upper Nile and the African tribes in Uganda,
then called the kingdom of Buganda. Missionaries, soldiers, and trading
companies had united to pronounce the Africans "savages" and to pre-
empt any possibility of the traditional tribal chiefs ruling their own territories. In 1886, the Germans and the British carved up east Africa between themselves, the British taking the northern portion (Kenya) and
the Germans the south (Tanganyika). When they announced the results
to the sultan of Zanzibar, who was left with only his island, there was absolutely nothing he could do about it. In 1896 the British laid a further
claim to Uganda. The young Churchill, who had been first to Africa with
General Kitchener's army up the Nile in the 1890s, enthusiastically en-
joyed the rituals of meeting the various tribal leaders, who were brought
like anachronistic relics before him. He relished the pomp while they
were lined up in ill-fitting uniforms, laden with odd medals, their outfits
mingling British military gear with feathered tribal dress. But he was ever
the imperialist. Going through his mind, without cease, was a search for
an answer as to how the wild region might be ultimately subdued and
what its potential was as a "White Man's country."

He settled on the issue of clothing. "It is unquestionably an advantage," he observed, "that the East African negro should develop a taste
for civilized attire. In no more useful and innocent direction could his
wants be multiplied and his desires excited, and it is by this process of
assimilation that his life will gradually be made more complicated, more
varied, less crudely animal, and himself raised to a higher level of economic utility." This was yet half a century before tribespeople would
dress up in their traditional war paint and ceremonial garb purely for the
benefit of the tourist photograph and in exchange for spare change.
Churchill observed tribal chiefs in their more natural, traditional form:

> In his war dress the Kikuyu, and, still more, the Masai warrior, is a
> striking if not impressive, figure. His hair and body are smeared
> with the red earth of his native land, compounded into a pigment
> by mixture with the slimy juice of the castor-oil plant, which
> abounds. Fantastic head-dresses, some of ostrich feathers, others of
> metal or leather; armlets and leglets of twisted wire; stripes of white
> clay rubbed across the red pigment; here and there an old pot-hat or
> some European garment, incongruously contrasted with leopard
> skins and bulls' horns; broad, painted cow-hide shields, and spears

with soft iron blades nearly four feet long, complete a grotesque and indecorous picture.

Yet Churchill wanted to change things, for he had the European's ethnocentric view of linear progress.

> The course of these reflections has carried me a good deal further than the politics of Nairobi would seem to justify; and I hasten to return to the question with which I started: 'Can the Highlands of East Africa be made a white man's country?' Let us examine this by fresh process. As one rides or marches through the valleys and across the wide plateaux of these uplands, braced by their delicious air, listening to the music of their streams, and feasting the eye upon their natural wealth and beauty, a sense of bewilderment overcomes the mind. How is it they have never become the home of some superior race, prosperous, healthy, and free? Why is it that, now a railway has opened the door and so much has been published about them, there has not been one furious river of immigration from the cramped and unsanitary jungle-slums of Europe?

The countries Waugh traveled through in the late 1950s, Kenya and Tanganyika (now Tanzania), were then still colonies ruled in the traditional imperial manner by governors sent from Britain with white-skinned district commissioners answering to them. Waugh also spent time in Rhodesia (now Zimbabwe), which was then still a white-ruled apartheid state. But the thunder clouds of coming changes loomed too ominously to miss. Waugh might offer amusing commentaries about native African tribespeople; in southern Tanganyika he encountered a village of the formerly Hehe tribe, who once defeated both a German column and the Masai. But "now they mostly go to work in the copper mines and return dressed as cinema cowboys. There were many of them swaggering about the streets with spurs, ornamented leather work, brilliant shirts, huge hats." Earlier he had been introduced to a nonogenarian Dervish, a local leader in a sect of fanatical Muslims "who looked like a black Father Christmas." Waugh observed on the wall of the man's home a framed picture of King George VI with an inscription signed by a former governor in the name of His Majesty "as a record of the valuable services rendered by him to his own Country and People and to the British Government in advancing the Moslem religion. It seemed," noted Waugh, "an odd tribute from the Defender of the Faith."

Waugh's quaint anthropological observations notwithstanding, a traveler by his time was ready to acknowledge a shared humanity with Africans not much credited earlier. Accompanying this was even some notion that they were, in fact, his hosts. One evening, Waugh was a guest of the paramount chief of the Chagga tribe near Arusha in northwestern Tanganyika. As he recorded it:

> Dinner that evening was highly enjoyable. R., the brigadier and an English accountant and his newly arrived wife and an elderly Greek doctor and his wife comprised the party. Marealle (the chief) was in anything but tatters and rags; a dandy with great social grace. His house, not fifty miles from the nearest Masai *bomas*, is of a date with everything in Moshi, entirely European in design and furniture; tiled bathrooms with towels to match their pastel tints, a radiogram in every room, the latest illustrated papers from England and the U.S.A., a grog tray on the verandah. Only the cooking was African, two delicious curries. I cajoled the accountant's wife into asking our host to turn off the wireless.

Waugh, without being quite a sharp social critic, acknowledges the humanity and the tragedy of the last great chief of the Matabele, Lobengula. He argues persistently against theories that the ruins of Great Zimbabwe could have been left by anyone other than Africans. And he makes a case for better preparation of blacks to run their own show, as inevitably they would.

How different these three books are, appearing over a mere century. Burton is overwhelmed by the continent and, in the face of tremendous difficulty and life-threatening odds, must explore it. Churchill enters a continent covered with a veneer of European order and, with a thoroughly parochial bent, sees the chance for further exploitation. "It is no good trying to lay hold of Tropical Africa with naked fingers," he wrote, arguing for investment and modernity. "Civilization must be armed with machinery if she is to subdue these wild regions to her authority. Iron roads, not jogging porters; tireless engines, not weary men; steam and skill, not sweat and fumbling: there lies the only way to tame the jungle—more jungles than one."

By the time Waugh arrives the dream has progressed, has been fulfilled you might say, to the point where all is almost spoiled. Africa has been saddled—either through the colonial dribble-down effect, or through the minds and dispositions of the Europeans who have ended up there—with the worst of Europe. The effect is a combination of silly and tragic. Certainly, in Waugh's acid opinion, the towns of colonial Africa offered the worst of Europe. He spends a night in Rhodesia at an "English Pub." "I left my bags in a sad little, stuffy bedroom, lit by a single faintly glowing bulb, and I wandered out. Attracted by a neon sign which read: 'TAVERN. OLD ENGLISH ATMOSPHERE,' I descended concrete steps to a basement-bar, softly lit and pervaded by 'background music.' The barman was white and wore his hair in a Teddy-boy style. A white lady, whom I took to be a tart, sat before him. She had an odd look of Mrs Stitch. Four or five youngish Rhodesians were drinking with her. The old English atmosphere was provided by chair and tables made to look rather like beer barrels."

The continent that a century before could be entered only with the adrenalin of bravado was now stifling with petty bureaucracy. Arriving into Northern Rhodesia, Waugh had to stop and fill out elaborate entry forms, a fact that irked him and drew forth his considerable sarcasm. "I say the usual official forms, but one was unique in my experience. In order to spend one night in transit at Ndola I was required, among other things, to inform the Federal authorities of the names, ages, sexes, dates and places of birth of children not accompanying me, date and place of marriage. What European languages could I write? The oddest demand was to state 'sex of wife.'" He spent some time filling out this and accompanying forms, and then

> Looking at the form again, I see I was too conscientious. Visitors for periods of less than sixty days need not have affirmed pretensions to write English. Rhodesians have good reason to be suspicious of English journalists, but it is, surely, naive to suppose that it takes sixty days to compose an article traducing them. Nor need I have stated that I was free from infectious or communicable diseases. That seems odder still, for it is one of the few sane questions. No country welcomes the plague-stricken. In fifty-nine days an active carrier should be able to broadcast his diseases liberally.

Waugh, unable to contain his irony, reaches the conclusion: "Here fully displayed are the arts of modern government for which, it is popularly believed, the native races are not yet far enough advanced."

A third of a century later, the lands entered by Burton, Churchill, and Waugh have changed dramatically again. Lest I appear to be bowing too obediently in the direction of linear progress, I should say that my first trip into Africa, in 1992, was actually more like Burton's than Churchill's or Waugh's. The changes having taken place in the part of Africa I was to visit were not ones of obedient improvement in either comforts or atmosphere. I was to be part of a television documentary crew shooting in Angola. Angola was then a dangerous and chaotic place. Thirty-five years after Waugh, not only had colonialism completely fallen in upon itself, but the brief generation of independence, too, had in many places turned sour. Angola was a case in point. Back in 1958, the traveler to this country would have found road and communications systems among the best in Africa and cities that looked unabashedly European—the Portugese who colonized Angola made no apology for building a more prosperous, grander version of what they had at home. But by 1992 it had been through thirty years of war. Fifteen years of a war for independence had chased the Portugese colonials out; that was followed by fifteen years of civil war to see who would run the new country now that they were gone. On top of this, Angola was one of those unfortunate places that the Soviet and American superpowers had chosen as a surrogate battlefield for the cold war, each global ideology arming a different one of the tribal combatants. After fifteen years of brutal fighting, the basic infrastructure of a once-functioning country was in shambles; civic life was a disastrous chaos.

We flew from Harare, Zimbabwe, to land at night at a huge city airport in Luanda and found it in almost total darkness. When originally built, Luanda's airport was meant to be a JFK or an O'Hare, but for more than a decade it had been barely maintained. It was shabby, dank, dark, and dangerous. Once in the city, we found the hotels, streets, shops were no different. Over the course of fifteen days we stayed only once in accommodations that had running water. It would have been all right if these had been traditional African structures designed so that one finds water and lavatories elsewhere, but these were the ruins of western European architecture. Every room had all the fixtures: lovely, commodious sinks and tubs but in every case their faucets had been seized shut by rust and corrosion and neglect. The Africans had to make the most tedious compensation. In one hotel, in the central Angola city of Huambo, the chambermaid climbed five flights of stairs (the elevator had long since ceased working) carrying five gallon tubs of water on her head. She did this for each guest in the hotel, leaving her delivery in the bathroom that had, by my count, six faucets—none of them working—and a toilet that had long ceased to flush. Angola had telephones on which you could get through perhaps 4 percent of the time. Currency, traded by women on the street corner at a rate twenty times better than that of the national bank, inflated almost hourly. Because of the war, no roads had been repaired in fifteen years, and those that weren't seeded with land-mines were so broken up by deep, water-filled potholes that travel was worse than impossible on both body and vehicle, not to mention extremely dangerous. Unlike the ability of Waugh and Churchill to depend on safe systems and a reliable bureaucracy, we were back to Burton's practice of negotiating our way at every turn as we went—we piggy-backed on the goodwill of the U.N., foreign aid agencies, the churches, or local political operators. Danger was everywhere, either in the form of hidden landmines, bandits, or the two armies soldiered mainly by teenagers cockily dangling AK47's. In the dark airport, upon entry, I stood for ten deeply unsettling minutes while a boy—who would have been of about high-school age anywhere else—glared at me across his automatic rifle. He was examining my travel documents. After a few minutes, in an effort to be helpful, I leaned forward only to note, to my dismay, that the well-armed boy, unable to read, was looking at everything upside down. On the tarmac of the same airport a few days later, we witnessed soldiers brazenly pilfering from shipments of supplies meant for aid agencies and destitute citizens. When I asked a soldier where in the airport I might locate a toilet, he made an arc with his arm indicating the whole of the terminal and compound: "It is all a toilet," he said.

Africa has changed once more. Many of its countries now are run not by faraway colonial despots but by local, black dictators, equally ruthless and exploitive of both their land's resources and their people. Populations have mushroomed, and the countries have been urbanized. The old European colonial cities have been overwhelmed by massive African cities, financed perhaps by Western foreign aid or foreign bank-loan moneys but distinctly African in their operation. The non-African settlers have been terrified and humbled in Kenya by the Mau Maus and in Zimbabwe by the brutal war of independence. In Uganda many were chased out of the country, literally, by the 1970s regime of Idi Amin. Westerners now live temporarily in these countries, not as the governors or consuls of colonial days, but as professionals—doctors, lawyers, engineers, and scientists—ostensibly on loan to the local governments, with their salaries paid by the foreign aid offices of places such as Norway or the Netherlands.

In 1996 you can reach Nairobi in a jumbo jet from London in nine hours. You can fly anywhere within Kenya in another hour. The Mombasa coast is a string of Italian- and German-owned hotels and beach pleasure palaces. Tourism has increasingly become a funneling of Westerners (and a rapidly growing number of Japanese) into private, heavily guarded beach or safari theme parks. The wild animals John Hanning Speke and Winston Churchill enthusiastically hunted are so threatened with extinction they must be protected on game farms. The ferocious tribesmen who terrified and challenged the explorers are now industrial workers, or teachers, or bureaucrats. At their most dangerous, they are the pickpockets and muggers working the slums of Nairobi and Kampala. And, like Richard Burton, the modern visitor returns from East Africa with tales of the Africans—how these mysterious people we ostensibly went to visit looked back at us. One hundred and fifty years later real communication is still minimal.

7

Can Tourism Save
the Elephants of Africa?

Somewhere at about 39,000 feet over the Central African Republic, or over the southern Sudan, about an hour prior to landing in Nairobi, I am roused by a "welcome to Kenya" video that swirls onto the front-of-cabin screens. I look around at the other passengers on the British Airways 747 and sense that this is an appreciated diversion. Most of us are tourists, eager, as we get closer now to our destination, to be yanked out of the stupor that has been induced by eight hours of airplane food, airplane air, and cramped, fitful sleep; we are all anxious to get on with what we have saved our money and come all this way for. We sit up attentively and, as we watch, satisfaction comes quickly; bull elephants and herds of wildebeest fill the screen, underscored by full symphonic flourish. The stale cabin air crackles with a happy, electric anticipation; the prevailing images of east Africa are reinforced; we are put perfectly in the mood for the Africa of our dreams.

At the center of the video, though, is something not quite expected, something that catches many of us completely off guard. The host, dressed in bush khaki and wearing those impossibly short shorts African White Hunter types seem to favor, details all the fun we're going to have. But then, looking straight at the camera, he intones a presumptuous, rather astonishing pronouncement: "Your holiday," he says, looking us collectively in the eye and pausing for effect, "guarantees the future for wildlife."

None of us miss this; we sit upright, delighted by a kind of unexpected reassurance, aroused by a novel sense of purpose that had not remotely possessed us before. Not pausing to think this preposterous, I sense that everyone on the airplane suddenly feels better. Our expensive excursion vacations are no longer simply luxurious self-indulgences; there is an important job to be done, and we, apparently, have a role to play. Without us the future of wildlife would not be guaranteed. Richard Leakey, the guru and international hero of Kenyan wildlife, steps somewhat awkwardly in front of the camera to assure us stiffly that all the revenue from parks in Kenya, where many of the travelers on the airplane will eventually be headed, is directed to conservation and park maintenance. Then, before absurdly cute video clips of tourists sipping tea with giraffes and cuddling up for photographs with elephants and Masai warriors roll on the screen, Leakey puts in a stern word promoting the continuation of the ivory ban that is supposed to have stopped elephant poaching in Kenya.

Tourism is very much about images. The tourist image is frequently very unlike the other images of a place, especially the images that would be important to local residents. Do British industrial workers or cockney shop girls live by the image of the Beefeater Britain or the "Changing of the Guard" Britain or the thatched cottage Britain so important in luring visitors? Does an Athenian taxi driver live by the sun-splashed Greek island image that adorns his country's posters?

The best way to obtain a read on the tourist image is to examine the postcards that are available for sale to visitors to send back to friends and loved ones at home. The postcard images generally have little to do with the objective reality of the lives of the people who live in a country. They very likely have little to do with the actual experiences of the visitors either. Consider the proliferation of porticoed white mansion postcards in Georgia, or Mountie and Indian chief and black bear postcards in Canada. An Indian chief in full headdress or a Mountie in a red tunic and a broad hat seated astride his horse are not at all part of the daily reality of a Canadian. The vast majority of visitors as well will arrive and leave without seeing either in the flesh. Yet those are the big sellers among Canadian postcards. Image, first and foremost, is what tourism is all about.

Thus, in Kenya, it is large animals—elephants, lions, cheetahs, giraffes, zebras—and Masai people in full get-up. For three weeks at the beginning of my visit to Kenya, I remained firmly ensconced in the city of Nairobi, seeing no animals and Masai only in white shirts or business suits. Yet I bought squarely into the image; all the postcards I hurriedly mailed off to friends and family had elephants, big cats, and tribespeople adorning them. What was I doing? My reality was taxi cabs, rather boring hotels, noise, polluted air, and crowded streets full of people trying to sell me things. But it never occurred to me to want to reflect those things in the images I sent home. Even had I wished to, there was certainly nothing available in the postcard market to help me out. For the tourist, images of Kenyan animals, in particular the "Big Five"—elephants, lions, leopards, rhinos, and giraffes—are the draw. This powerful, irrefutable draw has been created by two hundred years of mythmaking.

In Africa there is a definite cause and effect between the mythologies and the visitor and tourist industry responses. One of the most recent chapters in Kenya's international mythmaking was the 1985 Meryl Streep, Robert Redford movie, *Out of Africa*. Streep, playing the writer and outdoors-woman Isak Dinesen, and Redford, bounding out of his little yellow biplane as Denys Finch-Hatton, provided the identical kind of spillover shot-in-the-arm for tourism that Harrison Ford and *The Mosquito Coast* provided for Belize. In 1983, there had been 300,000 foreign (mostly European and American) tourist visitors to Kenya; after the movie *Out of Africa* was released into cinemas in North America and Europe, the annual figure jumped to 800,000. A complicated seduction was taking place, no small part of it being a fantasy in hundreds of thousands of North American and European minds that by making the trip there themselves, some of the romance might rub off. If we couldn't be Meryl Streep or Redford, Isak Dinesen or Denys Finch-Hatton, we could at least dress like them. Perhaps some excitement in the midst of exotic danger would sweep us away too.

The painstaking construction of the East Africa myth goes back much further than *Out of Africa*, with several specific important turning points. A big part of the myth of the traveler in Africa is the notion of the intrepidness required within the character of anyone who will venture there. It is as if a journey into this continent is a kind of proving ground for the courage and wits of the traveler, a watershed moment during which one cannot avoid facing squarely the great issues of his or her life. The writings of every European traveling in Africa, going back to explorer Captain Sir Richard Burton searching for the source of the Nile in the mid-nineteenth century, and missionary Dr. David Livingstone, who mapped much of the middle part of the continent from the Zambezi to Lake Tanganyika, underscore this theme. Malaria, driver ants, and hostile tribes are faced as if they were nothing, shrugged off as a necessary price to pay because a greater goal must be pursued.

Today travelers to the "Dark Continent" still work hard to nurture this illusion. Even if you do not in the least like the idea of putting up with misery or encountering danger, you must not admit this. The fact that you might have to face danger and misery, and the implication that you are willing to, is still an important part of the deal. Even if you have gone the safest route, assured of a constant supply of First World comforts, the *Heart of Darkness* is not far back in the mind, and it is part of the impression every traveler to Africa is certain to implant with friends left behind. To appreciate how this influences, profoundly, everything from wardrobe to the medical kit of so many of the visitors, you need spend very little time at Kenyatta International Airport in Nairobi. Immaculate, matching, designer Jungle Jim costumes arrive on every plane, causing you to wince self-consciously as if caught red-handed, should you note any swatch of khaki or canvas as part of your own gear. We are all sucked in; I spent long minutes in the immigration line eyeing my fellow new arrivees and wishing I'd worn a business suit. Or perhaps a parka.

Along the way to reaching this state, the best of our Western myth makers have played the themes full bore; Sir Winston Churchill in 1908, and former President Theodore Roosevelt in 1909, each came to East Africa on extended hunting safaris. Roosevelt reportedly traveled with an entourage of 500 porters, all in matching blue uniforms, and didn't quit until he had bagged, by his own count, 296 trophies from a variety of species. Neither considered their job done until they had written about their trips and their deeds. The books on Churchill and Roosevelt's respective expeditions, published once they returned to the familiarity of England and America, did much to further publicize East Africa and to amplify the myth of both the hero and the animals.

The greatest macho mythmaker of them all, Ernest Hemingway, turned out two books—*The Green Hills of Africa* and *The Snows of Kilimanjaro*—as well as a vast increment to his own personal mythology, out of a 1933 safari. His back injury, suffered when his plane took a nosedive onto the African savannah, plagued him until his death. But it was nurtured—like a troublesome war wound the victim forever complains about but is secretly grateful to drag out at the slightest excuse. Every time famous personages, such as the Prince of Wales or the young Princess Elizabeth and the Duke of Edinburgh, went to East Africa, they did the right things: they went on safari. With the huge publicity that accompanied their visits (in 1952, Princess Elizabeth was watching wild animals in Kenya when she learned her father had died and she was now Queen) the legends of the land grew in the popular imagination.

What has the myth been translated into? And, going back to the video on our British Airways flight, what does it mean in reality for the populations and the species of wild animals? Tourism has become *the* major industry in eastern and southern Africa. In Kenya, where in 1990 it took in $443 million (in U.S. dollars), it is consistently the main earner of foreign currency. A thousand miles to the south, in Zimbabwe, tourism brings in less money than tobacco or minerals, but it is growing more quickly than any other economic sector. What's more, as other aspects of the economies collapse or decline, tourism continues to be encouraged and remains the growth industry, the one invested with a true belief that it holds the key to the economic future and economic salvation. Animals, in all the equations, are indispensible. In both Kenya and Zimbabwe as well as other eastern and southern African countries such as Tanzania and Zambia, Uganda, Botswana, and now South Africa as well, animals are the supporting cast for this critical and highly valued industry. In Kenya, though some visitors go to the Indian Ocean beaches of the Mombasa coast, the big draw is, unarguably, the national parks and the game parks with their herds of everything from antelope to elephants, their prides of lions by the water holes, and their giraffe grazing the boughs of the acacia trees. North American visitors, especially, head out of Nairobi in seemingly endless caravans to the Rift Valley and the Masai Mara as well as to the Serengeti, across the border in neighboring Tanzania.

The animals are the draw, and their value has not gone unnoted. Wildlife economist Kreg Lindberg, in an assessment of the economics of nature tourism for the World Resources Institute (*1991*) estimated the "visitor attraction worth" of a lion at $27,000 per year. The visitor attraction value of an elephant herd is $610,000 a year. Animals are a major natural resource, and this is critical to their conservation. As long as the tourists keep coming, the animals will be protected—because they are earners. They are much more valuable alive than dead, as Lindberg put it bluntly: when wildlife pays, wildlife stays.

To consider what this means requires a broad and comprehensive consideration of very complex factors. Both the animals and the tourists have to be put in context of the continent and the life of Africa and the Africans.

"All discussions about Africa," wrote Raymond Bonner in his book about the future of African wildlife, *At the Hand of Man*, "must begin and end with a recognition, however grim, of the continent's under-development and poverty." Africa is a continent of exploding population, civil wars, military coups, drought, and disease. The population of 650 million is growing at twice the rate of Latin America and Asia. This remains the case despite regular population-decimating catastrophes; hundreds of thousands die in single fell swoops like the 1994 bloody civil conflict in Rwanda; as many as a million perished at an only slightly slower rate in civil strife in Angola, Mozambique, Somalia, and the Sudan. African populations continue to increase despite the fact that of twelve million HIV-infected people worldwide, two out of three, or eight million, are in that continent; and despite the fact that the world's highest infant mortality rate means that one out of every seven children born in Africa will not survive to a first birthday. Because of drought and soil degradation caused in part by heavy overuse of land, food production in sub-Saharan Africa in 1994 was 20 percent lower than it was in 1970, when the population was half the size. There is an ongoing food crisis somewhere in Africa at any given moment, and one quarter of the continent's people are threatened by chronic food insecurity. The United Nations predicts that by the end of the 1990s there will be 200 million hungry and malnourished Africans. Only 37 percent of Africans have clean drinking water; there is one doctor for every 24,500 persons. According to *Time* magazine, "sub-Saharan Africa's 530 million people have a combined GNP of less than $150 billion, roughly the same as that of Belgium and its ten million people." A steady drop in the world prices for African exports since 1980 has, according to the *New York Times*, shrunk private investment flow to sub-Saharan African states by half. Foreign debts sit at the murderous equivalent of 106 percent of gross domestic product.

One might be too overwhelmed, in the context of this human pressure cooker, to think clearly about animals and wild habitat. To sit on a comfortable 747 and be assured by a video that your role as a visiting tourist is a conserving one requires an enormous leap of imagination, and perhaps some arrogance. But the animals are not trivial, and in the long run their connection to the well-being of humans is no trivial matter either.

A day with Ray Townsend starts early. At 5:30 I opened my eyes to find Oliver, the camp cook, standing just inside the door of my hut with a cup of steaming coffee. "Boss wants to leave at six," he said, in a polite whisper, as if he was the orderly in a particularly caring hospital. Through the stretched chicken wire that formed my window, I could see first light of dawn filtering softly through the bush and across the creek bed; its effect was to send twenty thousand birds into absurd cheerfulness. Oliver disappeared. I savored the moment; this was as gentle as it would get. Before the day ended, even before lunch, we would have pushed twenty miles by Land Rover through rugged terrain on what barely passed for trails, and then hiked another seven or eight miles on foot through six-foot-tall spear grass under a blazing sun. Ostensibly we were searching for elephant and cape buffalo.

In 1991 Townsend started a company called Chapungu Safaris (named after the Shona word for the batelur eagle). He bid for and was awarded hunting rights to some two million acres of spectacular Zambezi escarpment just above Lake Kariba in the northwestern corner of Zimbabwe. Under strict quotas and carefully monitored by the Department of National Parks and Wildlife Management, Townsend guides big game hunters, sixty of them a year from all over the world. Each of his guests, from Spain, Mexico, South Africa, America, Britain, and Germany, pays up to $1,000 a day for the privilege of sleeping in a grass hut and spending the day tramping the Zambezi wilderness.

In this area of northwestern Zimbabwe you are on top of the world. By mid-morning we found ourselves high above the Zambezi River with a view of forty miles in almost any direction. It was awesome. Though we were carrying weapons, they were for protection; we were not hunting to kill anything. This was just before the season opened; Townsend's "real hunters" would not arrive for a couple more weeks; and before they did, he wanted to scout the countryside to see what was there, and to investigate the routes and the possibilities for some new trails into even further reaches of the game area. The trackers, led by Mapene (who was always referred to as "Old" Mapene, though he is probably not more than forty) continued to lead us higher up sharp inclines where the trees became ever thinner and the view ever more spectacular. The heat of the day increased, but our guides continued to set a brisk pace. My colleague, photographer Cheryl Albuquerque, and I carried very little—her camera and a pair of binoculars. The guides, dressed in blue coveralls and floppy hats, transported guns and large containers of water. Although we had sturdy hiking boots, one of the younger fellows, I noticed, had his bare toes sticking out from holes in his cracked canvas shoes. Ray Townsend, wearing the white hunter's traditional short pants, what the Australians might call "stubbies," carried a two-barrel 450-calibre elephant rifle that must have weighed thirty pounds. The beautiful antique, a Webley-Scott rifle made in England at the turn of the century, had been given to him by an octegenarian guest from Michigan in gratitude after his last safari, when he had had to be carried to the hunt like a sultan in a sedan chair. Townsend, a stocky white Zimbabwean, has a claim that is as valid as anyone's on this land. He has lived his life in the countryside and knows and loves the bush. He is of an age to have fought, during the prolonged Rhodesia to Zimbabwe war of independence in the 1970s, on the opposite side of many of the men who are now his guides and employees. But all that seemed to be behind them now.

Hunting, like fishing, is primarily process. This is why, like the term "fishing," the term "hunting" is active; it emphasizes the activity of looking or searching, and takes nothing else for granted. On a viewing safari, in a game park or even a national park, we would have seen dozens of animals by the time the sun was high enough to stop for breakfast. But on the whole distance between the Zambezi Escarpment and the distant Matusadona Hills, we saw only a few scattered impala and a lone sable antelope. He was hidden in the trees, and it required a careful look with binoculars to make him out. It was the end of the rainy season, so the water holes that would become important gathering places as the country dries up (an elephant requires fifty gallons of water per day) were less significant and certainly not predictable spots for sightings. We searched them out and found them, one after another, vacant.

We didn't see animals, but we looked for and saw, rather, evidence of animals. Broken trees. Flattened wallows where the night had been spent. Evidence of grazing; grass and green branches chewed off. I was learning a lot about being a hunter. Hunters are patient people; for a hunter, this gathering of evidence is almost as exciting as the actual, real sighting, because it builds an anticipation that will leave one almost apoplectic should consumation occur. There was to be no instant gratification here; we would learn patience and immense amounts of savannah lore. When we were in the vehicle moving through grass that was taller than us, the trackers in the back would thump gently on the roof at any sign, any piece of evidence that something might be present. At these moments, Townsend would bring the truck to a quick halt. Sliding his not inconsiderable bulk out gracefully, in a motion that would do dancers proud, he would quickly drop to a crouch, his rifle to his shoulder. We became spoor experts, learned in the science of scatology, able in short order to differentiate the droppings of an elephant from those of a buffalo. (Both leave amazingly prodigious quantities.) And we received a seminar on how to gauge the freshness or the age of the spoor—hence determining how recently the animal had passed by. For the hunter, this is a critical tracking skill; for the non-hunter it is still excellent trivia, useful at countless dinner parties back home. By mid-morning I had learned to differentiate our quarries by smell alone—the elephant leaves something much more pungent than does the buffalo, for example, the strong pachyderm odor lingering in the breeze over an area that seems to cover acres.

At the end of an exhausting day, we had seen no elephants. On the way back to camp Townsend handed Cheryl his shotgun and pointed her in the direction of a covey of guinea fowl that were just disappearing over the side of the trail. She fired twice and had a plump one to bring back to Oliver to contribute toward supper. We had seen no buffalo either—but we had seen ample evidence of both them and the elephants. Townsend, opening a bottle of wine and settling himself in a comfortable cane chair, confirmed that he knew now exactly where to push his new trails to be ready when his season would swing into full tilt.

In Zimbabwe the elephant herds are growing; lions and buffalo are healthy. But an animal that remains in danger from organized poaching are the rhinos, both black and white. There are only about 300 rhinos left in the entire country (as there are about 500 in Kenya out of an estimated 20,000 twenty-five years ago). Even the Department of National Parks and Wildlife Management strategy of de-horning—where game officials corral a rhino, sometimes by helicopter from the air, sedate it with a tranquilizer dart, and then cut off its horn to end its appeal to poachers—is having only limited success. The poachers, who seek the rhino horn for sale to Far East Asian aphrodisiac merchants or to Yemeni knife makers who want it for the dagger handles, are still a threat; indeed, they are winning. Because the stakes are so high and the money involved so lucrative, a war is still going on.

We saw no rhino when we were out with Ray Townsend. But a week later, on an early morning game drive during the first day at a very different kind of safari lodge, I was startled to see a gray form on the savannah, about a hundred yards from the trail. It was about the size of a garage. Our driver, a young game guide named Kevin, pulled to a stop.

"Is that what I think it is?" I whispered.

"Yes," he said.

"Do you think we'll get closer, or should I try to take a photo now?"

"No, no," Kevin said. "Just relax." Then he stood up in the vehicle, an open-topped Land Rover, and he shouted over the chill, early morning stillness, "Here Clemmie, Clemmie, Clemmie!"

The rhino's massive head, fully horned, lifted in the air; her little ears perked up. And then, like a bus running late, two tons of leathered flesh commenced at a fast trot toward us, and before you could say Jack Robinson, Clemmie's prehistoric head was thrust full onto the front seat, happily sucking up the apples that Kevin had thoughtfully brought along for the occasion.

Pamuzinda Safari Lodge is as different from Ray Townsend's Chapungu camp as a Mercedes is from a Land Rover. This is not for hunters who relish rugged hardship, but for passive tourists who want pleasant comforts. It is not for the patient searcher who sees significance in a broken tree or a pile of reasonably recent shit. This is for people whose cameras demand results. There are pros and cons, of course, to both. But differences between the two places are definite and startling.

At Pamuzinda a tourist can see giraffe, zebra, warthog, and wildebeest; a wide variety of the antelope family including dyker, kudu, eland, tsesebe, impala; monkeys, bush babies; birds, from the impressive gray heron to the smallest warblers. The crowning glory are the four elephants, and Clemmie and her partner, the two black rhinos, sightings guaranteed. Pamuzinda is owned by the Cresta Hotel company, which has broad interests in ten hotels and lodges throughout Botswana and South Africa as well as Zimbabwe. But it is not two million acres, like Ray Townsend's wilderness on the Zambezi escarpment; it is, rather, 2,500 acres, a couple of hours south of Harare, surrounded by rich tobacco and cotton and dairy farms. The resort and game preserve is separated from the surrounding farmland by an eight-foot-high fence (though the kudu can jump over even that). The effect of the fence is to create a psychological separation as well. Pamuzinda is one of the most comfortable places I've ever been. Twelve luxurious grass-roofed huts surround an elephant wallow. The gentle thumping of a drum announces everything from teatime to game drives to dinner. The modest price of about $100 a day includes everything from your laundry crisply pressed, folded, and waiting for you within an hour of your having left it to gut-packing gourmet meals with three choices of entree and ample wine, served by

Patrick, the head waiter, at a communal table in the thatch-roofed but otherwise open-air dining room. My first reaction was to decide that, were I stricken with any terminal disease, this is where I'd like to come to die, spend my last days until the money ran out, and then have one last look at the elephants across the pond.

What a visitor to Pamuzinda gets is not an adventure but a guarantee. Though it provides the semblance of wilderness, it is in reality an elaborate zoo. The elephants that we spent days looking for and miles trekking after under the hot sun with Ray Townsend were available to us within our first five minutes at Pamuzinda. Before we took our bags to our rooms, we went to the open-air bar for a cool beer; we happened to glance up toward the nearby pond, and there they were, four young pachyderms coming in for a midday drink. We, and all the other guests, set our drinks down and galloped to the steps and the deck for a closer look. Cameras started clicking. We needn't have hurried; the elephants would perpetually be around. They were on the payroll.

At Pamuzinda, explained Jealous Tsatsa, who has been manager for seven years, the elephants and rhinos were imported from other places in Zimbabwe. The elephants, all young males, were orphans from culling operations in the south at Gonorezhou; the rhinos had been brought from the Zambezi Valley where they were in danger from poachers. At a place like Pamuzinda you'd think they would at last be safe. This is not the case. Both the rhinos and the elephants are followed twenty-four hours a day by armed guards to keep them out of trouble and to keep trouble away from them. Poachers, Tsatsa claimed, would climb the fence into the Pamuzinda property quick as a wink if they weren't watching, and would off Clemmie for her horn. Though the elephants were on their own when I first saw them, I soon realized that they, like the rhinos, had company. I became accustomed to looking out from my balcony across the dugout and seeing them marching down for a drink with the following guards hanging on to their tails.

In the zoo-like atmosphere of Pamuzinda, the animals were assiduously protected. Their presence and their protection was definitely for the benefit of the tourists, and the cost was covered by the guest fees of the tourists. But just what are the mechanics of animal salvation in Africa, and what is the tourism connection? Would Belize-style baboon sanctuaries thrive or have a place in Africa? Wild animals in Africa are regarded very differently by Africans than they are by Europeans and North Americans. I don't know what the African staff of the safari resort thought of us visiting tourists engaging in our various rituals, including the exaggerated one of the twice daily sightseeing game drive. Perhaps we amused them; no doubt they thought us bizarre. Maybe we were feared or despised if we witlessly threatened some deep-seated cultural view. Or, at the least, we were seen simply as passing numbers; a job, cogs whose revolving presence served as a pay check, a source of income. Our practices were strange. Almost everything we tourists did revolved around either the elaborate preparation of photographic equipment, or the follow-up telling and re-telling, around the dinner table or the bar, of the anecdotes and observations. I felt a tugging embarrassment when a vanload of Germans arrived and I noted that an additional job for poor Patrick, the head waiter, was to slip from his white serving uniform into an elaborate masked headdress and feathered skirt. Picking up a spear, he hurried to the parking lot to perform a welcoming war dance to the boisterous applause of the Germans, who were all dressed in *their* costumes: identical, overly crisp, spanking clean safari outfits. As quickly as he had left, Patrick scampered back and changed once more to take up his other role, serving lunch.

But on the question of animals, the gap between the visiting westerner and any, particularly rural, African, is vast.

Westerners have always romanticized and idealized especially the large African animals, and, of late, have lobbied emotionally to protect them. The great nineteenth-century French zoologist, Georges Louis Leclerc, compte de Buffon, wrote about the European fascination with wild animals of which "only vestiges of their once marvellous industry remain in far deserted places, unknown to man for centuries, where each species freely used its natural capacities and perfected them in peace within a lasting community." Africa, in the western imagination, was such a place. Westerners decided to aggressively protect at a distance what our ancestors had destroyed at home, an expiation for the fact that you cannot now find a wild buffalo in America or a bear in France. It is no small irony that the main threat, for the most part, never came from the Africans; demand for ivory and ostrich plumes originated in Europe and America, as did the sport hunting of big game. The missionary-explorer Dr. David Livingstone reported that 30,000 elephants were shot in 1841, a number which by 1880 was up to 70,000—all by Westerners. When Europeans started to open farms in Kenya, Uganda, Tanganyika (Tanzania), and Rhodesia (Zimbabwe), lions were poisoned or trapped or shot because they were considered "vermin." But no matter, westerners will lead the saving as well; whenever news of any threat arrived, the western impulse shifted into a highly idealized view, and a panicked, protectionist stance.

The African attitude is quite different and probably more natural. There are possibilities of connections that are spiritual, kindred, or mystical, but those notwithstanding, animals were (and are) real, daily parts of the lives of at least rural Africans; they posed and pose regular threats to life and safety, or nuisances to crops and travel. The western approach takes little into account of this real life of Africans. To tell a poor peasant that an elephant that tramples his crop or a lion that steals his goats and might even kill him or his children is a thing of abstract beauty to be preserved for its own sake is an example of cruel urban humor. One day we were taken by a University of Zimbabwe sociologist to the end of a hilly back-country trail. There, past an out of the way village called Tafirenyika, we finally arrived at the tiny homestead of Taylor and Elizabeth Shingirayi. A small, neat patch of red and white flowers around a name post introduced three wattle-and-thatch huts, a pen for goats constructed from poles and sticks, and a farm that consisted of six bumpy acres of maize and pumpkins—not to mention one of the best views in the world, looking over the hills of far western Zimbabwe toward the distant Mana Pools National Park. The spectacular view was wasted on an agitated Mr. Shingirayi, his brow shaded by a bright blue cloth hat. He took us immediately into his maize field to show us the damage the elephants had done. Six of them had come a few nights before, rambling in from the hills, and they had had their way with the crop. Broken stalks of maize and crushed pumpkins lay everywhere. The remains of a small crop, close to harvesting, was scrambled in sorry disarray. The Shingirayis had done what they could to frighten the intruders off: "We lit torches and waved them around and made noise and tried to scare them away," explained Elizabeth, "but it was no use. Once an elephant enters a field, it stays until it is satisfied." The Shingirayis were luckier than their neighbor, a seventy-year-old man named Mr. Mazambara who, the year before when he had tried to chase marauding elephants from his field by banging on a tin pot, had been killed when the elephants turned and trampled him. But this was the second time the Shingirayis had lost a substantial part of their crop; a year before, bush pigs dug up their ground nuts. Wildlife, for the African farmer, is an adversary, an enemy.

The outsider view is different. The animals, statistics tell us, are in danger and so need protection. The primary outsider or western solution to animal protection in Africa is the national park. The system of national parks operating throughout Africa now is strictly western in its origin, and uses the U.S. national parks as a model. The western idea of the national park came at the same time, in the late nineteenth century, as the popular creation of zoos, a notion, according to philosopher John Berger, that coincided with the disappearance in western civilization of animals from daily life. "The zoo, (and by extension the park)" writes Berger, "to which people go to meet animals, to observe them, to see them, is in fact a monument to the impossibility of such encounters."

When the parks were organized, moreover, African people were left out. They were largely excluded from what should have been their own parks. The first national park, Albert National Park established in 1925 in the Belgian Congo (now Zaire's Virunga National Park), was closed to everyone except scientists (white and European) who wanted to study mountain gorillas. The initial conservation declarations by European conventions in the late 1800s were designed to conserve African wildlife from over-hunting by white sportsmen. The assumptions underlying animal conservation and the creation of national park systems have always been, according to Raymond Bonner, that the Africans, first, didn't count, and later, could not be trusted. In 1933 the *Convention Relative to the Preservation of Fauna and Flora in their Natural State* was signed in London by nine European powers that had African colonies. As Major R. W. G. Hingston, who had scouted the situation through Britain's East and Central African colonies—Northern Rhodesia (now Zambia), Nyasaland (Malawi), Tanganyika (Tanzania), Kenya, and Uganda—told Britain's Society for the Preservation of the Fauna of the Empire, "The unique fauna of Africa must be preserved. Its disappearance would be a crime against posterity." The London conference laid the groundwork for national parks systems, placed seventeen species of animals on protected lists, and restricted aircraft, balloons, and cars in the reserves. No black African person, however, was present to participate in the discussions or put ink to the agreements.

To this day, African people remain suspicious of western conservation moves. When they kill animals for protection or for food, they are labeled poachers. They see protection of animals as something not for their benefit, but for the benefit of western tourists; they view national parks as vestiges of colonialism with little or no connection or meaning for them. This makes a program started in Zimbabwe in the late 1980s all the more interesting.

On a sweltering afternoon, Cheryl and I were invited by Steve Kaseri and Liz Rihoy, two young people, one African, the other British, who work for the Zimbabwe Trust in Harare, to travel with them to the countryside. Our destination was Muganje, a market town and the center of the Hurungwe District in northwestern Zimbabwe. This rolling country with its reddish soil is a typical farming area in the Communal Lands, the areas where blacks were forced to live when Zimbabwe was segregated Rhodesia and where about 60 percent of the population still live today, on 40 percent of the country's land. If you were a commercial farmer, you wouldn't want most of these lands; they are hilly and stony, with marginal soil. Yet most people feel they have little choice but to try to scratch a living from the earth. We were taken to the council office, a low plastered concrete building set back behind a bit of a dusty square in the middle of town. In a big, airless, meeting room with smudged green walls, twenty-two village chiefs, headmen, and other leaders were gathered poring over mimeographed sheets of numbers and figures. Overhead, ancient ceiling fans turned languidly, moving nothing. Outside the open window a tractor trundled by, followed by an ancient ox cart loaded with heavy sacks. Women with basins and boxes of produce balanced on their heads waited for the bus to Harare. But it was not their agriculture that the chiefs were thinking about that day. By the time they closed the meeting, they would have divided up the equivalent of $120,000, which they would then carry back to their villages—most of them clusters of thatched, mud huts at the remote ends of rutted hillside trails—earned from quite a different crop, their wildlife.

CAMPFIRE is an acronym for the Communal Areas Management Programme For Indigenous Resources that, though it bears an unwieldy title, is arguably one of the most creative conservation undertakings in Africa. It is also one of the most controversial. CAMPFIRE was set up as an experiment to change attitudes of rural Africans toward wildlife and—in the words of one of its founders, Rob Monro of the Zimbabwe Trust (Liz Rihoy's boss)—"to help people who suffer from wildlife reap some benefit." In five years its quite dramatic success has helped it grow so that it now operates in half the rural districts of Zimbabwe and stands as a model for both conservation and local control in southern Africa. CAMPFIRE makes use of a region's animals, either through hunting safaris, what they call "consumptive tourism," or forms of "nonconsumptive tourism" to make money for local people. In turn, this is seen as the route to guarantee the animals' conservation.

The practice of looking at his country's wildlife in commercial terms, as an economic resource, started with Rowan Martin, the National Parks Department wildlife guru who has been around Zimbabwe so long that he is an institution. Under good management, Martin believed, it was feasible to realize returns from wildlife of over $10 per acre. This, he predicted, would be better than returns from commercial beef ranching and possibly twice as valuable as traditional cattle systems.

The idea of wild animals as a commodity was revolutionary and remains difficult for many western conservationists to swallow. But it is precisely what makes CAMPFIRE work most convincingly in the eyes of the Zimbabwean villagers, the rural Africans who were gathered in the council room that day and who had previously been shut out of considerations completely. When we were at the homestead of Taylor and Elizabeth Shingirayi taking stock of the crop damage done by the elephants, Lovemore Muchidzagora, one of Hurungwe District's animal reporters, was also there, listening carefully and taking notes. In another time, a farmer's instinct would have made him go after the elephants and hope to kill them. Now the Shingirayis will be compensated by CAMPFIRE. Perhaps money will be available to build an electrified fence around their field. The elephants will be saved for the tourists, and the tourist money will pay the Shingirayis.

The theory, as Kreg Lindberg pronounced, stays simple: if wildlife becomes a source of tangible benefit, then it likewise becomes deserving of protection. An elephant killed out of anger or for revenge is worth nothing, except maybe a couple of acres of maize saved; an elephant poached is worth a jail sentence (or an instant death if wildlife officers happen upon a poacher in the act). But an elephant kept for a trophy for a foreign hunter on an approved safari, or preserved for viewing in the context of a tourism resort, is worth a new village grinding mill, a coat of paint for the school, supplies for the medical center, or a payment that can equal half a family's annual income from all other sources.

What CAMPFIRE has done is take the benefits of tourism directly into the homes of African villagers. Tourism, though it is abstractly important in the grand balance of trade and foreign exchange of many African countries, often remains totally alien to the immediate lives of local people and local villagers. But when it comes into their homes and their hands in the form of cold cash that has been given in exchange for a visitor and their animals, it changes their relationship, changes their attitudes, and, among other things, convinces them that conservation pays. In a country where family cash income averages $200 a year from five or ten acres of maize and pumpkins, any extra money means a substantial difference. At the end of the meeting we sat with Ray Townsend while he had a beer with Ivan Bond, a lanky young researcher for the World Wildlife Fund. Bond had questions about Townsend's safari business, mainly concerned with the numbers of people he employed and what they did. "How many trackers have you got?" he asked. "How many guides? How many weeks will they work this year? How much do you pay them?" Chapungu Safaris is a CAMPFIRE project. Bond wanted to put together numbers that would show that, as well as putting thousands of dollars from visiting tourists into villager hands, Townsend also provided employment for up to thirty people who would otherwise have no jobs. CAMPFIRE, most importantly, is a symbol that the elephants, buffalo, warthogs, and baboons that inhabit the hills and forests around the communal farmland plots are not simply a danger or a nuisance, but something that can bring income and benefits, in a variety of ways, to villager's families. By becoming part of CAMPFIRE, villagers become partners in their country's tourism. The day-by-day education of being involved begins to show them the benefits of conservation. By providing incentives, the strategy promises to save wildlife infinitely better than any approach built on threats and punishments. For one thing, the greatest enemy to wildlife is loss of habitat. But if game can compete economically, as Rowan Martin figured, with cattle production, habitat that would otherwise be turned over to farming can justifiably be saved, and the animals will flourish. Poaching, in many of the twenty-two rural districts where there are CAMPFIRE programs, has been drastically cut according to Brian Child, senior ecologist with the Zimbabwe Department of National Parks and Wildlife Management and a zealous supporter of CAMPFIRE. In Guruve District in the north of the country, an area that has marginal agriculture but a rich wildlife base, Child recounts that each household averaged $800 from CAMPFIRE income. This was on top of new local employment with increasing numbers of jobs for wildlife managers, problem-animal reporters, game guards, tourist operators, and administrators. In that community poaching has all but been eliminated. "Snaring of animals is no longer tolerated by community members," Child says, describing how the local council sentenced a man who had killed a wild pig to two months of carrying out garbage for the clinic and took away his CAMPFIRE dividend for two years. In another community, the chief, while distributing dividends, singled out a man who had been convicted of killing a buffalo and proclaimed in front of the whole village, "if you had not poached that buffalo, there would be even more money for us all."

One thing CAMPFIRE had to do, though, was deal with the volatile issue of big game hunting. Trophy hunting, like that offered by Ray Townsend at Chapungu Safaris, is a huge part of CAMPFIRE's tourism program. The local council, through a strict quota system and a license granted to a safari hunter by the department of wildlife, effectively sells off one of its big wild animals. The hunter pays a hefty trophy fee— $10,000 for an elephant, $1,000 for a cape buffalo. By tradition he takes only the animal's head as his trophy, leaving the meat for the villagers who also get, after the various license fees are deducted, about half the money the hunter has paid. In Hurungwe District, safaris that bring in big game hunters provide 95 percent of the district income. So CAMPFIRE was confronted with a significant philosophical and public relations question. It might seem odd, if not a disgrace, to a European or a North American that elephants are protected only so they have a chance to be hunted later. This was the thorny question that faced both CAMPFIRE and the tourism planners.

The writer, aviator, and woman-about-Africa Beryl Markham once wrote, "It is absurd for a man to kill an elephant. It is not brutal, it is not heroic, and certainly it is not easy; it is just one of those preposterous things that men do, like putting a dam across a great river, one tenth of whose volume could engulf the whole of mankind without disturbing the domestic life of a single catfish." Markham would know: she was one of the first and few female elephant hunting guides in Africa. Until not all that long ago hunting, most of it for big game, was basically the only form of tourism in Africa. It was an exotic undertaking, and it was restricted to those with a great deal of money, people like the Prince of Wales, Winston Churchill, and Ernest Hemingway. Beryl Markham also wrote: "The essence of elephant hunting is discomfort in such lavish proportions that only the wealthy can afford it."

But the slaughter and the consequent game shortages caused it to lose its luster until, in many eyes, it had no luster at all. In 1977 Kenya banned hunting, as Tanzania had done four years earlier. The sympathies of non-African conservation and animal rights lobbies supported those decisions, just as they were strongly behind the later decisions to ban the sale of ivory in order to attack poaching. In Zimbabwe, however, hunting was never made illegal, and hunting safaris have continued on the well-researched argument that animal populations there, as in neighboring Botswana and South Africa, are not in danger. In fact they are so healthy as a result of good management, say observers, that without hunting and culling, populations would quickly outgrow their habitat. Still, Zimbabwe has had to fight a public relations battle. Brian Child acknowledges that his department's policies upset Western sensibilities. "We are utilizing wildlife. Our programs, like CAMPFIRE, are not of animal protection, but of conservation through utilization." Because CAMPFIRE supports hunting, the Zimbabwe agencies behind it—like the local chapter of the World Wildlife Fund—have had to buck the strong anti-hunting opinions of their international parents.

But the jury on big game hunting, far from delivering a conclusive verdict, might be changing its mind. Hunting may be on the way back in, even in Kenya and Tanzania. As more information becomes available, hunting has an increasingly favorable reputation as a route to conservation. Raymond Bonner writes, "From a conservation standpoint, it might be wiser to promote hunting over tourism, however preposterous the proposition might seem on first examination." He goes on to make an argument that tourists, "speeding across the plains in their minivans in pursuit of a lion pride or rhino, tearing up the grass and in rainy periods cutting ugly ruts," are more destructive of the environment than are hunters. There is something definitely unsettling about the horrors of herd tourism. There is nothing either romantic or noble about a convoy of forty minivans loaded with camcorder-armed passengers racing toward a pride of lions. The expectations of the tourists and the hunters, and their results, are very different as well. The stereotypical tourists expect amenities, accomodation, cuisine, comforts, and service that are consistently of resort status. Those willing or seeking to "rough it" are rare exceptions, and the stereotypical tourist wants instant gratification. "A tourist who drives all day and sees only five animals is disappointed, if not angry with the driver of the van," says Bonner. A proper hunter, on the other hand, is a student of the environment, expects a minimum of comforts, and, to be satisfied with his expedition, needs to see only one animal of the sort he is pursuing.

"Very little research has been done," reports Bonner,

on the impact of large numbers of tourists on the wild animals, but what research has been done should disturb anyone who believes unquestioningly that tourism is the panacea for conservation. For one thing, tourists are taking some of the "wild" out of animals and Africa. A visitor can practically pet the elephants in Amboseli Park near Nairobi, Kenya. As recently as the 1970s, the lions in Ngorongoro Crater in northern Tanzania would hide from tourist vehicles; today the lions have become so accustomed to man and his car that they yawn and pose. But the consequence of too many tourists may be far worse than the taming of the wild. 'Harassment of the lions by camera in Serengeti has led to so many kills being missed that lion cubs sometimes starve,' Norman Myers, a British conservationist observed, and that was twenty years ago, when the number of tourists was a fraction of the numbers today. Cheetah have been seriously harmed by camera-clicking tourists. The cheetah hunts in the daytime, and tourists love to follow one as it stalks a gazelle or an impala. The vehicles often scare off the prey, and the cheetah itself will react to the vehicle by either lying down and waiting until it leaves or running away from it; either outcome deprives the cheetah of its meal.

Recent observations suggest that the presence and interference of so many humans is causing some cheetahs to alter their habits: they are becoming night hunters in order to avoid the tourists.

Because of these considerations, people like Dr. Richard Leakey, the director of Kenya's Wildlife Service until 1995, when he left the post to enter politics, reportedly was contemplating allowing safari hunting in parts of Kenya as it exists in places such as Zimbabwe or Zambia. This move is likely to alter substantially his reputation as the darling of the international animal rights and conservationist set. Economics as well as ecology certainly seems to be a deciding factor. A 1989 study predicted that hunters could generate $20 million annually for Kenya; they would pay $4 million to the Kenya Wildlife Department for license fees alone. Zimbabwe's license fees and CAMPFIRE concession agreements require each hunter to fork over a trophy fee of $10,000 for an elephant. A buffalo is worth about $1,000; a bush pig $50. Safari hunting requires a less expensive infrastructure than that demanded by other forms of tourism, with fewer roads and lodges. The per capita return is much higher; safari hunters still have to be well off, prepared to pay $20,000 to $50,000 for a trip that a non-consumptive tourist would expect to have for $2,000 to $3,000.

But what about all the tourists who do not want to be hunters, and the increasing demand from more of them for more tours into more

places to experience more animals? What about those who are not able
or willing to spend $20,000 or more on a trip into Africa? Will Africa re-
turn to being a destination for only top-of-the-line safari hunters?
Should it? What does this mean—for animals, for villagers, for the countries? What, returning to the premise of the introductory video, is the
tourist's role in the wildlife of Africa?

The CAMPFIRE coordinator for Hurungwe District is a vegetarian, an
angular, middle-aged British woman named Cherry Bird. She has a degree in physics, came to Africa first as a teacher, and is supported in her
present job by Britain's charitable VSO (Volunteer Services Overseas).
Bird's cluttered office, off to the side of Magunje's council building, is
dominated by charts, maps, and printed proposals. She and her assistant, Mr. Banda, are at the service of the region's village chieftains, trying
to get them to maintain agreement on what kind of programs they want
to have and trying to keep the benefits fairly distributed. Bird and Banda
and the chiefs are also trying to expand and diversify the programs beyond trophy hunting.

On the morning when we visited, a squat, soft-spoken man named
Steve Pope, clutching a sweaty leather hat, was speaking to Cherry Bird
about his hike-in camp for photographic safaris. The district council,
through CAMPFIRE, had given him a concession to 15,000 acres around
Chitake Springs adjacent to the Mana Pools National Park. There live an
abundant population of hippos, elephants, baboons, wild pigs, and a
small herd of Zimbabwe's few remaining wild rhino. Pope had a crew
busy breaking trails for his season's first group of tourists, Germans who
would be arriving in a few days. He talked excitedly about building first a
tent camp, and then eventually a small lodge. Pope employs local workers in all capacities—construction, guiding, cooking; and returns 15 percent of his gross earnings, through CAMPFIRE, to the neighboring villages.

A myriad of small projects, like Pope's, were coming into being.
Cherry Bird described a venture one of the villages had on the drawing
boards that would allow visitors glimpses and experiences of local Shona
culture. At Sunungukai local people were building an extension to their
village, more huts where small groups of tourists could spend a weekend,
be looked after by the local people, and be taken on an exended tour of
local life and history. These projects, Bird said, should have the added
bonus of keeping young people at home in the rural areas, "instead of
rushing off to the cities where they get into trouble." If CAMPFIRE, she
pointed out, could diversify the forms of tourism offered and become

less firmly connected, especially in the foreign mind, with the thorny
question of hunting, it will be better for everyone.

Approximately five billion human beings populate our globe. This is almost twice as many as in 1950, a short forty-five years ago. There is no
shortage of talk and no shortage of concern about the issue of the population explosion; but despite all talk and all concern, the number of the
world's humans continues to grow, expanding ever more rapidly. We are
told to expect seven billion in the near future, early in the next century,
and to anticipate what seems unthinkable, twelve billion, before there is
any hope of things leveling off. A lot can happen, of course, on the way
from five to twelve billion people, but the point, as trends continue, is to
consider the residual impact of all these humans. As the human population of the Earth increases, what also increases are the pressures on the
planet's other populations, such as her wild animals. Through a combination of use, killing for sport or food or hide and, more detrimental,
loss of habitat, we humans have placed animal species, like the elephants and rhinos of Kenya and Zimbawe, the tigers of the Indian sub-
continent, or the jaguars and the howler monkeys of Belize, one after
another, under ever greater stress and in more and more danger of extinction. We ask ourselves what can be done to move at least a little distance in the direction of creating or ensuring balance. As the CAMPFIRE
experiment in Zimbabwe tries to determine, we also ask whether tourism
really has any role in securing a balance. Can tourism truly have a role in
saving the animals of Africa or Asia or Central America, or anywhere else
for that matter? And, going hand in hand, with saving animals does it
have a role in saving the economies of the local peoples?

   In Africa, for some individuals, tourism and the tourist industry have
been a route to careers and economic betterment. Jealous Tsatsa comes
out of his office behind the dining room at Pamuzinda Lodge. Immaculate, with his trimmed moustache and pressed shirt and slacks, he joins
his much more roughly clad group of guests, who are sipping tea under
the acacia on the lawn while they wait for the afternoon game drive.
When Jealous Tsatsa was a young boy, he decided that there was an individual future for him in the tourist business. A bright student, he left his
village and enrolled in hotel school in Bulowayo, Zimbabwe's second
largest city. The early 1970s were still pre-independence, and Jealous is
black. But this most careful of men saw the future: hospitality and
tourism would be his country's growth industry. This was where oppor-

tunities lay for a person to make his mark, no matter where he had started. In his case, it would take him from a first job as a busboy all the way to management, with stops at every stage along the way. Tsatsa cannot say for certain what percentage of Zimbabwe's employment is in tourism fields, but his own lodge is sort of the paradigm. Pamuzinda maintains a one-to-one ratio between guests and staff, and all of their twenty-four staff are Zimbabweans.

A question larger than individual careers is who controls the tourism industry in African countries and which segments of society get the real benefits, not to mention future benefits as the industry grows. In Kenya, a criticism is that the tourist economy mirrors the old colonial economy: whites hold the senior positions in the conservation organizations, and whites or Asians own and operate most of the safari companies and camps. Africans are secretaries, cooks, and drivers. If a tourist leaves behind $250 or $300 for each day in the country, where does that money end up? What proportion ends up back in Europe or America in the profits of the foreign-owned hotel chains or tour companies? In both Kenya and Zimbabwe, until recently, laws specified that hotel bills of foreign visitors had to be settled in foreign currency. This ensured that foreign money made its way into the country's economies (though, the rule puzzled me because, as a tourist, even to pay in the local currency, I would have brought my foreign currency into the country and exchanged it at a Kenyan or Zimbabwean bank). A troubling thought gnaws at you when you are spending your money: you know that only pennies will trickle down to the people who serve you drinks or the people who make your bed or the people you see on the streets. The largest portion by far will either leave the country, flowing into the accounts of airlines, tour companies, and hotel chains headquartered elsewhere; or it will go to the "vampire elite," the corrupt, over-rich, upper political echelons that have a stranglehold on so many developing countries.

Probably the biggest question affecting the connection between tourism and animals is the issue of revenue sharing. In Belize the villagers at Bermudian Landing and the farmers who have agreed to make their lands part of the Baboon Sanctuary, see immediately even the small amounts of tourist income. CAMPFIRE, in Zimbabwe, has turned into such an exemplary and effective venture because it is built on spreading the revenues from tourism around. By doing this, both programs underline dramatically the connection between animal conservation and economic income. A substantial proportion of the money spent by foreign hunters at Ray Townsend's safari camp, for instance, goes directly to the local people. This happens first through the wages Townsend pays to the thirty employees who work for him as guides, trackers, skinners, drivers, and cooks; and then through the supplies he buys, the licenses he purchases, and the levies for each animal killed. CAMPFIRE, explained Brian Child, "is a community development program; it uses elephants to get small rural economies started." The World Wildlife Fund recognizes this, and, when I visited, it employed ten staff in a multi-species project to conduct research on wildlife as an economic resource in Zimbabwe. Over the long term, they would develop analyses and provide wildlife management training to local community people.

Beyond Zimbabwe and beyond CAMPFIRE, revenue sharing is a thorny issue. Most often, local people who live adjacent to parks and reserves see little, if any, direct income from the fees of the tourists. This has its repercussions down the line. If the resource is considered a local one, but the exploitation of it is national with only meager or no local benefits, tensions between conservationists and the local communities are bound to erupt. Writer Graham Boynton recounts the story of the Shangaan tribe in southeast Zimbabwe. For centuries, their tribal culture incoporated a conservation ethic toward the local wildlife—only a few trained individuals were hunters, and both the hunt and the division of the spoils were controlled by the village chief. The tribe's survival depended on wildlife's flourishing, "and flourish it did." When colonial rule arrived, however, the new rulers ordained that all wildlife belonged to the Crown. Boynton, quoting Zimbabwe wildlife expert Clive Stockil, writes: "at the stroke of a pen, these people who were living in perfect harmony with the animals were transformed into poachers. It was like closing down all the supermarkets in Manhattan and telling the inhabitants to fend for themselves." Later, when the area was reserved as a national park, the Shangaans were removed and their huts were torched. The government needed the land for tourists and the money that would bring in. The Shangaans, dispossessed and angry, logically concluded that if there were no animals, there would be no tourists, and things might return to the way they had been. They initiated a poaching campaign to rid the country of the animals they had once so carefully shared it with.

In Kenya the KWS (Kenya Wildlife Service) identified revenue sharing as a priority as early as 1989. But it was easier to identify it as a priority than to achieve it in a full and useful and fair and agreeable manner. The goal of sharing 25 percent of the revenues proved impossible to meet. Although in 1992 the KWS set up a Community Wildlife Service charged with helping communities "promote socio-economic development through conservation and sustainable management of Kenya's natural resources," according to a report to the Ecotourism Society, "the program raised unrealistic community expectations, while at the same time generating internal political conflict. Clear revenue-sharing guidelines were lacking. Disbursements of funds were delayed, and the community was involved in revenue sharing in only a limited way." To its credit, Kenya was at least saying the right things and making a start. But its goal of ensuring conservation by making certain that revenues generated by wildlife tourism were paid, as with CAMPFIRE, to those people and villages who bear the burden of co-existing with wildlife still had a long way to go.

Zimbabwe, its CAMPFIRE program notwithstanding, still struggles with the issue of getting National Park gate revenues either even obliquely connected to wildlife conservation, or into the hands of villages neighboring the parks. In 1994, parks monies in Zimbabwe still went back into general government coffers; out of the $95 million Zimbabwe earned from foreign tourism, only $6 million was allocated to the country's parks. The rest went into the national treasury. For people who wanted a more deliberate and direct connection to animal conservation, the issue of the parks being allowed to retain and invest their revenues remained a battle they still had not won.

It seems that the theory "if wildlife pays, wildlife stays" can hold true in Africa when all the wrinkles of administration and all the issues around who should justifiably share the revenues are worked out. But part of what also should happen is a rethinking, on almost everyone's part, of some definitions. The effect of a safari game park such as Pamuzinda, and the growing number of others like it, may be to save the animals, but one isn't long in such a setting before developing a casual attitude. When the animal sightings are all but guaranteed, they lose some value. Out in the wilderness with Ray Townsend we tramped for most of the day up and down hillsides, over rough terrain, through spear grass and thorn acacia brush, under the heat of the sun. The fact that we spent our entire first day without seeing any large animals was, in fact, not a disappointment. A sighting would have been a thrill, but the hunt and the work it entailed, learning about spoor and scent, broken trees and flattened grass, was what was important. At Pamuzinda, although it was

marvelous to watch the young bull elephants feeding on the other side
of the dug-out or wallowing in the mud by the dam, the fact that their
driver could deliver them close enough that one of the other tourists, a
woman from Australia, could regularly feed them vegetable scraps from
the lunch table depressed me. After two days it was old hat, and I found I
wouldn't even bother to leave my hut for them. It became predictable.
The dispiriting possibility is that the price of saving animals will be to
turn a whole continent into the kind of zoo described by newspaper
travel-writer Jeremy Ferguson upon returning from a Kenyan jaunt: "The
safari is like a zoo in that something is roaming and something is caged,
only the something caged comes festooned with zoom lenses."

Another problem of definition involves the species of animals themselves. In Africa, everybody talks about five big animals; lions, elephants,
giraffes, rhinos, and leopards. You could throw in a few additional popular brands; cape buffalos and hippos come to mind and so, perhaps, do
ostriches, zebras, gorillas, crocodiles, and certain species of large antelope. But that is the limit, and the governing view in both the mind of
the tourist consumer and the tourist provider is of species, certain
species that exist in some kind of splendid isolation and are to be pursued, seen, and checked off a list like purchased groceries.

This, however, ignores the fact that everything in nature is part of an
inter-connected and interdependent system. I engaged in a conversation
about this matter of the "Big Five" with James Makau, a slender, good-
natured game guide with a chipped front tooth, one evening in front of
a campfire in the Kenyan bush. Makau is a naturalist who was working
for the East African Ornothological Safari out of Camp Delamere, a game
preserve carved from private farmland in Kenya's Rift Valley north of
Nairobi. James stirred the embers of the fire and smiled, "What about
the small five thousand?" he demanded. For a while I was the only guest
at this pleasant tented camp, so Paul, the senior guide, and James had
taken me under their wing. James could identify by sight or by sound all
the hundreds of birds at Delamere and knew all the stars in the Southern
Hemisphere sky. He was twenty-nine, but claimed he knew what he
wanted to be ever since he was a ten-year-old boy scout in Nairobi and
would run off every weekend to nature classes at Ngong Park. "I never
wanted to have a job where you have to go in at eight o'clock and be
choked by a necktie," he explained.

The secret for the future success of tourism in Africa, suggested James

Makau, will be to expand the base of interest from the Big Five animals in the big parks and include all the little camps, like Delamere. Throughout eastern and southern Africa there are a growing number of very comfortable, very interesting, and very individually attentive private reserves such as this one, with twenty-four guests, thirty employees, and all the fauna the average Westerner has only remotely heard of. The only large animal we saw at Delamere, except for two tame giraffes, was a formidable cape buffalo bull encountered on a night game drive when we rounded a clump of trees on the trail and surprised it. It suprised us too, turning with its ferocious, lowered head to stare down our vehicle. We had been prepared to view only small animals and to that point the excitement of our night had been a mongoose slinking along the edge of the bush. We had seen also a herd of thirty zebras; dik-diks (the smallest antelope); Thompson's gazelles; impalas; elands (the largest antelope); reed bucks; stainboks; water bucks; skunks; African hares; spring hares; baboons; big, ugly undertaker-look-alike maribu storks; ibis; hornbills; and guinea fowl.

The next morning James took me to spend a couple of hours perched in a tree-house lookout where we waited for and then observed a small herd of eland at their water hole. Paul, who stated modestly that he can identify 1,700 species of birds, seemed pleased when I told him we had plovers back home in North America. He then asked me to name which species of them are to be found there!

Tourism in Africa will not be stopped. The mythologies are too strong and too deeply implanted; too many people have adopted into their imaginations the desire to go. African countries have an ever-growing infrastructure of hotels, resorts, tour companies, parks, and staff. The desire of the host countries to grasp this method of securing foreign exchange is too urgent.

Hunting safaris may return to Kenya and Tanzania, and they may become an even more important part of the foreign-exchange earnings of Zimbabwe. But they will not replace the non-consumptive tourist: the hiker, the photographer, the game-drive sightseer, the camcorder carrier who dresses like a hunter. The pressure of the herds of minivan tours will not abate either. What African countries and other places must do, though, is be attentive to turning the tourism impulse toward the benefit of two aspects of their societies, two facets of their societies that habitually have been undervalued, badly cared for, and overlooked. They must look after their local environments, which include all indigenous species of animals and their habitat; and they must consider their local peasant and village peoples. These local peoples must have a role in setting the rules and must benefit from them. If this doesn't happen, Africa will turn first into a theme park, and then a strip mall.

8

Tourism in the Middle of Nowhere: North Dakota, Minnesota, and Manitoba

There were twenty-two buses, all lined up like snoring brontosauri, in the parking lot of the Shooting Star Casino in Mahnomen, Minnesota. This was a Wednesday afternoon, a fact that is possibly irrelevant; like other waystations in the world of gaming and gambling, the Shooting Star Casino knows no days, as it knows no nights. Nothing ever stops, nothing ever pauses. The dealers stand by their tables, the machines hum and blink, the money rolls and clatters day and night, night and day, twenty-four hours a day, seven days a week. The players are crowded like inmates into the dim, purple, luminescent confines of the casino. When, one might wonder, is Christmas? When is the Fourth of July?

If there is any differentiation of time, it is through other markings. This particular day, for example, was "Seniors' Bus Day," which explained why the 2,100 bodies pushing for places in front of the one-armed bandits appeared to have an average age of about eighty. Among the private automobiles and the giant tour buses stationed in the parking lot was a small fleet of petite medi-vans that had come directly from hospitals or from personal-care homes to dispatch their passengers to the blackjack tables. Nothing was going to stop these determined folks from rolling their dice. On the casino floor you had to be careful lest a careening wheelchair ran you down.

I have to explain my prejudice right off the bat. Gambling bores me. I can't remember the rules of a card game from one day to the next, and I hate to lose money. So I have a hard time understanding the attraction a casino holds for so many people. I've poked my head into a number of the world's great gaming palaces; I've been to the casinos in Monte Carlo, Atlantic City, Estoril Portugal, Nice, Nairobi, and in the American midwest. Always, I've been perplexed; inevitably a wave of lethargy settles over me like a cloud. The appeal remains a mystery. I've tried to give it a fair shake. On my first visit to Nice (until then uninitiated), I was genuinely excited by an invitation to go to a famous casino. I borrowed a tuxedo and, as I left my passport with the guard at the casino's front desk, I was feeling truly cocky; I fancied myself a bit of a James Bond—ready for anything. The blinking lights were overhead, and all the glamorous people of the Riviera waited inside. A couple of hours later I left in what was close to a depression. There had been no glamor; no one was beautiful. Nobody seemed even to be having a very good time. Rather than an enchanting corner of the world, I felt like I had been to a mental ward on another planet.

Gambling seems to be not very much fun unless—probably especially if—you are addicted to it. But I must be one of very few people who feel that way, for casinos—my opinion notwithstanding—are inevitably jammed and busy places. And they invoke a conventional wisdom: that a casino is the surest ticket to tourism in tough-sell spots. This is why you find them on Indian reservations all through the Midwest.

This particular twilight zone of blinking lights, whirring high-pitched musical machine noises, clinking coins, pushed by the wide-eyed momentum of chance and greed and held tightly under the folded-arm watchfulness of the dealers and security personnel, was the dream-come-true of a little band of tribal council leaders of the White Earth Chippewa Nation. The Shooting Star sits on Chippewa Indian reservation land, and the Chippewa people seemed to have adapted, almost overnight, into the croupiers and blackjack dealers, hotel administrators, waiters, busboys, and security guards required to keep such a place humming.

The founding elders, whose idea for a gambling palace had miraculously transformed the fortunes of this otherwise-backroad-of-America place, were tribal heroes, celebrated in large photo portraits that adorned the hallway running between the casino and the always-full and still-being-built hotel. They were jolly, beefy, fellows who had been laughing uproariously when their photos were snapped. Someone had told a good joke. They were labeled with nicknames like "Chip," for Tribal Chairman of the White Earth Reservation, Darrell Wadena; and "Poncho," for Jerry Rawley, the tribal council's secretary-treasurer. They looked as if they might have just finished enjoying a great plate of lasagna with their casino-management business partners, Angelo Medure and his cohorts from Gaming World International, who had discovered northern Minnesota despite the fact that it is a very great distance from Philadelphia. But these jolly-looking men were visionaries; their idea, their initiative, had brought jobs, and it was the only initiative anybody had undertaken in a long, long time that held any promise of bringing an economy to their reservation.

Mahnomen, Minnesota, is an unlikely place to have a twenty-four-hour-a-day casino. Mahnomen is definitely one of the world's "middle of nowheres." It sits in rolling northern Minnesota farmland perched on the balance between indifferent and marshy. Highway 59 comes up from the resort area of Detroit Lakes, an ice-fishing haven in the winter, and, after passing through the 1,600-square-mile White Earth Indian Reservation, keeps going through Thief River Falls and on to Canada, where it ends at Winnipeg, three and a half hours later. Minneapolis–St Paul is 240 miles in the other direction.

The land was given to the Chippewas for a reservation in 1867. This was in the midst of the roundup of all the plains tribes. Outgunned by the U.S. Cavalry and overwhelmed by white settlers, they were offered brutal choices. If they didn't agree peacefully to the lot of the reservation, they faced starvation or sure attrition of a quicker, more horrific manner. So they took the reservation. In the intervening century and a quarter, much of the Chippewa land in this part of Minnesota was sold off, so that the towns and farms are now as likely to be inhabited by whites as by Chippewa people. This was a dismal exchange for both sides: the Chippewa were squeezed onto smaller parcels of land, and the fortunes of the whites took no more than a desultory turn—they couldn't prosper on the poor land either. Both Chippewa and whites had to struggle to make a living out of the economically depressed thinness of their isolation.

Mahnomen, consequently, is the kind of prairie farm town that looks as if time had stopped in 1949. It has two grain elevators, a dusty main street with the requisite Ben Franklin store and Rainbow Cinema, and more stuffed deer heads than customers in the Red Apple Cafe. Its proudest claim to fame, boasted on billboards at both ends of town, is that it was home to the state football champions in the successive years of 1991 and 1992. To picture at the edge of such a sleepy town, soaring like a cathedral-of-tomorrow against the flat prairie sky, a 210,000-square-foot, twenty-four-hour-a-day, seven-day-a-week gambling palace, you must push your imagination. But there it is, the Shooting Star Casino, its parking lots loaded with more gigantic buses, out-of-state cars, and block-and-a-half-long smoked-glass limos than Mahnomen could previously have imagined seeing in a lifetime.

It is one thing to invest $25 to 30 million to build such a monster in the middle of the prairie, but quite another to make people come and spend the money that will make it succeed. All those buses must come all those miles from Minneapolis and Fargo and Illinois and Canada. Yet that is what the tribal elders achieved on the White Earth Reservation. U.S. law allows casinos to operate in Nevada, Atlantic City, on riverboats, and on Indian reservations. The tribal elders went with what was available to them. To bolster a flat economy, they needed whatever gimmick they could come up with to get people to come to their community and leave money behind. To emulate them is what dozens, or hundreds, of other out-of-the-way economically deprived Indian reservations and small towns in the middle of nowhere all across the middle of America and Canada want to do. They want to attract tourists. How can they get people to come and see them and spend good money in their community? To pull this off, they all want to build on whatever gimmick will work best.

"Friendly" is the word that Manitoba prints on the 779,000 license plates that are attached to the midwestern Canadian province's cars, trucks, and buses. So when they are wandering the roads—not only at home but all across North America—this will be the message of the rolling advertisement. No one is certain if the promise meets truth-in-advertising standards; people in Manitoba are generally friendly, though probably no more or less so than people anywhere else. But you go with what you've got, and Manitoba decided to go with "friendly." Previously, license plates advertised one-hundred-thousand lakes, (ten times the number Minnesota advertised on its license plates, a difference that became a matter of chagrin for the state to the south). Then Manitoba abruptly dropped its water advantage and went with "friendly" instead. And no one was certain whether it was working.

"Manitoba needed an identifiable profile," explained Madeleine Arbez, who is the manager of marketing for Travel Manitoba, a branch of the provincial government's Industry, Trade and Tourism Department. Arbez has the job of turning the events and the people and the sites and the landscapes of her home province into a tourist draw. The pressure is on her to capitalize on her province's strengths and minimize its weaknesses, to figure out what might appeal to whom, and lure them in. To do this, she needed a thesis, a statement giving the bottom line of the product she would be trying to sell. She handed me a sixteen-page document entitled "Travel Manitoba Marketing Plan." On page seven in bold type it stated, "Manitoba is friendly people, safe environment, outdoor adventures, cultural and historical events, diverse geography."

Across the border in North Dakota, Tracy Potter is assistant director of tourism. His task in Bismarck is equivalent to Arbez's task in Winnipeg. His view of the challenge facing him was pretty much the same. "In order to attract tourism, North Dakota first needed an image," Potter told me. "We didn't have a bad image; we just didn't have any image. Even in the minds of people as close by as Minneapolis in neighboring Minnesota, North Dakota was just this blank spot." So he and his staff had to get busy; after five years' worth of image advertising beamed by television into Minneapolis as well as into the neighboring Canadian provinces of Manitoba and Saskatchewan, Potter seemed satisfied that his state had at last achieved a visible identity. "We've moved from being a vague blank spot to something," he said.

When the tourism promoters give their state or province an image, it may or may not have anything to do with reality or with what the rest of the citizens perceive themselves to be. What North Dakota chose to be, in the words of Potter—the picture of relaxation in golf shirt and sneakers in his office at the state capitol—was "a mythic west." North Dakota, he pointed out, has a history that includes cowboys and bandits as well as farming settlers. Indians and explorers and cavalry figure big in the story, and so do railroad builders and miners. North Dakota took the theme of its early settled history and, in Tracy Potter's words, presented "a dreamy, ghostly place where you could come to walk in the footsteps of . . ." he paused, "I hesitate to call them heroes, but . . ." Potter trailed off because he didn't quite know how to present the fact that, besides Lewis and Clark and Teddy Roosevelt, General George Armstrong Custer's house was also on the North Dakota tourist trail. But after the mythic west promotional campaign was initiated, visits by out-of-staters to the North Dakota Badlands increased by 18 percent.

Manitoba, too, chose to push a kind of fuzzy history. In 1992 it spent big money on television ads that evoked a kindly version of a hundred years ago: pioneers, explorers, French Canadian fur trade voyagers, Great

Spirits, buffalo hunts (minus the slaughter), and Indian tribes. Its television ads were done in soft focus, turning out liquid, light images of actors pretending to be Indians as they paddled canoes up the Red River, or making like the village blacksmith hammering a horseshoe over a glowing forge. "We decided to clean up all the imagery about Manitoba," explained Madeleine Arbez, "and be consistent. We wanted to invoke a warm feeling toward the Manitoba product and yet be consistent with what was recognized as the trend in travelers' desires." Manitoba produced one set of television ads that emphasized a sense of history, and another set of ads that promoted going to the beach—those 100,000 lakes. Test markets at home liked going to the beach; test markets outside the province liked the history. The new slogan became "Explore Manitoba; Discover a Place That's Hard to Leave and Impossible to Forget." Scrapped, because "it didn't help with brand awareness," was the former slogan that had been used for only a brief time: "Manitoba, A Place in Your Heart."

If tourism, traveling to places for recreation or entertainment or sightseeing purposes, is going to be the economy of the future and the industry of the twenty-first century, which places will get traveled to, and which will not? How will people make their decisions, and what will be the deciding factors? Can tourist and travel draws be manufactured out of nothing? Can they be the creations purely of advertising? Can any place become a tourist attraction and have a tourist industry simply by wishing it to be so? Can flat landscapes in the middle of a continent with less-than-astonishing natural features, less-than-marvelous climates, no great histories of artistic or cultural production, places far from concentrated centers of population become tourist meccas? Do they require only good planning, creative image building, and tireless marketing? Or are these places foolish to even indulge in such dreams?

It is intriguing to watch North Dakota and Manitoba, these two landlocked territories in the middle of the North American continent, eyeballing one another's tourism strategies and then coming up in the end with similar marketing schemes. The tourism industries of North Dakota and Manitoba are built largely around swapping visitors with one another. North Dakota is the biggest source of foreign and U.S. visitors to Manitoba, and the same is true in the other direction. North Dakota, Minnesota, and Manitoba, along with, perhaps, neighboring Saskatchewan on the one side and Northwest Ontario on the other, all in large part feed one another and depend on one another. They live in a rarified, touristic equivalent of an ecosystem, mutually dependent. Their tourism industries consist of their citizens crossing state or provincial or international boundaries to visit one another; their advertising energies are directed at luring one another; their tourism statistics consist of counting one another. According to U.S. Customs and Immigration, 3.4 million people cross the international boundary between Canada and North Dakota each year. "Most of our visitors arrive on rubber," explained Tracy Potter in Bismarck, meaning buses and cars. "They come here from two sources, Minnesota and Manitoba." According to Lenore Laverty, who keeps the numbers for the Manitoba government, Manitoba gets 600,000 visitors from the United States each year; 220,000 of them are from North Dakota, 190,000 from Minnesota. "Ninety percent of our tourists," said Laverty, "come by buses and cars."

These neighboring provinces and states compete to see who can get the other to come and visit more frequently and leave behind more money. It is a fierce competition with a continuously changing set of circumstances and rules. Shopping is one thing that always attracts Canadians to the United States because of generally lower prices. As people in Manitoba are accustomed to explaining, "things are so cheap there." Beer, liquor, cigarettes, and gasoline, as well as more substantial items such as clothing and school supplies all appear to a Winnipegger, living about an hour from the border, to be well worth the trip to North Dakota—customs duties and currency exchange differentials notwithstanding. Carloads of Manitobans regularly trek down Highway 75 and across the border to Grand Forks or Fargo for a weekend of nothing but shopping. While there, they stay in a hotel, eat in a restaurant, and leave a lot of money. But it can go the other way too. Sometimes the comparative value of the Canadian dollar falls so low that Americans can't resist bringing their stronger currency to shop in the stores of Winnipeg. Canadian prices might be higher, but the exchange differential more than makes it up.

Another perennial attraction, taking people in both directions across the border, is gambling. For a few years, when betting on horse races was not allowed in Minnesota or North Dakota, Winnipeg's race track, Assiniboia Downs, did very well with American visitors. Many of the cars in its big parking field bore out-of-province plates. Ample U.S. currency went through the betting windows. When the border states changed their betting rules and opened up tracks closer to home, Assiniboia Downs realized it was in trouble. It was in even more trouble when gambling tastes and opportunities shifted. Government-sanctioned casinos, lotteries, and video-display gambling terminals opened up and horse racing dropped correspondingly. In the 1990s the big draw became casino gambling. The places where casinos and bingo palaces are built and the decisions about who will control them are fought over fiercely. In 1989 Winnipeg opened a government-controlled casino in the Fort Garry Hotel, an old dowager of a railroad hotel that was otherwise threatened with demolition. The Crystal Casino hoped both to keep Canadian gamblers and their money from going to Las Vegas, and possibly to attract some American gambling tourists to come to Winnipeg. At about the same time, Indian reservations in the northern United States—Michigan, Wisconsin, Minnesota, and North Dakota—started building casinos on their reservation lands. It did not take long for Indians in Canada, having seen the glamorous palaces, the jobs, the cash, and the tourists flooding into the establishments of their southern brethren, to start lobbying ferociously to get permission from the governments that control gambling in Canada to let them do the same thing. They suffered from severe economic problems; tourism and gambling, they postulated, would solve those problems.

The first big billboard I encountered when I entered North Dakota from the north on Highway 3—after the International Peace Garden that was built to commemorate the happy relationship between Canada and the United States along their endless border—advertised "the World's Largest Buffalo." This could be seen at Jamestown. So I got out my "Discover the Spirit" official highway map to find Jamestown and realized I probably wouldn't be there for a couple more days. First I had to drive through Rugby, "Geographical Center of North America," a town of two dozen houses with a map of the world on every signpost. Then I proceeded through Towner, "Cattle Capital of North Dakota." When I finally got to Minot, among the barrage of signs and billboards at the edge of North Dakota's fourth largest city, was one for the Best Western Safari Inn, complete with the kinds of lions, giraffes, and zebras I liked to see in Africa. I didn't stop to check whether they were really in Minot.

Every little center in Manitoba and North Dakota seems to have a visitor gimmick—something that somebody, some developmental organization or chamber of commerce or board of trade committee, believes will make their place stand out, will make outsiders take note enough to want to make a trip and come and visit. This is all a product, I was told, of a strategy developed during the 1980s. In other parts of North America the 1980s might have been the apex of the yuppie, leveraged buyout, fast dollar, Reaganomics boom. But in the middle of the continent, in the Dakotas, Minnesota, and Iowa, those years meant not boom but rather an almost devastating depression. As things went up everywhere else, here—in what used to be fondly called "the heartland," "the breadbasket," and other such sentimental terms for a land of distances and weather and respect for an honest day of back-breaking labor, things all went down. During the 1980s there was a prolonged drought and an agricultural-products price crisis. The region's other natural resource, energy—oil, natural gas, and some coal and hydroelectric power—became surplus. Prices fell and development slumped. The region was devastated. People went broke and their children moved away.

Everyone began to wonder, quite desperately, how they could salvage their lives and their communities and their livelihoods. Seemingly at the same moment, they came up with an idea: tourism. "All over the state of North Dakota," Tracy Potter told me, "people started to figure, possibly not always correctly but nonetheless convincingly, that tourism could save their communities." If they built a waterslide or a museum, or started a festival or opened a casino, people would come. The money these tourists would leave behind during their visit—for meals, hotels, tickets, gas, knickknacks—would grow into a whole new economy, one that would replace wheat and cattle and natural gas and lumber. And, by golly, it worked. Tourism for the 600,000 people of North Dakota is now the third largest industry, and it is growing more quickly than anything else. In the last decade tourism in North Dakota grew 18 percent faster than inflation. In neighboring Manitoba, tourism was also number three, behind mining and agriculture.

To get to all that required a massive injection of pizzazz (some might say cornball) into places and communities, onto the landscape, and into people's thinking. People who were farmers had to learn to understand a form of show business. Shy, basically reticent people had to become outgoing and hospitable and learn to treat perfect strangers as though they were old and cherished friends. They had to understand that they were doing this for commercial rather than sincere or genuine reasons. People who had a no-nonsense relationship with the land had to learn the skills of gimmickery. After endless days of driving across the rolling North Dakota steppe, I reached Jamestown and the World's Largest Buffalo. It was made of cement.

History lies still, like a thin mist, ghosting the landscape. Driving along the expansive, treeless brow of the Missouri Coteau, it does not require a farfetched extension of imagination to picture the thundering buffalo herds gathering in the valleys, the dust of their milling hanging in the air like a curtain. From the leeward side a band of Sioux hunters might approach, ponies silenced, bows and arrows at the ready. Occasionally you come upon the markers; a statue for Sacajawea, the Shoshone woman who guided the explorers Lewis and Clark on their trek between the Missouri and the headwaters of the Yellowstone River in 1805 so they could continue their journey of exploration westward. Turn a corner and there is a sign pointing twenty miles to the house General George Armstrong Custer and his wife Libby inhabited at Fort Lincoln until the fateful Sunday of June 25, 1876, when Sitting Bull and the Sioux struck and put the lights out on Custer's grand, egomaniacal dream. "Let no man call it a massacre," Sitting Bull is said to have protested, "it was merely an incident of war. We did not go out of our own country to kill them; they came to kill us."

Indian chiefs in full warbonnet are still silhouetted on the road signs of North Dakota, the highway numbers printed at about upper cheekbone level. But the land has surely changed. Surrounded as everything has become by the fast-food and fast-sleep chains—the Perkins', Hardees, and Comfort Inns—and geriatric people on bus tours, you can barely hear Teddy Roosevelt's Rough Rider yell. The noble image of Sitting Bull, who defeated Custer, has succumbed to the subsequent images when Indian Agent James McLaughlin, exploiting the great chief's later poverty and desperation, dressed him up and carted him off to the East as a freak in Wild West carnival shows. Alas, any real feeling of the historic past has vaporized entirely.

Even the more recent past has seemed to evaporate. On the brows of hills one occasionally sees the rusting hulks of old threshing machines, left over from the days when what is now called "agri-business" was still known as "farming." The recent urban past, likewise, is a brittle memory. Bill Bryson in his hilarious yet touching book, *The Lost Continent*, describes how you can't find towns now if you travel through America.

> It used to be that when you came to the outskirts of a town you would find a gas station and a Dairy Queen, maybe a motel or two if it was a busy road or the town had a college. Now every town, even a quite modest one, has a mile or more of fast food places, motor inns,

discount cities, shopping malls—all with thirty foot high revolving signs and parking lots the size of Shropshire. Carbondale (Illinois) appeared to have nothing else. I drove in on a road that became a two-mile strip of shopping centers and gas stations, K-Marts, J.C. Penneys, Hardees and McDonald's. And then, abruptly, I was in the country again. I turned around and drove back through town on a parallel street that offered precisely the same sorts of things but in slightly different configurations and then I was in the country again. The town had no center. It had been eaten by shopping malls.

It seemed all towns in North Dakota are like this. When I finally reached the World's Biggest Buffalo, I found it at the edge of Jamestown, a city of 15,600 people. I could see it from the I-94 highway, looming on a grassy hill beyond low buildings and chain-link fences while I was assaulted by more signs and billboards promising now, as well, a "live buffalo herd," as if in compensation for having fooled us with the concrete statue. But, as is becoming increasingly the case in much highway driving throughout America, especially on the big interstate expressways, seeing something and knowing it's there is no guarantee that you are actually going to be able to get off the freeway in any useful way to get to it. Before I could find an exit to the World's Largest Buffalo, I was a mile and a half further along, and the big buffalo was in my rearview mirror. Eventually I found a place to turn around and was able to come at it a couple more times from different directions. Finally, in exasperation, I gave up and took an easy exit to a Perkins restaurant. Unlike tourist attractions, fast food and fast motel outlets are not difficult to get to off America's highways—this being part of the whole philosophy. Before I knew it, I had a placemat and a menu staring me in the face, both faithfully promoting and picturing the "World's Largest Buffalo," and the "live buffalo herd."

The attraction I'd been seeking for the last two days proved to be the inevitable disappointment. It was sad and awkward and kind of awful. The statue weighs sixty tons and is forty feet high but looks like the kind of clumsy thing a kid in the early grades might model out of plasticine; neither appealingly abstract nor quite realistic. An information plaque, describing how long and how difficult it was to construct and hoist it up there, did nothing to improve its appeal. I hesitate to admit to anyone that all this time I was really expecting the world's largest LIVE buffalo. But, what could I have been thinking? This was America and this was the business of tourist attractions; what is real pales in comparison to what can be manufactured. The live buffalo herd accompanying the statue was even more disappointing and disheartening, if that could be possible. A few of the noble beasts were supposedly out in a field, though they couldn't be seen as they were hiding amongst clumps of trees and bushes. I was directed instead to a makeshift corral sandwiched between the National Buffalo Museum, the Jamestown municipal water plant, and an RV park where overweight people in funny holiday outfits were enjoying a few brief moments of real air outside their air-conditioned motorized homes. These "live buffalo" consisted of three animals and a calf standing in the mud. In an adjoining pen were two llamas, who knew they were marooned far from home, and a morose pony.

It is perhaps too easy to make fun of the tourist attractions that are thrown at us in places like North Dakota or Manitoba, or the world over for that matter. But if people are going to put them there and advertise them, if they are going to expect folks to drive hundreds of miles to see them, expend valuable days and weeks of holiday time in the journey and, most of all, spend money both on the trip and in looking at the things, then they should have to stand the test of criticism. Sometimes so-called tourist attractions seem like ironic jokes, with the perpetrators waiting to see how long they can get away with them before anyone catches on.

In the cause of attracting tourists, some of the goofiest constructions possible have been put up across the great plains of North America. The Jamestown North Dakota buffalo is only one of these. In Cut Knife, Saskatchewan, a little town northwest of Saskatoon, there is the world's largest, you guessed it, tomahawk. It is forty-five feet long, made of fiberglass and mounted at the edge of town so as to be caught in mid-swing slicing through the top of a twenty-foot-high teepee. Not to be outdone, Vegreville, Alberta, has a giant Ukrainian Easter Egg and the tiny nearby hamlet of Glendon, also a settlement of immigrant Ukrainians, has built the world's largest perogy, an ethnic potato dumpling, out of doughy-looking white plaster and then has stabbed it through with the world's largest fork. An appetizing construction indeed. The folks of Glendon were able to get a government grant of $58,000 to help build their perogy, and a local mechanic composed the official "Perogy Song"—sung, to the tune of "Volare," to all visiting tourists.

Another government grant of $9,000 went to help the people of Torrington, Alberta, a little town northeast of Calgary between Olds and Equity, put together their Gopher Museum. Gophers, formally known as

Richardson's Ground Squirrels, are common and sometimes overly populous throughout the prairie grasslands. The small creatures average about six inches in length, are vegetarian, and look a bit like chipmunks. They live in huge, underground colonies, burrowed beneath the prairie or under a farmer's wheat field. In Torrington, residents decided to capitalize on what was otherwise considered a nuisance or a pest. Numbers of the little beasts were captured, killed, stuffed, and then placed on display in the Gopher Museum dressed in Royal Canadian Mounted Police costumes, or like tiny characters out of children's stories. Their bright button eyes and smart little faces made them look like illustrations in Beatrix Potter books, but they were very much dead.

The bizarre and decidedly morbid character of the gopher museum received national television news coverage, after which Torrington and the museum were both criticized and ridiculed. Big city people made fun of them; animal-rights types were appalled. The publicity, however, didn't faze the locals in the least. "This fuss is all free publicity," they said. "It can't help but put us on the map and attract tourists."

Americans are even better at this sort of thing. La Crosse, a small city on the border between Wisconsin and Minnesota, boasts "the world's largest six pack"—a half dozen gigantic silos filled with beer; and Escondido, California, has the world's largest champagne glass—at the Lawrence Welk Museum. Seguin, Texas, has the world's largest pecan; Gardner, Massachusetts, has the world's largest chair; and Blackfoot, Idaho, the world's largest Pringle potato chip. Obviously no one cares that they might drive halfway across the country to see something that turns out to be totally corny, or perhaps visitors share the crazy tastes of their hosts. Even places whose natural beauty and splendor should make them "seeable" and attract visitors on their own merit get tarted up with awful additional "attractions." In that same state of Wisconsin, the dells on the Wisconsin River are a series of lovely islands and cliffs of richly weathered sandstone rock. But a visitor can go there and never see the rock or the river, so busy are you looking for Elvis or Marilyn Monroe in the Wax World of the Stars, or playing a round at Old River Adventure Golf, or visiting the Pirate's Cove or the Biblical Gardens or Crazy King Ludwig's Adventure Park. Or the Ho-Chunk Casino. Niagara Falls, one of the great natural wonders of the world, is overwhelmed with so much junk—horror museums, rides, and fast-food outlets—that the falls themselves are the last thing many people notice.

In Manitoba, when tourism in the countryside started up in earnest a

couple of decades ago, small centers attempted to get the edge on neighboring communities through whatever gimmicks seemed available to
them. They went the theme route—like an imaginative hostess having a
party—selecting something that could from then on be identified with
their community. Many places took the theme they had selected and
then attempted to attract tourists at specific times of the year by building a festival around it. Some of the early ones made authentic sense;
they were tied to a community's history or to the ethnic background of
its settlers. Canada's National Ukrainian Festival, for example, was set in
the town of Dauphin where, at the turn of the century, many Ukrainian
immigrants had settled. Islendingadagurinn, or the Icelandic Festival of
Manitoba, happened in the Lake Winnipeg town of Gimli, which had
been so exclusively Icelandic when it was settled in the late nineteenth
century that it had been known for a time as "New Iceland." Other
places celebrated their crops or their harvests: the town of Portage la
Prairie created an annual strawberry festival, the town of Morden celebrated its corn and apple harvest. But, as usually happens in situations
where people try to get an edge on their neighbors, the edge can't last
long because the neighbor soon copies or tries to outdo in order to catch
up. So before long, every little town and crossroads in Manitoba had a
festival; there were enough of them to fill two pages of small print in the
government's *Provincial Vacation Guide*. Some of them had to reach far:
the people in the town of Miami (no relation to Florida, and no beach)
decided to have an annual Mule Derby; the community of Boissevain, in
the southwest of Manitoba, organized turtle races and called the event
the Canadian Turtle Derby. There were Frog Follies in St. Pierre, Hoof
and Holler Days in Ste. Rose du Lac. The little crossroads of Dugald decided it should be the place where the annual Canadian Wellington
Open Boot Throwing Championship was held; and Pine Falls, a pulp
and paper mill town on the Winnipeg River, instituted a Paper, Power,
Pickeral and Pea Festival. Roblin, near the Saskatchewan border, had
Moonshine Daze [sic]; and Seven Sisters Falls, on the edge of the Canadian Shield wilderness, had Trapper Dan Days. I could go on, but you get
the picture.

Each of these festivals became welded into an annual event and then
was aggressively promoted as a tourist attraction. In short order, they
attained legitimacy; each with its own spot in the province's calendar of
special events, its own billboards, its own lore, and its claim on public
tourism promotion dollars. Each event—each trout festival, corn and

apple festival, and winter carnival—became, in the minds of its organizers and in the minds of the people in little places with names such as Flin Flon, Morden, and Leaf Rapids, a reason for people to travel a quarter of the way across the continent to see them. The visitors, each little burg believed, would come for the events, appreciate the unique local gifts, and, most importantly, drop money into the local economy.

For rural Manitoba, these festivals became tourism incarnate. The organizers of each did a follow-up calculation when the event had ended to determine the ratio of costs to benefits for the local or the regional economy. Each event persuaded its host community of its indispensibility; its value in putting and keeping the community on the map, providing identity and, more importantly, producing spin-offs in terms of business, jobs, and money.

Some tourist-attracting ventures make it only halfway there, as if something important has been forgotten or a critical page has been torn out of the "how-to" book. There is a small village north of Winnipeg, in the Manitoba Interlake, called Komarno. The Interlake is low and boggy and, at certain seasons of the year, thoroughly insect infested. Trading on this, Komarno took the mosquito as its mascot. At the edge of town, the citizens erected a statue of a gigantic, ferocious mosquito, proboscis poised. The draw worked; friends of mine reported that they once drove miles out of their way to see the Komarno mosquito. When they got there, they discovered that Komarno delivered only what it promised—a mosquito statue in a field of wet, tallish grass. They might have been pleased and gratified, but they were in fact disappointed. It was like a job only half done. It wasn't in the least a proper tourist trap; there were no souvenir stands to capitalize on the attraction, no theme park or irritating insect gallery. "Nobody wanted to sell us anything," my friends complained. There was no Mosquito Bar and Grill wanting a few dollars for lunch, and no Proboscis Motel inviting them to stay over and get another look by the dawn's early light. There was just the mosquito statue; you came, you looked, you left. The entrepreneurs of Komarno had missed the boat; they had sold themselves short.

According to Tracy Potter in North Dakota, this is a common problem among rural midwesterners who are just figuring out the tourist game. "A lot of rural areas don't understand all the things urban people are willing to pay money for," he said. "There's a lot of room to move in that area; we have a very low level of infrastructure. You can go to a lot of wonderful places here and not find a cash register to leave your

money at." A lot of the so-called attractions that, in the mind of someone steeped in the tourism business, should have dollar signs attached to
them, are free; for country people they are just things that they do, and
they wouldn't dream of charging money for them. To turn an event
from simply something that people do to something that is an industry
requires a substantial leap. Potter used bird-watching as an illustration.
"If someone in North Dakota wants to watch birds, he just goes. He takes
his binoculars, and parks along a back road near some woods. But if
someone in New York City wants to watch birds, he understands that he
might have to hire a guide, rent a car, book a motel, and make a two-day
expedition of it. It's a different way of looking at everything." Potter postulated that people in his state, and in Manitoba too, would have to
learn how to think and operate differently, in ways someone from New
York City might understand, if they were going to make tourism into the
industry that could truly take up the slack where the rest of their economy had left off. If they were going to use it as they wanted to—to save
their communities—along with everything else, they would need to
understand better what things they could make money from. "It may
only turn into a few jobs," said Potter, "but in a town of a hundred
people, twelve jobs is big!"

I should point out that from an economic standpoint, the mid-
continent—Manitoba and North Dakota—probably deals with some of
the worst kinds of tourists in the world, those who come but don't spend
any money. If you happen to be the Winnebago dealer, you'll make
some money from these people, but after making that major expenditure, it seems to be a matter of pride to take everything with them and
avoid spending a cent on the road. I've seen motor homes equipped
with extra fuel tanks so that they didn't even have to fill up with gas on
a thousand-mile trip. Americans in such traveling bungalows are cursed
by Canadian resort owners in the lake- and river-laced wilderness country, who call them "pork and beaners." "They drive on our roads, park by
our lakes, eat their own groceries, leave their garbage behind, and take
all our fish home to the States."

But, that little aside out of the way, there is something plaintive, almost heartbreaking about tourism in the mid-continent. There is such a
long way to go. Despite the increased awareness and the massively increased strategizing and marketing activity of the last few years, North
Dakota was still forty-ninth out of the fifty U.S. states in terms of its
tourism industry; Manitoba remained seventh out of the ten Canadian

provinces. This adds a dimension of poignancy to the optimism and the earnest efforts of these mid–North American landlocked entities. Could anything they do really succeed? Was it worth it? Were they on the right track, one that would produce prodigious fruit at some magical moment down the line? Or were all their assumptions wrong-headed; were their hopes built on sand? On the other hand, was the situation so desperate that they had no choice? Was an economy built around tourism their last hope even if it turned out, in fact, to offer no real hope?

In the United States as a whole, travel and tourism in 1995 represented 10.5 percent of gross domestic product ($870 billion according to research by the WTTC, World Travel and Tourism Council and the U.S. Travel and Tourism Administration). Five hundred and thirty-five billion dollars of this was spent by U.S. citizens traveling within their own country. Overseas visitors brought $76 billion into the U.S., which was $25 billion more than Americans spent traveling abroad. The United States is the largest producer of travel and tourism in the world, followed by Japan, Germany, France, and the United Kingdom. And it enjoys a healthy tourism trade surplus.

The situation for Canada is very different. Tourism in Canada is a $26 billion a year business. In terms of international balance of trade, unlike the United States, Canada has a perennial deficit (about $6 billion in 1994); a great many more Canadians choose to visit the rest of the world than do foreigners elect to come to Canada. This is no doubt a function of many things, not the least of which is that in a competition for foreign-tourist money, the United States frequently wins out over Canada.

Canadians and Americans travel for similar reasons: to escape winter; to make a ritual visit to Europe, for example, to experience old culture, old history, and old architecture; to make return visits to relatives and friends left behind in "Old Countries": the Philippines, India, Hong Kong, and China as well as countries of Europe. Both, too, are well off relative to most peoples of the world, and therefore can afford to travel for adventure and life experience. However, the Canadians who trek in Nepal or go on safari in Africa or visit ruins in Guatemala do so without many reciprocal tourist visits to Canada by Nepalese or Kenyans or Central Americans.

The tourists who come to Canada come for quite different reasons. In Manitoba, for instance, the tourism office identified visits of foreigners to that province in 1991 as being for the following purposes: 237,000 for pleasure or to shop; 113,000 to visit relatives or friends; and 98,000 for business or to attend conventions. In Manitoba, tourism is worth $833 million. But, as in Canada as a whole, there is a deficit vis à vis those leaving and those visiting. More Manitobans leave each year to go somewhere else than foreigners come to visit in Manitoba. In 1990, Manitobans traveling within their own province spent $407 million; other Canadians coming to Manitoba dropped $186 million; Americans brought $109 million to Manitoba; visitors from other foreign countries, $33 million; and Canadians outbound, $98 million. This last is a curious category, identified by Manitoba tourism statistics as "those expenditures made in Manitoba by Manitobans and other Canadian residents for goods and services related to trips to U.S. or other foreign destinations or enroute to the U.S. or other foreign destinations." The statistical breakdown as to how the money was spent in 1990, or which segments of the economy received it, was as follows: $124 million for accommodation, $388 million for transportation, $153 million for food and beverages, $52 million for recreation, and $116 million for miscellaneous purposes.

These are numbers that you or I may not care about one way or another, but to the tourism bureaucrats they are like mantras; recited, reported, and pored over. There is probably no industry in the world that employs more bean counters or activates more varied and creative ways to interpret numbers than the tourist and travel business. Part of this is because it is still such a new industry, and its definitions and understanding in the gross-domestic-product scheme of things are still being worked out. Part of it is the players still trying to figure out how the grand chain of things works and what makes an impact on what—they are trying to understand just how far the ripples may go from any particular action or transaction. A third reason is so that the industry can argue about having a solid place in the economy, which is necessary if they want to justify appeals to governments for grants, investments, and tax breaks. If you are going to fashion an industry, tell people what makes an impact on what, and pitch governments for concessions, you have to know your numbers, and you have to have your ammunition at the ready.

Neither the assumptions nor the accounting systems, however, are by any means standard or shared across the industry. The North Dakotans, for example, care about tourism only as something to bring money from outside into their state. Thus they keep no track of their own citizens going to visit the next town. "Our mission is to create new wealth; our role is to bring tourists here," explained Tracy Potter. In Manitoba, by contrast, Lenore Laverty, who shepherds the numbers for her government, acknowledged readily that 70 percent of her numbers, by volume, were Manitobans moving around in their own province. That was fine with her. "If you are eighty kilometers (fifty miles) away from home, we consider you a tourist," said Laverty. This means that even people driving out of the cities to go for the weekend to their lakeside summer cottages got counted into the tourism statistics.

In the department of calculating impacts and benefits, North Dakota is also straightforward. "We used to apply a multiplier factor of 1.8 to each dollar," said Tracy Potter. "But we dropped that and now just keep track of direct spending. $800 million comes into the state from outside. Period. That's what we care about." Manitoba, again, does it differently. Tourism Winnipeg, the bureau that promotes and keeps track of tourism in the province's one large city, uses a formula that might be either extraordinarily complicated, or extraordinarily sohisticated, depending who you are talking to. But what it does is allow the bureau to produce sheafs and reams of statistics and data and reports that, if nothing else, make their point by the sheer persistence of their volume and weight. Grant Meder, who is manager of research and information for Tourism Winnipeg, attempted to explain to me all the variables, factors, impacts, industry outputs, and generated taxes that go into the computer model he uses to analyze, and in large part justify, his city's tourism initiatives. The $30,000 computer model is called TEAM. TEAM is used by the Conference Board of Canada and the cities of Toronto and Vancouver as well as Winnipeg to assess the impact of tourism on the local economy. "It uses sophisticated input/output methodology and econometric modeling techniques," explained Meder. "It also uses the latest tax structure and input/output matrices to ensure reliable, conservative analysis and reporting. The model is designed to calculate either the demand or supply side of a tourist sector."

This is a lot to absorb. If you are, say, a senior citizen from Duluth or Des Moines clambering off a Greyhound bus in front of Winnipeg's downtown convention center for an international conclave of square dancers, you probably don't even know that you and your actions are being counted and analyzed in this way. Your involvement with official tourism will be more immediate. When you step off a chartered bus in Winnipeg, officials don't step forward to place a lei around your neck as they would if you were arriving in Honolulu. Tourism Winnipeg's official mascot is a character in a fuzzy, moth-eaten owl costume, who is marched out to descend on any visiting group larger than three. They may giggle at the time, surprised and overwhelmed by the attention, but I wonder how many elderly folks return home plagued by recurring nightmares of being waltzed into the lobby of the Holiday Inn by a character wearing a great, horned head and a dowdy, musty suit.

All the elaborate analysis and number crunching is neccessary, explained Meder's boss, Janet Walker. "Tourism is unlike any other industry; there are so many crossovers. You can't analyze or understand it under any of the traditional umbrellas." Walker, a spirited redhead, described her attitude four years earlier, before taking her Executive Director job: "I had a suitcase and traveled, and I thought I knew what tourism was all about." But she soon learned how simplistic she had been. Her earlier attitude hadn't included the kinds of analyses TEAM is obsessed with, and which would come to absorb her.

Walker's $1.5 million budget and fifteen staff members run a visitor's center at the Winnipeg International Airport, but otherwise they are engaged in research, marketing, and sales. They busily use their computer printouts to razzle dazzle various governments into supporting tourism initiatives. "If we can show the province (of Manitoba) that it will get $11 million in taxes from $600 million worth of conventions, then we can persuade them that it is in their interest to put up a million dollars to support such events." Walker said their formula was that an investment of a million dollars in tourism would yield $11 million in taxes to the city, and $53 million to the next level of government, the province. But to arrive at those numbers requires leaps of imagination and calculation that presume cumulative and ripple effects all up and down business—manufacturing and retail—industries (with taxes paid at every stage) stemming from every actual dollar spent by every real, live tourist. Winnipeg's prototype for this kind of analysis was set when the city lured the national football championship Grey Cup game in November of 1991.

The Grey Cup football game provides an interesting paradigm to show how a modest local community in the 1990s examines and evaluates its tourism. It shows how the industry both manipulates and responds to events and eventualities. It is also a good illustration of tourism active in a community, raising questions that both tourists and host populations should be aware of. It is also, since I lived in Winnipeg, the only example that I, usually the traveler, have of what it's like to be the recipient/host/victim of tourism. The Grey Cup event gave me an idea of what it might feel like to be a resident of a Caribbean island, or of a European town with a cathedral; what it might be like to be in a village on the edge of the Masai Mara, or Jerusalem at Easter, or in Pamplona Spain when the bulls are about to run.

Gathering information like crazy and pouring the data into their computer, Grant Meder and his helpers came to the conclusion that Winnipeg residents and tourists visiting Winnipeg would drop $9.75 million by the time the Calgary Stampeder and Toronto Argonaut football players left the field—the winners to guzzle champagne, the losers heading for the showers. But they also speculated that an additional $5.5 million would move around in the city economy directly because of the game, as retailers stocked $2.75 million worth of football merchandise, as $1.57 million was spent on capital improvements—including an expansion of the football stadium—and $1.29 million was spent organizing and holding a week's worth of Grey Cup Festival events. The total economic activity generated because of the Grey Cup event would be $33 million for Manitoba, $29 million of that in the city of Winnipeg. Five hundred and eighty jobs, 530 of them in Winnipeg, would be supported, at least for a short while, by the Grey Cup championship and festival events. All of this activity would reward governments with $8.25 million in taxes.

Not all of this was strictly tourist, since many of the people going to and spending money at the Grey Cup game and during the week of events preceding it were people who already lived in Winnipeg. But Meder figured that 45 percent "of the total industry output"—that is, all the numbers, including taxes—would come from tourist spending or spending by people who wouldn't have been in Winnipeg were it not for the fact that the Grey Cup was being played there that cold, late November week.

To make their case for the Total Economic Impact, Tourism Winnipeg showed a chart with a Demand Side that included the Direct Expenditures (every dollar put out for a Grey Cup–related ticket, souvenir, hot dog, or bottle of beer by a Winnipegger or a visitor). Then they multiplied those by Economic Multipliers, Input/Output Matrices (the things North Dakota refuses to use). Through this they achieved an Economic Impact that they added to their other Economic Impact, the one that calculated the business and capital expenditures from the Supply Side also multiplied by their Economic Multipliers, Input/Output Matrices. The results were too dazzling for any layperson to refute. The CTS (Canadian Travel Survey) and ITS (International Travel Survey) methodologies were employed to estimate average expenditure per person, a process that carefully eliminated multiple counts. "For example," they explained, "accommodation expenditures for two persons sharing one hotel room would, through this method of survey, be evenly distributed." There would be no phoney inflating of the numbers. "CTS (which is used by Statistics Canada) evens out those odd cases where persons will spend far above the average: stay in a downtown hotel, eat at expensive restaurants, buy many Grey Cup souvenirs, and those cases where persons will spend below expectation: stay with relatives, eat only at home, buy few souvenirs." This evening out is achieved by virtue of the "Normal Distribution Principle."

I live in Winnipeg. I didn't go to the Grey Cup game, though I watched it on television. I'm a little ambivalent about football. What's more, as a resident of the host city I don't know how much, if any, of that economic impact trickled down as far as me. I suspect not very much; probably none. Maybe I actually suffered a deficit after my taxes paid the salaries of the bean counters. What I do know are entirely different things. During the Grey Cup parade, the day before the game, my street was closed off for four hours, and in order to get home, I had to park my car in a Safeway supermarket lot three blocks away and walk. There was also serious evidence that as the parade was marshalling itself into form, some Calgary Stampeder types must have had their horses on my lawn.

For eight or nine hours after the game was over, the downtown area of the city, where I live, remained crowded, busy, and noisy. There were rowdy and loud people in the streets, traffic was congested, car horns honked either out of celebration or out of frustration; it would have been impossible for anyone to get any sleep or have a nice quiet time reading a book. The football game ruled the day; it would have been impossible for anyone to have a life that was not severely influenced by the football game, by the city's event of that day, by Winnipeg's tourism of that moment.

I don't say all of this just to be a sourpuss. I raise it because this will be as close as I'll ever come to identifying with the folks whose little houses are in the back streets behind the hotels and night clubs of Acapulco, or who teach at a junior high school around the corner from Disneyland, or who manage the woodlot and do a little farming on a few hectares of land along the road leading from Fussen to Neuschwanstein Castle. Tourism is good for the tourist businesses and quite possibly for government tax accounts. The holding of the Grey Cup game and the preceding week of partying generated nice big numbers for tourism bean counters and brought broad smiles to the faces of civic luminaries. But what did it mean for me and my neighbors? Or what did it mean for anybody else and their neighbors? What does it ever mean, anywhere: in Thailand and Jamaica and Rome and Costa Rica as well as in Winnipeg? Is my life better because the Holiday Inn was able to fill all its rooms?

The Grey Cup is part festival, the kind of natural, almost spontaneous celebration required by any community to keep alive in its culture the ability to share and celebrate. The championship game has been played every year since 1909, so, unlike the U.S. Superbowl, which was a media event from its beginning in 1967, it has a history that predates the economic opportunists. But over the years it has been transformed, like the running of the bulls in Pamplona in Spain, from spontaneous community ritual into an infinitely bigger phenomenon. There is something tangibly artificial about its becoming that. Like the concrete buffalo statue in North Dakota and the cornball weekends that have been invented for small towns all over Manitoba, it is now also a tourist trap. The Grey Cup was a more elaborate form of the St. Pierre Frog Follies or the Mule Derby in little Miami Manitoba or the Wellington Boot Kicking competition of Dugald. The moment it became a tourist trap was the moment that launched around this football game the elaborate effort to justify it as an economic enterprise: to identify it as a creator of jobs, a lure for money to be spent, a source of tax revenues. The promotions operators have always rubbed their hands together around such events, but the moment that government-supported computers started cranking out economic impact analysis data, the week, the football game, and all the people it was hoped would show up for it became commerce of the most calculated kind.

Turning visiting, community ritual, and celebration into commerce seems to me to create a couple of substantial problems. The first is: at what cost or what price? The second is: where do you stop?

The tourism industry is constructed on a vast, capital-intensive infrastructure. It costs a lot of money to have airlines and bus lines and airports and hotels and restaurants, and they are only the tip of the iceberg. This necessary infrastructure also includes roads and map-printing services, travel agents and advertising and credit systems. It can be a huge part of an economy; there are many jobs to be had both building and maintaining it. But once in place, it has a huge mouth to fill. In the case of a place like Winnipeg, the city could get ready to handle ten or twenty or thirty thousand out-of-town football revelers; it could have enough of an infrastructure in place to bed and feed and entertain them. But if the Grey Cup football celebrants filled the hotels and restaurants and bars for one particular 1991 November week, who was going to fill them the next week? This business of building infrastructure, as it is so mechanically called, creates its own urgencies. They are not purely private ones, reserved for independent private entrepreneurs (ask any citizen of Montreal who, almost twenty years after a flamboyant mayor brought the Summer Olympic Games to that city in 1976, still finds the payments of the debt added to his or her taxation bill). The data and analysis that are becoming an increasing part of the tourism enterprise have one great purpose: they will justify prying loose public money. If governments, at all levels, can be persuaded of positive economic impacts and tax benefits, the tourism operators hope in return to get larger public participation to help their enterprises: investments, grants, tax breaks, or secondary support systems such as advertising or visitor services. We taxpayers and our children—who inherit the government's debt—share not only the burden of the cost of the public stadia, convention centers, or whatever other drawing card may be built, we also share the urgency that the privately owned Holiday Inn remain filled and profitable. Because if it doesn't, it and any other enterprise that is an integral part of the infrastructure will stiff us for the incentives and tax breaks that lured it to be built in the first place. It is plainly much easier to see where we all share in the potential problems than the potential profits and successes of the community tourism venture. And did anyone ask us?

The second question, where do you stop, is equally urgent. In southern Germany, the town of Oberammergau has a unique public pact amongst its citizens that dates back over three hundred and fifty years. Every ten years, they all become part of the town's tourist attraction. In 1633, Oberammergau miraculously escaped the plague that ravaged almost all of the rest of Europe. So, as an act of thanksgiving, the townspeople agreed they would regularly, in perpetuity, enact a Passion play of the suffering and Easter story of Christ. Members of the town to this day voluntarily dress up and play roles in this Passion Play Oberammergau has been putting on since the seventeenth century. The baker becomes Judas Iscariot, the nurse at the hospital become Mary Magdalene.

The auto mechanic might be Jesus; the local teacher gets to be Pontius Pilate.

At first, the performance was put on solely for the benefit of God. But now it is an attraction that lures tens of thousands of tourists and is an important cog in the economy of both the town and of the tourist numbers for southern Germany. But the Bavarian citizens of Oberammergau, as well as making the play a total community venture, have decided how to put a limit on it; they restrict it, by long unwavering custom, to once a decade. But if one of our communities, through an aspect of its landscape or its history or culture or through some artificially engineered attraction, turns into a tourist draw, where do we as citizens want to be in that? Have we agreed where our privacy starts and ends, particularly if we do not have jobs somewhere in the tourist economy?

Do we agree with, or have any part in deciding, the image of our community that is presented to draw tourists? The city of Winnipeg has long hung its tourism hat on the peg of its ethnic variety. Winnipeg is made up of peoples from all over the world; the ethnic variety of Manitoba leads the Canadian mosaic. The community's ethnic and civic leaders decided to capitalize on that. Each summer tourists are drawn by the busload to a festival called Folklorama. They come from rural points in Manitoba, they come from the American Midwest, they come from Saskatchewan. All over the city the festival goes on—in churches, neighborhood halls, and ethnic clubhouses. People dress up in Old Country costumes, cook and serve ethnic foods, and perform traditional folk dances for the visitors. The event is huge. It's also hard to criticize; it's nice to be an ethnically and culturally diverse place, everybody putting on the face of getting on in harmony. But the question for those of us who are citizens of this city is, did we all agree that that is how we'd like to be marketed? Do I want to buy in to that? If I don't, do I want to put up with a tourist stopping me on the street to complain because I don't look appropriately ethnic? It's the same question for anybody, anywhere in a tourist environment. How do the farmers of North Dakota feel about their task, to live in "the dreamy, ghostly place where people walk in Custer's footsteps"? How do the people of Mahnomen, particularly the non-Indian population who stand to receive precious little economic reward, feel about living on the doorstep of a casino culture? Do citizens of the cathedral towns of Europe wish continually to be seen as "quaint"? What do the island folk of the Carribbean think of the constant pressure on them to appear happy-go-lucky and simple in order to fulfil the tourist expectation?

The decisions, and their implications, about who we will be, what we will do, and how much of our public money and energy should be spent to lure the tourist economy raise themselves daily. In 1995 the city of Winnipeg wrestled with the question of the future of its professional NHL hockey team. The Winnipeg Jets had been part of the National Hockey League for twenty years. They were regularly a mediocre team and perennial money losers. As big-league sport becomes more and more ludicrously expensive, the consensus was that to keep the Jets in town and to keep them playing in the National Hockey League would require two things, both of which would eventually involve large dips into the public purse. A new arena would have to be built at a cost of, maybe, $140 million, and the team would have to be purchased from its owners either outright, or with its losses covered. Those losses showed no sign of abating; with astronomical athletes' salaries, major league sports are becoming an increasingly expensive proposition. Could a mid-sized city such as Winnipeg compete with the big markets such as New York, Toronto, and Los Angeles? Should it? In 1996 an agreement was reached for the Winnipeg Jets to move to Phoenix, Arizona.

Those who argued for the team's staying frequently made the tourist attraction case. Without a major-league hockey team, Winnipeg, they said, would be Nowheresville. If the team left, the city would be diminished, in its own eyes and in the eyes of potential visitors, convention-goers, and tourists. Besides, a hockey team's losses are not really that; the hockey team red ink doesn't take into account the ancillary economics: the Demand Side, the Supply Side, the Economic Multipliers, Input/ Output Matrices that would show how well off the city really was, in tax revenues generated and general economic activity.

Those opposed argued that a city such as Winnipeg couldn't afford a luxury like the Jets. The hockey team was bleeding the city dry in order to support a minority of sports fanatics and tourism dreamers. The taxpayers should not be held hostage to fulfill fantasies for a few.

So it goes; the up-side considered, the down-side pored over. The debate engaged. Stan Beardy, who is president of something called the Northern Ontario Native Tourist Association, dreams of the day when visitors from places such as Germany and Japan might come to the native Indian communities in his part of the world to experience life in teepees and get lessons on how to skin rabbits. The Ojibway of northern

Ontario inhabit a land of pristine fish-filled lakes and rocky pine-shrouded islands, where loons call in the morning and moose wade in the shallow bays. When the tourists from Germany and Japan discover this land and the villages of the Ojibway people, Beardy argues to his fellow Indian leaders, they will leave $7 million behind on the forty-eight Indian reserves across that region. But the elders tell him they are worried about their culture. What will happen to it if the tourists come, if the sweat lodge or the sundance or the pipe ceremony is put on at the bidding of snapshot-taking visitors? They are worried. Are they right to be worried? Their customs are all they have left of a culture that has been under full assault for over a hundred years. They don't want it to be commercialized. They fear that would be the final nail in their culture's coffin.

Across North America, tourism is seen as a solution for economically depressed areas. Sometimes this is a pipe dream, an unrealistic panacea. Other times it is a form of real salvation, a solution that keeps people living with self-respect and independence in their communities. It is a solution that keeps them at work offering genuine pleasure, relaxation, and edification to visitors, and provides the reason for their children not to pick up and leave at the earliest opportunity. In Maine, when the value and the importance of the forest industry dropped off abruptly, tourism gathered up the slack. From 1977 to 1989, while the traditional employer in that state, the timber industry, was laying people off, the value of tourism to the Maine economy grew by 5.1 percent a year. In the southern Appalachians, a chronically impoverished part of the United States, tourism and recreation brings in $379 million annually.

All kinds of people benefit from the jobs that tourism creates. The Shooting Star Casino might be on a Minnesota Indian reservation, but so many of the gamblers going to visit it are Canadians that a major beneficiary has been a Winnipeg tour promoter named Wayne Flett. By chartering buses and running them exclusively between Winnipeg and the Mahnomen casino, Flett, whom the Indians have nicknamed "Mr. Canada," turned a $300 investment into a $10 million business in two short years. Flett, in turn, supports companies that charter buses to him, and employs drivers, mechanics, and young women like Wendy Williamson and Kathy Hradowy. A couple of times a week Hradowy, who is otherwise a nurse in the palliative-care ward of a Winnipeg hospital, and Williamson, a journalism student, don purple-and-teal "Mr. Canada's Touring Network" track suits with the company logo of a

Canadian moose on the back and "You're the Moost" emblazoned as the slogan on their sleeve. Then they head to the depot for their part-time jobs as hostesses on Flett's buses. For the three-and-a-half hour trip down and the three-and-a-half hour trip back, they entertain whoever is on the bus—be it a group of senior citizens, an ethnic club, or an office party. They answer questions, tell jokes, lead songs, show movies, or, if people can't wait to start gambling, hand out bingo cards. The day trip gives them each a hundred dollars. Income-supplementing money. Tourism money. It is money they would not otherwise have.

But there are many questions, it seems to me, that don't get answered, or even asked, in the predominantly economic sytem of considerations about tourism. We have the numbers for the tax benefit and the hotel and restaurant receipts, but did Winnipeg become a better place by holding the Grey Cup Championship game? Is Mahnomen, Minnesota, a better place for having its gambling casino? Are they better places in all ways, or are there hidden costs that are going to turn out to be serious in the long run? Are people having a good time? Did anybody, on either side—visitor or visited—learn anything?

How close are these concerns to the mind of someone like Janet Walker as she sits in her office in the Winnipeg convention center and ponders the possibilities for marketing her (my) city? "An important thing is knowing what kind of destination you are," she told me. "Can you be all things to all people? If not, what kind of city are you going to be? Are you a casino destination? Multi-cultural? A meeting place of history?" Are you a winter city? Can you turn the mosquitoes that plague your summer into a tourist and economic advantage?

The last point: there is, according to Janet Walker, no way to calculate saturation, to know when you've had or offered enough or too much. She shrugged when I asked her that question. "You gotta know that you don't know all the answers."

9

Traveling in a World of Tourism

Perhaps all this mass movement, all these people getting on and off airplanes and cruise ships and sightseeing buses, is a passing phase. A friend of mine, on his way to the airport in Toronto where he was going to board a plane for Guatemala, encountered a woman who exclaimed, "Travel, what an interesting way to see the world!" As if it had never occurred to her. Travel is, in fact, hard work as a way to see the world. This woman experienced the world as much as she wished in very different ways: through books, through movies, through television. Despite all the hype, advertising, and promotion of an industry that can get us almost anywhere almost instantly, this woman remained resolutely unmoved and unmovable; she was charmed by the idea of actual traveling as if it were a thoroughly novel concept, interesting but not something she would ever do herself. Perhaps, in the end, we will agree with her; we will come to believe we do not need to travel—just as easily as we came to believe we did need to. Or, as the supersonic jet surpassing the sailing ship has altered our world, a new technology will alter our experiential context so much that travel, as we know it now, will cease to have any meaning.

In the very near future, we are told, we will be able to consume an experience of travel simply by going into a room and putting on a virtual reality helmet connected to an interactive computer program. Video, computers, and the simulations that are possible through combining them, are the growth industry that may well supersede travel and tourism. As I write this, one such enterprise—called the Human Interface Technology Laboratory (HITL), in Seattle—is busy developing the technology to bring enhanced armchair travel to consumers. In the HITL scheme of things video cameras, some of them fitted to robots (presumably for the hard-to-get shots), will be sent touring through foreign countries and exotic locations. What the photographers and the robots recover will be fitted into computer programs. The customer or consumer (or former traveler), donning a virtual-vision visor and headset and climbing into an audio-visual chamber, will start his or her trip. Computer-generated signals will cause sensors to reproduce sensations, sounds, smells, and sights, and the customer will find him- or herself awash in a shark-clogged coral cavern, or dodging traffic on a noisy street in Istanbul—with all the sensory illusions of actually being there.

The changes these possibilities hold for human activity (certainly not for human experience—though perhaps for human anti-experience) are quite astounding to consider. Those in the know try not to cause alarm by taking us too far too fast. Virtual reality, caution promoters, will be a sales tool at most, serving in the travel agent's office as a taste of what a real trip *could* be like, improving on what a brochure can show—possibly making the brochure an anachronism. But what is to prevent it from becoming a substitute for the trip itself? Much mass tourism, we already note, is simply clever marketing; why couldn't virtual reality, cleverly marketed, not have a brilliant future? By the end of the century, it is predicted, the Disney empire will have become one of the world's major travel entrepreneurs. Wouldn't virtual travel fit perfectly into the Disney mix where everything is entertainment anyway?

I'm betting, however, that no matter how brilliant its future, virtual travel won't replace or supersede real travel. I suspect that humans have more complex needs and urges than the creators of virtual reality technologies can comprehend, amazing and clever as their inventions are. And part of the complexity of human urges is the urge to travel actually rather than virtually, to move from one place to another on our globe.

When Darwin was examining the world's flora and fauna for his studies of the evolution of man, he noted that for certain species of birds the urge to migrate was stronger even than their maternal instincts. If autumn came before they were quite ready, the mother would nevertheless leave the nest and abandon the fledgelings rather than miss the moment for the long journey south. This conflict of instincts sometimes plagues humans as well. Bruce Chatwin, in his book *The Songlines*, where Darwin's observation is recounted, develops his theory around the conflict between the sedentary and the wanderer in the human character. Without deciding clearly whether the wanderer and the settler are opposed parts of each of us individually, or are opposed parts of our society— some of us wanderers, some of us settlers—Chatwin declares himself unequivocally predisposed in favor of the wanderer. He blames most of the ills of history, including all aggressions starting with Cain against Abel, on the settler impulse. The wanderer impulse, by contrast, is freeing: "as a general rule of biology, migratory societies are less aggressive than sedentary ones. There is one obvious reason why this should be so. The migration itself, like the pilgrimage, is the hard journey: a 'leveller' on which the 'fit' survive and stragglers fall by the wayside. The journey thus pre-empts the need for hierarchies and shows of dominance. The 'dictators' of the animal kingdom are those who live in an ambience of plenty. The anarchists, as always, are the 'gentlemen of the road,'" says Chatwin.

It is worth being reminded that the great religions of the world were founded by prophets who were itinerant travelers. Buddha, Moses, Mohammed were all wanderers; Abraham was a nomadic tribal chieftain. Christ's most memorable instruction to those who would follow him was to give away all but one cloak, and not worry where they were going to lay their heads when night came.

There are theories, cited with relish by Chatwin, that emphasize the healthful mental and physical properties of travel. Robert Burton, who wrote *The Anatomy of Melancholy*, cited travel as a cure for the depressions brought on by settlement. "There is nothing better than a change of air in this malady [melancholia], than to wander up and down, as those Tartari Zalmohenses that live in hordes, and take the opportunity of times, places, seasons." Burton linked the human urge for movement to the patterns already established in the cosmos, and postulated that movement must thus be ordained. "The heavens themselves run continually round, the sun riseth and sets, the moon increaseth, stars and planets keep their constant motions, the air is still tossed by the winds, the waters ebb and flow, to their conservation no doubt, to teach us that we should ever be in motion."

Chatwin goes also to the Danish theologian, Søren Kierkegaard, for some further advice on the mental health benefits of ambulation. Kierkegaard, in 1847, wrote to a friend, "Above all, do not lose your desire to walk: every day I walk myself into a state of well-being and walk away from every illness; I have walked myself into my best thoughts, and I know of no thought so burdensome that one cannot walk away from it . . . but by sitting still, and the more one sits still, the closer one comes to feeling ill. . . . Thus if one just keeps on walking, everything will be all right."

Not all of us who travel, of course, are as eloquently thought out or as articulate about why we travel as Kierkegaard or Robert Burton. The urge to travel, nevertheless, is possibly one of the purest of human urges—it is the urge to see the world, the urge to meet other people and see how they live, the urge to see the world's great and famous wonders. It informs us and it possesses us. The possibility of looking over the next hill or seeing the other side of the world is irresistible to most of us. Many of us nurture the dream of taking a trip for years, and, if we are not rich, we assiduously save our pennies for it. My mother, a farm wife, had no opportunity for any far-flung travel until she was almost sixty years old. But she had carefully nursed two dreams: to visit the Holy Land, and to witness a performance of the Oberammergau Passion Play in Germany, the land of her ancestors. When she was sixty, she was able to fulfill both dreams, and they formed touchstone moments in her life. For years afterward she showed her slides, taken on those trips, to her family, to church groups, to anybody who would sit still to watch.

Those of us who have been invited to sit through our friends' slide shows or home videos of their trips understand the delicacy of the equilibrium we are in with the returned traveler: they have been where we have not been, they have seen what we have not. Sometimes there is a strain. Not always are we swept into the orbit of their enthusiasm. The journeys of the great traveler-explorer Marco Polo resulted in a total change of the world after the thirteenth century with the opening of the silk road and the spice routes. But as he lay on his death bed in Venice, he complained with bitterness about the reception he had received upon returning from his adventures. He had been called "crazy" and a "liar," and, in Genoa, he had been thrown into jail. Though broken by his disappointment at the small-mindedness and the lack of imagination of his fellow countrymen, he stuck to his story. "I have not told half of what I saw," Marco Polo stoutly protested.

Travel changes us. As it did for Marco Polo, it may separate us not only from who we used to be, but also from others who have not gone with us, who have not seen what we have seen, who have not looked over the top of that next hill: who don't understand. So sometimes we feel we dare not tell them too much. But the important thing is to have had the experience of the engagement and to understand how the travel and the engagement might enlarge and change our lives. My mother's trips to Germany and the Holy Land were the pilgrimages of her life, undertaken with awe and innocence. Her attempts to share her experiences afterward were her way of letting people in on a little bit more of who she was.

We forget easily, in the gloss of commercial promotions and in the mechanical systemization of the industry, how precious the experience of travel is for most people, and how innocent and enthusiastic most people are about their travels. This happens in spite, I might add, of the sometimes cynical or snobbish tone of a lot of travel writing. Sallie Tisdale, writing in *Harper's* magazine, vents her annoyance at some of the more famous of today's travel writers because she finds the tone of much modern travel writing—"as opposed to the traditional travel books of writers like Mary Kingsley (marvelous), Evelyn Waugh (precise), or Robert Byron (adventures I read simply for the way the language flowed)"—to be pompous, snobbish, and often narcissistic. The height of snobbism, according to Tisdale, is the preoccupation of those who like to consider themselves "travelers" to distinguish themselves from "tourists." Modern travel writers seem exceptionally determined to do this. "A particular distinction between travel and tourism marks modern travel writing, which sometimes goes to acrobatic lengths to frame it. The self-annointed traveler despairs of the nearness of other visitors, the tiniest evidence of travelers having passed this way before, and is touchy indeed at being mistaken for one of the crowd. What he hates most about tourism is tourists." She goes after Paul Theroux, one of my favorite writers, first for his grumpiness: "Paul Theroux, on the other hand, filed an amazing number of peripatetic dispatches from around the world, not liking much of anything." Then she attacks him for something he said in *The Happy Isles of Oceana*, his book from the South Pacific. "Tourists," wrote Theroux, "don't know where they've been, travelers don't know where they're going." This is a clever, snappy phrase, but it attempts to pick a fight where none should happen.

Tisdale is particularly snappish at Paul Fussell (editor of the *Norton Book of Travel*). "Paul Fussell calls tourism 'egalitarian,' but with that word he detests it. He longs for the days when traveling was the province of the few." The modern-day traveler, and by extension the modern-day travel writer, is, in Tisdale's opinion, far too precious and is thereby, in fact, dangerous. "He goes alone where no one he knows has

been, and then comes home to talk about it. It's the new colonialism."
Better they should experience the trip in the manner of most tourists,
who are infinitely less self-important. She tells the story of her father's
excitement when he finally got to see the Panama Canal, after having
dreamed about it since World War Two. "I was struck," she says, "by his
unapologetic enthusiasm, his apparent lack of concern for who might
think his cruise ship vacation silly or inappropriate or just not cool.

"There is nothing like a trip," says Sallie Tisdale, "to cure a swollen
head."

I agree with Tisdale though I'm afraid I am guilty also of the feelings
harbored by the writers she criticizes. I know the feeling of not wanting
to be part of the herd and not wanting to be confused with the herd. I
have nurtured the desire to be mistaken for a local and loathed being
lumped in with the gang of my contemporaries—American and Canadian tourists. I am quite familiar with the urge to walk the other way
when I see a tour group coming up a street or a village road. I know the
panicked feeling of not wanting to associate with them, of not wanting
to be caught in the restaurant crush with them, of not wanting to be
mistaken for one of them. I have said to myself, "I did not go halfway
around the world in order to hang out with more North Americans."

But then, why *did* I come halfway around the world? Who do I think
I am? If I feel I cannot be who I am, then who am I? And if those
thoughts do not shame me, then what am I learning? Tisdale, again,
writes, "What's the point of going somewhere different to pretend to be
someone different? Travel should be a mirror; and when I look in a mirror I see a bloody Yank with a poor command of languages, a map unfolded on the street corner, lost again."

Perhaps the problem is that since the travel experience is so special,
we correspondingly want to think of ourselves as too special to be who
we really are. We enter into and persist in indulging an extended fantasy.
We insist to ourselves that we are not like other people, and since we are
not doing what we normally would do every day, neither are we quite
ourselves. But travel is not the way for us to forget or deny who we are; it
should be, rather, a means of reminding us who we are. We, too, can be
foreigners, can be unilingual and insecure. The purpose of travel should
be, indeed, to make one a foreigner and to make us feel what that is like.
This will not happen if we go only to Disney-controlled environments.

In the Oxford dictionary one of the words grouped in the definition
of *foreign*, along with *alien* and *dissimilar*, is the word *irrelevant*. I like this.

I can think of nothing more difficult for my ego than to think of myself as irrelevant. Yet that is exactly what I am when I am walking down the street in some foreign town, in Djibouti, say, or in Mexico City. It matters not then, to the hordes of other people on the street, whether I am a traveler or a tourist. I am confronted at every turn with my irrelevance. It is not my life that is happening around me on all sides; that life would be happening with or without me. I am a foreigner. Yet it is exactly that, my foreignness, that I must embrace. I like the idea of the humility we must submit to every time we are forced to do that, every time we are forced to understand ourselves to be irrelevant. If humility, to paraphrase Benjamin Franklin, is the doorstep to wisdom, how blessed we must then be. When we have no power, then we have no choice but to turn to a kind of childlike trust. "As a foreigner," wrote Tisdale, "one is both conspicuous and invisible; you can't blend in completely, and you won't be recognized either. To be a foreigner is to surrender somewhat. It requires a certain kind of trust, a willingness to play the fool for awhile." Or, as Flaubert put it, "travel makes one modest, you see what a tiny place you occupy in the world."

I am struck by how the act of traveling has changed the lives of individuals I know, and also how their enthusiasm for it never disintegrates or even diminishes. It is *not* something you do in order to get it once and for all out of your system. A friend of mine has had a job for fifteen years as a flight attendant for a major airline. So she has been in a position to see much of the world without having to pay full fare for the privilege. You might think that after a diet of foreign hotel rooms, early morning wake-up calls, restaurant and airline food, and 737 cabin air, Bonny would want to spend her time off sitting on her front porch with her feet up. Rarely so. Given a few days' holiday, she will usually be off once more, frequently on her own: to Egypt to see the pyramids, to India to see the Taj Mahal, to New Zealand to visit a friend, to England to indulge her passion for gardens. It was she who offered this quote from John Steinbeck: "A journey is a person in itself; no two are alike and all the plans, safeguards, policing and coercion are fruitless," wrote Steinbeck. "We find after years of struggle that we do not take a trip, a trip takes us."

"I can't better express the way one's life and travels seem to be connected or guided by some inexplicable force," Bonny said. "At least mine are. Sometimes disappointments occur, but none have been important enough to remember after they are past. For the most part, I have had such incredible opportunities that more than once I have had to stop, step back, and disassociate myself from the crowd or situation for a moment to fully appreciate the magic of it all."

For Bonny, the majority of these moments have occurred when she was traveling alone, without benefit of—or distraction from—an accompanying group. "At first I dreaded traveling by myself," she confessed, "but I was forced to do it. Now I go willingly, avoiding groups whenever possible, anticipating with excitement what lies ahead."

Travel (and possibly love affairs) provide for the main great adventures available to most of us. These two, uniquely, provide our chances to turn ourselves over to something or someone largely beyond our control. When we embark on a love affair, we enter into an adventure of discovery, discovery of the other and discovery of ourselves. We enter a world of wonder, high in risk because of the very high likelihood we will get in over our heads, but full of promise too because of what we are likely to discover, even when we are over our heads. Travel, as John Steinbeck postulated, is like that too. The trip takes us and the most exciting thing is that it takes us where we almost certainly could not have predicted we would go and into the arms and the care and the hospitality of those we could barely have imagined to exist.

One of the bittersweet beauties of the travel experience is that it reminds us of our vulnerabilities, of how much we must depend on other people, of how much we don't know—how much we don't know yet, and how much we will never know. When I travel I am constantly at the mercy of strangers, and the great, edifying surprise of it all is how well placed my trust turns out to be most times when I have no choice but to place it. My friend, Bonny, tells about being en route to Cairo, on one of the first of those solo journeys, and finding herself the only woman in the airport departure lounge in Amman, Jordan in the middle of the night. This unsettled her. But she took a deep breath and, after she calmed herself, she found the helping hand offered itself. "Miraculously, there was always someone to take me under their wing and guide me in the right direction," she says.

What she had done, despite her apprehensions, was move from needing to be totally in control to giving herself over, making the transition from fear to trust. This, perhaps, is the main lesson of travel. I habitually travel without advance hotel reservations. Some people consider this rash and think it shows that I am badly organized. They can't understand how I would want to live with such uncertainty. I like it, however, because it gives me the latitude to move freely, to follow my whims, and to take up the offers of people I meet along the way. Rarely have the experiences been unpleasant. There have been, I admit, some nights I would rather not have had. I will never forget getting off the train from Paris to Barcelona in the middle of the night. This was in the 1970s, not long after the death of Franco, and Spain was still a dark and medieval kind of place. Outside the train station it was a wet and chilly January. I was young, traveling with a friend, and since we had no other plans we felt we had little option but to take the offer of one of the station platform hucksters. Soon we found ourselves following through a labyrinth of darker and ever more ominous streets. Eventually we arrived somewhere—we had no idea where we were—and reached in our pockets to hand over eight or ten dollars so we could be taken into a glum-looking building and down a hallway past some rough-looking card players raucously jabbering in a strange language. Cigarette smoke and the heavy odors of cooking sat like some unwelcome uncle in the airless halls. I felt I was being led into a dream from which I might never emerge.

We were given a room: one that was about the size and shape and temperature of a refrigerator. The ceiling was high above our heads, and the walls crowded in so close to the saggy bed that we could barely move around it. A bare light bulb, hanging high above us, flickered a shadowy light. We settled in and agreed that my job for the rest of the night, as my friend attempted to sleep, would be to sit guard at the door.

I have no idea, in retrospect, whether the fear that kept me awake and alert all night was merited. Probably it was not; in the morning everybody and everything, even the grim hallway, seemed quite benign. The strange language I couldn't place with the aid of my Berlitz Spanish phrase book was, in all likelihood, Catalan; my friend and I were very young and knew next to nothing. But the point is that I recall nothing, through many, many subsequent nights without Holiday Inn reservations, ever being any more ominous—and certainly even that one was not so bad. Rather than stumbling into bad experiences, I have, by contrast, been offered incredible hospitality, safety, and assistance by total strangers who wanted nothing from me in return other than a conversation, a tale about my country, or perhaps the opportunity to bestow their kindnesses. I have been taken on duck hunting expeditions by cowboys encountered in a restaurant in a small town in the middle of Guanajuato state in Mexico, and on safari by a camp owner in Zimbabwe. In both cases, my hosts were people I had known less than half an hour before the offer was made. Hospitality always, in my experience, is more available than trouble.

Even when bad things happen, they are frequently accompanied by redeeming factors that instruct us amazingly about human nature. Friends of mine were in Turkey. They had rented a car and were driving on back roads in a far corner of the country. In a blinding rainstorm they had an accident; their car bumped a pedestrian who was walking by the side of the road, knocking him into the ditch. It was really a minor accident, but it soon turned into a debacle. The man was all right, but when my friends stopped to help him out of the ditch, they were set upon by a group of passersby who, infuriated by what they took to be carelessness, wanted to beat them up. My friends, barely able to understand all the shouting that was going on around them, were terrified. One of them had his glasses broken in the scuffle. The other had his nose bloodied. It took an hour and the arrival of a policeman to calm things down. But eventually things were sorted out, and my friends, shaken, were back on their way.

They didn't, however, as some of us might do, hurry themselves out of Turkey, shaking the dust, so to speak, off their feet in relief. They stayed on. For the rest of their trip every Turk they met took care of them, deliberately doing something to make up for the horrors they had suffered during their frightening hour. When an optometrist in the next town heard the story of how my friend's glasses had been broken, he repaired them without charge. "Nothing like this should happen to visitors in our country," he exclaimed. When they told their story to a hotel keeper, he gave them a meal and insisted they stay for free: "Nothing like this should happen to visitors in our country!"

Travel is catastrophic, changing, uplifting. But it doesn't happen unless we embrace rather than recoil from the position of being a stranger, giving ourselves over without choice but also without reserve to our vulnerability.

In human terms, the possibility of engagement is the critical element pushing almost all our travel. This is why I believe that virtual reality helmets and cyber travel and computer programs will never take the place of real traveling, any more than computerized cyber-sex will take the place of real-life love affairs. If anything, we are more likely to move in the other direction. The masses may be criticized, but most people as individuals are not stupid. In the past people put up with a lot because they believed their alternatives were limited. Now many people's travel desires

and demands are becoming much more sophisticated. For the same reason that there will not be a huge stampede toward the cyber-travel
booths, we are beginning to see a groundswell of rebellion against the
barrenness and manipulation and the sanitized nature of much of our existing travel options, especially the old tried-and-true package tour.

Not long ago I spent a morning with a woman who for five years has
been my travel agent. I wanted to ask her about the changes she has witnessed in her business, not so much in the industry, but in the demands
and the requests of her customers. Ruth Wiebe has run a small, independent travel agency for eighteen years. The business as a whole has certainly changed: in volume, in possibilities, in the kinds of people who
travel, and in the places they want to go. She is caught in the middle,
she says. "From the corporate side there is more technology—starting
with computerized booking—and a great deal of pressure for the agent
to be simply an order taker." But from her customers, the pressure is in
another direction. "They want to talk to somebody who cares about
their trip. And they more and more want you to help them *do* something." There is not a full-scale revolt among her customers, Ruth Wiebe
tells me, but there has been a shift of about 30 percent among what used
to be her package—eighteen European countries in twenty days—travelers who are now demanding more intensity and a great deal more local
interest. "They want to spend a week walking through the Cotswolds;
they want to plant trees in Costa Rica."

Often those of us who travel a little bit differently criticize the pack-
age-group traveler, accusing him of lacking imagination. This is arrogant, and it wrongly places the blame. I suspect more and more that
what we identify as the sterility of a lot of tours is not the fault of the individual traveler. From dozens of conversations and hearing hundreds of
stories where the teller's eyes light up, I know that most of us crave engagement. People's travel stories are never about how well-organized and
efficient their airport departures were. Ruth confirmed this. The tourist
has to overcome the vast, stupefying power of the corporate approach.
This is a system, like any other conveyer belt, so the natural thing in the
corporate approach is to get the horde out there, assure them of their
safety, give them an opportunity to take photos, get them home, and
collect their money. People who defy this system, who want to define
their own options, who want "air only" for example from an excursion
package, who want to leave the beaten path, are looked upon as rebels
anywhere might be. They stand in the way of the system's smooth func-

tioning; they stand in the way of maximization of profits. It is not in the interest of the corporation, whether that be the tour company, the airline, or the hotel, to encourage them. But they will not be stopped. The industry has had to respond to accommodate them. Travel is not a corporate experience; it is a human experience. "Experience" is the operative word. It is not a commodity simply to be consumed.

The human and the experiential in travel is what we must all hope will ultimately prevail. The corporate and the industry component, we must all hope, will have to listen and respond. Another travel agent, Sandra Janzen, is part of the second generation of a family-owned tour business that for twenty years has been taking people across North America on bus package tours. When I asked her to identify the main trends in the travel business from her standpoint, she didn't hesitate. Her travelers wanted more. More trips, for sure, but they were also demanding more within those trips: more adventure, more participation, more engagement. "We can't just put people on a bus and send them somewhere. They are making much more specific demands about the experiences they want, and we have to respond. People will not be passive lookers through the window."

10

The Problem with Tourists

In an out-of-the-way restaurant, some distance from the noise and bright lights of downtown Nairobi, Kenya, I waited, as I had been requested to, for Stephen Ole Senteu, Mark Ole Karbolo, and Charles Ole Sonkoi. It had taken several days and two intermediaries to set up a meeting with these three Masai elders, and I wasn't sure what to expect. The restaurant was dark and very warm. The smells were the heavy, steamy ones of maize meal cooking backed by the sharp whiff of braised goat meat. Tables, covered with oilcloth, were crowded and the chatter of tribal languages predominated over English. Presently my contacts arrived, not quite as "elder" as I might have anticipated. Two were in their early thirties and the third, Mark Ole Karbolo, was perhaps forty. The first thing I noted was how they were dressed; in this part of Africa, even on the streets of big cities and especially at places like the open market that happens every Tuesday on a wide empty field between two busy thoroughfares and the skyscrapers of downtown Nairobi, one can see Masai men and women in their traditional garb. The Masai are tall, their bodies, slender as willows, wrapped in bright, red cloth; their heads are closely shaved. Heavy bracelets weigh down bare arms, and necks and shoulders are encircled by necklaces of endless loops of colored beads. The most startling aspect of Masai get-up, as we know from decades of *National Geographic* photographs, is the work that has been done to their ears: the lobes are first pierced when they are quite young children, and then they are stretched, on both men and women, into huge dangling

loops in order to accomodate elaborate rings of heavy, colorful, uncom-
fortable-looking beads. Traditional people wore all handmade orna-
ments, but Masai in contact with the modern, urban world have been
known to accessorize all manner of additional materials into their decoration. I saw one elderly fellow who had strung bright yellow, empty
Kodak film canisters on his earlobe. A friend reported seeing a person
who had incorporated pork and bean cans.

But these three men, though they had come from a distant village in
the country, were in smart, dark, business suits, which made them odd
indeed. There is a moment of doubletake when you encounter men
whose earlobes are pierced and stretched, extended open loops flapping
like spinnakers, who also wear business suits. But I suppose when you
are scheduled to meet government officials and then a foreign writer,
you dress for the part. We shook hands and, after ordering a tray of Coca
Colas and plates of maize-meal ugali, a dish that everyone traditionally
eats by eagerly scooping it up with agile fingers, they began their story.

They explained first how far they were from home. To have come
from the Masai Mara to a suburban restaurant in Nairobi, without doubt,
placed them psychologically much further from home than I was,
though I had traveled all the way from North America. I had crossed an
ocean; they had transgressed a cultural divide. Their particular corner of
the land was known as the Loita. The Loita, a forest area of 1,000 square
miles inhabited by villages containing 20,000 of their people on the east
edge of the Masai Mara is, I had been told in preparation for meeting
them, the last refuge of traditional Masai life. The world there is still a
place where cattle and trees are the centers of spiritual and cultural as
well as economic existence. When you greet a traditional Masai, cour-
tesy demands that you ask first how his cattle are, and then you inquire
about his family. "Our forest is the only thing that is of value to us," explained the men without the least hesitation. "We graze our cattle in the
forest and have our *bomas*, or homesteads, there. We have our cultural
ceremonies and rituals in the forest." The forest is mountain forest stud-
ded with hundred-foot-tall cedar trees, eighteen and twenty feet around.
The Loita Masai are nomads. In the dry season they and their cattle
share the forest with elephants, buffalo, leopards, colebus monkeys, and
hundreds of species of birds, reptiles, and insects. In the rainy season
they move, with their cattle, out to higher grazing grounds. Life is isolated from the outside world. The village that Stephen, Charles, and
Mark had come from is seventy miles from both the nearest post office

and the nearest telephone. To get to the road that would bring them to Nairobi for meetings with their big-city lawyers, the government, and with me, they walked five days through the forest. But these well-spoken, serious men explained that they felt they had no choice but to come to Nairobi because that life back home in the forest is threatened, about to change dramatically. "We don't like to spend so much time in Nairobi," said Stephen, the de facto spokesman for the group. "We are completely rural people. But if our forest disappears, then we will be in Nairobi permanently because we will have no home."

The great fear that drove them to Nairobi was that their forest will disappear because their land, like the rest of Kenya's Masai Mara, is about to be given over to tourism. It is appealing land. It has all the desirable elements for tourism development: the Mara is haven to great herds of the large animals—elephants, wildebeests, and lions—that tourists like; it is within hours of Nairobi and an international airport; the existing lodges are busy, lucrative, and overcrowded. So the Masai are vulnerable, and they have no ready protective champion. The political tale is long and complex, filled with the usual elements. There are foreign conglomerates with ready cash and political intrigue that sounded to me both universal and, simultaneously, of a uniquely Kenyan variety with elaborate in-fighting, intertribal rivalries, and perceived treacheries by the very people the Masai believe should be standing up for them: their own local politicians and county councils. Through it all, because of their vulnerability, these community spokesmen had become desperate. They hoped, they confided to me, to change the government's plan through any method available: they were filing a lawsuit on behalf of the Loita Enaimina-enkioyio Trust and were appealing to world opinion. Should those strategies fail, they feared—no doubt correctly—the last bastion of traditional Masai forest life would be lost forever.

The development plan for the Loita forest threatened to inundate their isolated region with roads. Eight tourist lodges would be built by a South African company. The tourists who would come to the lodges are presumed to want to see elephants and lions, not herdsmen and cattle. So if the disruptions of the roads and development didn't destroy the life of the Loita Masai, the pressures for them to move out of the way would. "We would be denied our right to use the forest," the three elders complained, "which we have protected from time immemorial, for our cultural practices and for grazing our cattle."

This would not be the first time this has happened to the Masai. Once a great and feared people with reputations as fierce warriors, the Masai ranged over an area that stretched from the Indian Ocean to Lake Victoria, some 80,000 square miles covering the lands north to Mount Kenya and south to Mount Kilimanjaro. Arab slave traders, even as they were decimating the tribes in all the surrounding country, feared and avoided the Masai; writer Isak Dinesen described them as "chic, daring, and wildly fantastical." But the first squeeze on their territory and their nomadic roaming came in the nineteenth century when the British colonized East Africa and built the Uganda Railway. The British forced the Masai to move out of the way of the trains. They were placed on reserves, like Indians in North America, and pushed further south onto the Serengeti Plain in what is now Tanzania, and then into Ngorongoro Crater, the spectacular hundred-square-mile volcanic bowl. Then, in the 1930s, civilization caught up with them again. With an eye to a huge tourist and visitor potential, moves were initiated to turn the Serengeti into a protected wildlife conservation area. The Masai became migrants not only because of their tradition of following their cattle, but also because they were pushed to keep ahead of the pressures of development, land protection, and tourism. The half million or so of these tribesmen still left inhabit territories that straddle the border between Kenya and Tanzania, occupying the edges of the Serengeti and the Masai Mara game preserves. But the pressure is constantly on. In the 1970s they, with their cattle, were evicted from the floor of Ngorongoro Crater. In Kenya growing tourist development in the Masai Mara likewise made their world smaller and less secure. The Loita Masai now see it as urgent to make a last stand.

Tourism is the push that is chasing the Loita Masai, just as it is pushing indigenous, local peoples in many places of the world. Tourism development has the potential of being every bit as disruptive of peoples and cultures as industrialization would be—the building of giant factories or power dams and the accompanying transformation of agrarian or wandering people into industrial workers or urbanized paupers. In fact, tourism's insidiousness arguably makes it even more disruptive. Tourism, on the massive scale that the last decade has achieved and with promise of more to come, forms one of the great movements of people in the history of the world. As John Elkington and Julia Hailes point out in their assessment of tourism's impact on global environments and peoples, whenever relatively large groups of people traveled during history— whether it was the Crusades, the Mongol invasions, or the European colonization of America—havoc and devastation followed in their wake. "Entire cities were put to the sword, tribal peoples were wiped out." The fact that in mass tourism people move temporarily, perhaps only for two weeks at a time, is beside the point. Or perhaps it makes the impact even greater; a revolving movement of people is the same as a permanent movement with arguably more effect because of the constant, unrelenting intensity. Presumably the Mongols rested periodically; the American colonists eventually had to settle down. Tourists never rest; when a group has worn itself out, it returns home to be replaced by another wave at the height of their energy and enthusiasm. When such groups of intensely energized, holidaying or sight-seeking people move, all manner of change and disruption cannot help but surge before and follow them like a wake.

What the marauding army of tourists primarily leave behind is a radically changed culture. Riding in the travelers' suitcases, western, basically American culture—sporting its other self-appointed guise as world or global popular culture—intrudes everywhere. It is both cart and horse, in advance of and as a result of, tourism. In some ways, the culture precedes the tourists in order to welcome them, to make them feel "at home." If it is believed, for instance, that the American traveler will only go where he or she can watch CNN, as the British masses earlier would only go where they could get chips with their meals, CNN will certainly (and quickly) find a way to be there. There are few places in the world where you can't now watch CNN or British SKY television in your hotel room. This has two effects, the first being that it changes the culture of the places visited. The second effect is that for the visitor, it becomes increasingly impossible to get away. If you are American, it is more and more difficult ever to leave America behind.

On the other side of the world from Kenya and Tanzania, in Belize, March is the month when people plant their crops. In the fields of big plantations or on tiny, burnt patches cut out of the tangle of the jungle, corn, beans, tomatoes, and squash seeds are pressed into the warm earth. Along the Caribbean coast, March is the height of the conch season. Every daybreak, skiffs set off from village jettys praying to return home loaded with valuable cargoes of the fruits of the sea. Because the weather is starting at last to become swelteringly hot, this is also when people, both locals and visitors, flock to the cays, the string of tiny, crescent-shaped coral islands, to celebrate Easter, lie on the beach, or snorkel and dive off the country's glorious reef.

But in the last few years, March has also become the month for something else. It is when U.S. college basketball's national tournaments are played. In Belize "March Madness" is creating a truly unique aberration. Until recently the only people who paid attention, the only people who cared how Wisconsin was faring against Stanford or how Tulane might come off against Auburn were basketball crazies, the special afficionados and loyalists of the colleges and universities in the United States—students or people following their alma maters. The rest of the world didn't know anything was going on and presumably didn't care. But that was before ESPN, the all-sports cable television network. And that was before sophisticated electronic dishes and Earth-orbiting communications satellites made it possible to watch U.S. cable television virtually anywhere on the planet.

So in March, along with planting, conch fishing, and Easter visits to relatives on the cays, U.S. college basketball is now also a fixture in the life of Belize. In the communities where tourism's presence has demanded U.S. television in every hotel room as well as in most of the restaurants and bars, it is inescapable. On a sunny Saturday afternoon the sandy main street of San Pedro on Ambergris Cay is virtually deserted. The beach, except for a few desultory sunbathers, is empty. But the bars just off the street and along the beach, from the Holiday Hotel to the Purple Parrot, are packed to overflowing. Passionate, cheering, shouting, pressing crowds, visitors and Belizians alike, scream with excitement at the Arkansas Razorbacks or the North Carolina Tarheels. A young Belizian of about nineteen or twenty, whom I recognized as a guide on one of the tour boats, his eyes glowing with excitement, confessed to me that he thought the Arkansas team to be "superb!"

This basketball frenzy was totally unexpected for me when I was caught in San Pedro in late March. I watched the hoopla for a while on a big screen that had been placed in the lobby of the Holiday Hotel. Then I returned to my room where I switched on the television. Immediately, I encountered something else that ought to have been totally out of place: Tanya Tucker singing about losing love on TNN, the Nashville Network. This was on the shores of the Caribbean in sight of the ruins of Mayan pyramids. U.S. television is no longer U.S. television; as happened with Hollywood movies, the television version of American culture marches with as much self-confident authority as Caesar's armies when they went into North Africa and Gaul. By virtue of its technology and the peculiar audience-mesmerizing lure of "Oprah" and "Home Improvement," it has become imperial and global. It is impossible to escape. In Kenya each morning, government-run television in Nairobi gets out of the way for an hour of CNN from Atlanta. All this is a function of the last few years. It happened almost instantaneously in the early 1990s. But so quickly are the changes and incursions being implemented that by the time you read this it will all be even more pervasive and more profound. CNN is American television, CNN is also world television—American world television. And it is moving at the same speed as is the phenomenon of tourism itself, into the furthest corners of the globe, to change things irrevocably and forever.

In another country on another continent, foreign visitors to the new Marriott Hotel in Warsaw are met at the desk by staff who, in better than passable English, tell them to "Have a nice day." This is Warsaw, Poland. A decade after Solidarity, less than half a decade after the collapse of Communism, the restaurants in and around the Marriott offer burgers and steaks and, once a week, hold a Tex-Mex night. For any who might find this not "down home" enough, an American-style Pizza Hut has been constructed next door. By installing a satellite dish, the attentive folks of Marriott circumvented a chronic Eastern European frustration; guests get telephones that work and they can direct dial anywhere in the world without dealing with Polish operators or phone lines.

The world is homogenized like a carton of milk. For a die-hard traveler who might wish to experience other worlds, the very reason for going is negated; there are no other worlds. The smaller the world becomes, the more possible and the more likely is its homogeneity. A man who has a job as a tourist guide on one of Belize's outer islands told me that the television dish, not tourism, was changing the world. He was right—except he should have understood them to be the same thing. Television dishes come first to serve the tourist, or to serve what the travel operators believe to be the wishes and needs of the tourists. Once in place, they catch on with the locals as well. The locals get hooked and all is changed. In Harare, Zimbabwe, a young woman explained to me that her favorite program was WWF All-Star Wrestling and that she and her six-year-old son adored Hulk Hogan and the Million Dollar Man. Tourism and such cultural changes go hand in hand. Traveling visitors change a place first by their presence and then by their expectations of comforts and amenities like television and standards of transportation, restaurants, and hotels which must be created for them. All these are then left behind when they depart.

Local people are little more than passive pawns, often bewildered by
what is happening around them. Even if they like the ways their world is
changed, it still happens without their permission or their control.
Tourism's legacy is the Americanization or the westernization of the
world. If you don't like it, what can you do?

Sometimes, as might be the case for all of us, the local inhabitants get
angry. The pressure gets on their nerves, and they lash out at their visitors. Frustration spills over in explosions of random, rabid fury. Russian
youths in Moscow, not long ago, astonished visiting tourists by yelling
at them and making obscene gestures. Tourists, western newspapers reported, expressed shock and dismay. In Kenya a special police force has
had to be created to protect tourist visitors on game reserves from bandit
attacks. A couple of well-publicized murders set Kenyan tourism on its
ear but were also a pointed message from the locals.

In southwest England, Bath is an historic city that has been visited by
tourists ever since it was founded by the Romans in 54 A.D. For centuries
the visitors, first the Roman armies on their furloughs and then subsequent spa lovers, came to the natural hot springs on quests for health
and well-being. Some still come to Bath for the waters but, more likely,
they want to sightsee their way around almost 2,000 years of history,
from Roman baths to splendid displays of eighteenth-century Georgian
architecture. Though the locals have coped with the visitors for almost
two millennia, a few of them recently reached the breaking point. The
pressure of numbers has reached the point where open-top tour buses,
with their guides barking a running commentary over amplified speakers, pass through the main sections of Bath at the rate of about one every
seven minutes. A rebellion started when one man, at last pushed over
the edge, abruptly turned his garden hose on a tour bus and gleefully
doused the unsuspecting visitors. A kind of guerrilla campaign soon
spread; more hoses came out and other citizens, who also could take no
more, took to heaving apples at the buses.

There is growing cynicism and anger the world over on the part of
people who feel victimized by the events that change the country they
thought was theirs into something that appears to be mainly for the
benefit of somebody else. When the Masai were herded off Kenya's Mara
to make way for government game preserves, some of them tried to get
back at the whites and the authorities by killing rhinos. They were upset
by tourism and reasoned they could sabotage it most effectively by turning on the almost-extinct beasts they correctly concluded were being

preserved for the tourists, but at their expense. These people are not stupid; they are wise to what is coming down. "It is almost axiomatic," wrote peripatetic traveler and writer, Paul Theroux, "that as soon as a place gets a reputation for being paradise, it goes to hell."

The individual tourist is caught in the middle, unwittingly the cause and simultaneously the recipient of the bad feelings. For a long time I had wanted to visit Kenya. Like almost a million others who go there each year, I had been seduced by the romantic image of wild Africa yet available in a civilized and comfortable style. I believed I could find elephants and Masai tribesmen, but I knew I could also speak English and stay in familiar British or western-style hotels. However, there were a few things I didn't know. I didn't realize that to be a tourist in Nairobi makes one as much a pursued species as the animals you might want to go to see. As soon as I stepped from my hotel onto Kenyatta Boulevard the first morning, I was targeted by a phalanx of hucksters armed with pamphlets. Like jackals waiting in the bush, they all take off at once when a likely prospect appears. I was a likely prospect; three salesmen fell in stride—grabbing at my arm, jumping in front of me—persistently pitching a day trip to Amboseli Park or three days in a caravan on the Masai Mara. I picked up my pace; they kept in step, holding pamphlets an inch from my nose. I was annoyed and a bit frightened. I was just getting used to my surroundings; I suffered from jet lag, the beginnings of a sunburn, and the effects of my malaria medication. The doorman at the hotel had warned me to be careful out on the street, but I had laughed at him. I tried to keep a jolly smile on my face. "I don't want to go on a safari just now," I protested. The jackals paid no heed. "A minivan trip to the Rift Valley; a week on a bus to Mount Kenya." They stayed with me at a good pace for three blocks, never ceasing their patter. They had their job to do, which was to hunt me down as surely as Teddy Roosevelt ever hunted an elephant. At last, irritated by my lack of response, they backed off and I was left with the streets of Nairobi. This presented the next problem.

In Kenya the myth of wild animals, the legend of the savannah, is strong. It is ignited by stories we all remember from childhood and rekindled by glossy visitor brochures. But in reality, the animals are rather benign; certainly they are the last thing one needs to worry about. If you really want danger and adventure, you shouldn't go to the jungle; try instead to survive the streets of Nairobi. All the dangers and excitement requiring you to be agile and at the top of your wits are right there if you walk the impoverished, beggar- and thief-ridden streets of this dark, dangerous, many-storied city. Anything can happen to you. This tea-drinking former colonial town is now the jungle. Animals are a kind of idealized, curious, ironic backdrop to this other drama, the one you weren't prepared for. The animals stare out from postcard stalls, posters, safari brochures; but they are the least thing, the furthest thing, the most antithetical thing to life as you are experiencing it in this large, teeming city.

Tourists come now to Africa carrying cameras. They come to Kenya to hunt big game with Nikons instead of rifles. But when you are in Nairobi, you do not use your camera. If you don't become a target for thieves, you will become a target at least for the anger of all the people who do not want to be photographed by foreigners. I love to do street photography, to spend a day just wandering wherever my line of sight might take me, snapping away at all the color that crosses my path. Nairobi is not a good city in which to undertake this. Something has happened to the relationship between visitor and visited that is not announced in Kenya's tourism brochures, and the hostility toward cameras in Kenya is palpable. You can't snap pictures on the streets of Nairobi or even on the roadside in the country or in villages without fearing for your safety. At minimum you suffer verbal abuse, and you must be willing to shell out money. Perhaps this is as it should be; people have wised up. But it is a huge change from not so long ago. Winston Churchill on his African Safari in 1908 wrote, albeit with very much the eurocentric, imperialist eye, about how cooperative and eager the natives of Uganda and Kenya were when he met them during his travels. Evelyn Waugh was greeted and kowtowed to royally fifty years later. Not now.

The change is shocking to the unsuspecting tourist who feels he has paid a great deal already for his trip and should be able to snap away with impunity. But there is a great chasm between the tourist and the local. The local assumes the tourist is rich—and by his standard, anybody who can afford to travel surely is. So he feels exploited and angry when his workings and his daily life and that of his family are intruded upon by the stranger seeking the souvenir photograph, for he more than likely knows he and his family are getting nothing else from these visitors. My traveling companion in Kenya, a professional photographer, felt so intimidated and so confused by the insults and gestures hurled at her whenever she raised her camera on the street that she put it away while in Nairobi. Once in the countryside she felt she could relax. But the same thing happened again. In a tumultuous village market with abundant color and seemingly happy and welcoming faces everywhere, our Kenyan host asked her to put the camera away lest all the goodwill turn against us. After a stroll down a country lane, she returned in tears; women in their gardens had thrown things—stones and a tomato—at her. I was happily out one morning and passed close to a young boy, about eight years old, herding a small flock of goats. I couldn't hear what he was shouting at me as I raised my camera to bring him into focus, but I expected him to be good natured; I've rarely met an eight-year-old who wasn't. So I offered a friendly wave and got set to take a nice snap to show to the folks back home. When I got close enough to understand, I was able to make out the message of this cute second grader. "Hey Muzungu [white man]," he said, "give me ten shillings!"

No matter how much goodwill the naive tourist has, many encounters, at least in a much-visited place like Kenya, seem to end up like this. Things will only get worse. Little children across the countryside are no longer shy. Brazenly, they approach the visitor (even before we can brazenly approach them) with a blunt demand for money, or a chocolate, or a pen for school. Why shouldn't they, I wonder. There should be something in it for them to have to endure all these foreign, white people in short pants, lugging shoulder bags and cameras as we traipse through their lives.

As this happens, a wedge is driven deeper and deeper between visitor and visited. The tourist, out of fear or discomfort, starts to avoid the street, the countryside, and "real" local society. In order to protect himself he heads straight off to a resort with a fence around it. Here he will be guaranteed safety from attack or harrassment, and here he will be assured the freedom to snap away with his camera to his heart's content. There will be no impediments here to photographing the flowers, the birds, the monkeys, the waiters, or the gardeners who know it's in their best interest to stop and pose—or the game that is trotted by on the safari drives.

Stress between visiting tourists and host people, as the experiences of Moscow or Bath show, is not just a Third World phenomenon. Tourists everywhere, either by their insensitivity or by their sheer numbers, create stress. In every case, things move from bad to worse. In 1873, Winwood Reade observed that "Cairo, like Rome and Florence, lives upon tourists who, if they are not beloved, are welcome." By the 1890s, visits to ancient sites were starting to reach high numbers, and, correspondingly, tourists to Egypt were blamed for serious damage to the pyramids and other historic shrines. It was reported that "wall paintings were often defaced, and sometimes chunks of them were carved right out of walls as souvenirs."

Throughout an intervening century, all this has only been exacerbated. Sarlat-la-Caneda is a picturesque village of ancient stone houses and evocative narrow streets in the Dordogne region in southwest France, just inland from Bordeaux. But because it is so picturesque and because of its proximity to the famous underground Lascaux caves discovered in 1940, their walls covered with prehistoric animal drawings, Sarlat has become so overrun that even the tourists are put off. A writer in the *London Times* called his 1994 visit to what has long been considered an architectural treasure "the worst experience in more than thirty years of annual visits to France." What is happening to demolish Sarlat is the logical extension of forces put into play thirty years ago. In the 1960s Sarlat was chosen under the Loi Malraux to be one of the first French towns for protection and restoration as a heritage location. The idea had seemed splendid at the time; first the government of France would protect and refurbish heritage locations, then hope tourists would come to enjoy them and leave enough money to pay for them.

The heart of Sarlat was made a pedestrian precinct. Architectural codes went into effect and building restoration turned the town into a charming memento of its medieval past. Guidebooks, from the *Lonely Planet* to *Michelin*, touted the town as a "must see." The problem for Sarlat—and now for the visitors who seek it out—is that the plan worked only too well. Sixty million tourists now spend $30 billion in France. Some days it must seem like every one of these visitors is thronging the streets of Sarlat. The traffic jams and parking problems are mind numbing. The "authentic" shops in the streets jammed with camcorder-carrying tourists sell "rip-off" packaged foie gras and Bergerac wines made with only tourist consumers in mind. In the words of the visiting *Times* writer, "it is a nightmare; a town of real beauty is being destroyed by tourism and tourists." For the sake of tourism, Sarlat has become a parody of itself, a theme park of its own life, and through that it has negated the very reasons for its popular existence.

The impetus to resist or control tourism is growing as rapidly as the movements to expand and realize it. In 1995 in the United States, the people of Manassas, Virginia, faced down one of the Goliaths of the tourism and entertainment industry, the huge Disney Corporation. An hour south of Washington, D.C., Manassas is a picturesque town on the

edge of the splendidly scenic Virginia Piedmont. Despite its proximity to
such a major metropolis and the U.S. Capitol, this part of the country
has managed to preserve both a beauty of natural rural landscape—
undamaged woods and streams and stone fences—and an historic au-
thenticity. This is a region where some of the first colonial settlement in
America took place, so it oozes history. The rural villages still maintain
aspects of what they were 150 years ago, and among them are a smatter-
ing of the great homesteads of Americana. George Washington's Mount
Vernon, Thomas Jefferson's Monticello, and James Madison's Montpelier
remain in pristine shape and inhabit pretty much the environment in
which they were originally constructed. But a major historical connection comes, too, through a famous Civil War battle. In August of 1862,
the Confederate Army under General Stonewall Jackson, still strong and
on the offensive at that mid-stage of the war, arrived through the gap in
Bull Run to beat back the Union troops in the Second Battle of Manassas.
It was a bloody engagement, culminating in an almost total slaughter; at
the end of the day on August 28, 1,000 Confederate and 1,200 Union soldiers lay dead. One hundred and thirty-two years later, the people of
Manassas, along with serious Civil War historians, engaged in a battle,
less bloody but no less intense, to beat back a force more powerful than
either the Union or the Confederate armies: tourists and Disney.

Disney, which owns the massive amusement and entertainment
parks that bear its name in Florida and California, as well as the Euro-
Disney complex outside Paris, proposed Manassas, Virginia, as the site of
"Disney's America, A History Theme Park." The new venture, according
to an article in Condé Nast *Traveler* magazine would entail a $650 million
investment on three thousand acres. A little more than a hundred acres
would be covered by the theme park itself, and within it would be a col-
lection of show-business-style mini-parks encompassing the main the-
matic sagas of American history. For instance, in a corner called "Native
America," there would be villages of tiny wigwams. In "Victory America," guests would be able to "parachute from a plane or operate tanks
and weapons in combat and experience firsthand what America's soldiers have faced in defense of freedom." Other fabled moments of U.S.
history would be served up, including an opportunity in the words of
one executive, "for visitors to understand what it was actually like to be
a slave." The Civil War would be brought to life, of course, with "Civil
War Fort."

The rest of the 3,000 acres would be developed as a support system for the comfort of the Disney guests and the profit of the developers. There would be 1,300 hotel rooms, campgrounds, shopping centers, golf courses, and 6,600 new homes. The whole thing was scheduled to be ready for its five million guests by 1998.

Disney obtained early political and business support from local leaders who offered up $163 million in public bonds to finance road and other improvements to the area around the site. But opposition to Disney among local folks was also swift and pointed. People in the Manassas area took Disney's chirpy, world-famous symbol, Mickey, and started sporting buttons declaring "Fight The Mouse." The Piedmont Environmental Council voted in with a $600,000 commitment to the battle to oppose the development. Historians such as Shelby Foote fumed that Disney would do to American history what its movies and cartoon characters have already done to the animal kingdom, "sentimentalize it out of recognition." Civil War buffs, to whom battlefields are as sacred as cathedrals or martyrs' shrines, fulminated about "desecration of the region"; strip malls, they feared, would sit atop soldier's graves, and every evening at the precise moment when the battle had quieted, leaving the dead behind, Disney would send off fireworks to entertain the tourists. For their part, Disney made fun of the historians. Company chairman Michael Eisner told a group of *Washington Post* editors, "I sat through many history classes where I read some of their stuff, and I didn't learn anything. It was pretty boring."

A kind of trivialization of history aside, what the development would mean for the region of Manassas and the Virginia Piedmont was, according to the project's opposition, devastating. They pointed to Orlando, Florida, where Walt Disney World opened its theme and amusement parks in 1971, as the example of what would happen to their pristine, rustic, history-imbued corner of the country. In the twenty-two years after the arrival of Disney in Orlando, the population there had grown from 453,000 to 1,143,400. The number of passengers through Orlando airport leaped from 84,786 in 1971 to 21,500,000 in 1993, a 250-fold increase. The number of hotel rooms in Orlando increased ten times, from 8,000 to 80,000; and the number of McDonald's franchises in the adjacent county went from four to thirty-three. In an economic system predicated on the growth model, all this would be considered wonderful and virtually impossible to argue against. In fact, Disney executives protested that other communities should be as lucky as Orlando. But in tourism, as has happened in other sectors of society and the economy, blind growth is no longer the god it once was. People understand that growth has a price, and they recognize that that price must be reckoned.

By 1996 Disney, like the Union troops, had been routed at Manassas. The opponents of the Disney development had won the day, and Disney's America history theme park had been scuttled. No hordes of tourists would come to inundate the storied landscape; rural Virginia, at least for the time being, would remain as it was.

The incredible boom in tourism virtually everywhere in the world is causing pause, not just among the rebel thinkers who might have been spoilsports or party poopers in another time, but in the mainstream as well. Brian MacArthur, writing in the Travel Section of the *London Times,* in pages surrounded by advertisements for weekend getaways to Istanbul, affordable luxury holidays in exclusive seafront hotels, half-price trips to idyllic estates, oases of pleasure in South Africa, magical Spain ("thousands of people visit Spain every year, yet few ever discover the real country"), villas on Corfu, daily low-cost flights to Germany, etcetera, etcetera, dared to pose the question: "as we travel more often and more widely, is each of us destroying what we travel to see?" Not so long ago a writer in a major travel section of a major newspaper, particularly when surrounded by the kinds of ads that flanked MacArthur, would not have ventured to ask this question. A newspaper travel writer probably wouldn't even have thought of it. But there it was. "As aeroplanes get bigger and fares cheaper," MacArthur demanded, "will there be any secret places left in the world—any native cultures left uncorrupted—by the year 2000? Are all charter holidays going to be in sanitized tourist ghettos on coastal strips away from any contact with the local cultures that are surely the reason for travelling? Can the world sustain so much tourism?"

According to the World Tourist Organization, there were 450 million tourists in 1990. That number, it is predicted, will grow to 650 million by the end of the century, and become a billion by 2010. This projection has been developed by calculating the existing momentum, the capacities, marketing systems, appetites, and customer expectations, and matching them with world population demographics. The die for this level of growth has already been cast and unless something truly extraordinary occurs to throw it off the rails—a catastrophe—by century's end there will be 6 million tourists in Africa and a two-thirds increase in the numbers of those trooping through the castles and cathedrals of continental Europe. Part and parcel of all this is the draw from a host of hitherto unlikely places that now, too, want tourism. Places no one would have dreamed of a short while ago want now to place group-visiting by masses of outsiders squarely at the center of their national economic master plans. For instance, Libya, we are told, hopes it can become a tourist mecca; and North Korea, one of earth's most repressive, closed societies is reportedly constructing the globe's largest tourist hotel, 105 stories high. Vietnam, a destination not likely to jump to the front of your mind, nevertheless declared 1990 its "Year of Tourism." Burma, now having renamed itself Myanmar, is doing the same in 1996. Iran, less than a decade after the death of the Ayatollah Khomeini, was scrambling to alter its forbidden location image and lure (shudder) western tourists. By the end of the 1990s, Iran hoped to be earning $5 billion from visitors.

Nothing stops the dreamers. Not so long ago, when people in the Balkan states of the former Yugoslavia were killing one another off as a bloody national pastime and refugees were leaving Cuba on rafts made out of planks and doors, I stopped in at a tourism exhibition in Montreal. The first promotional booths I encountered were those of Croatia and Cuba. In Cuba, almost all forms of industry had been shut down, and sugar production and mining were disaster areas, which left tourism as Cuba's chief foreign-exchange earner. Despite all their problems, they thought it should continue to grow. So there in their kiosk, believing the rest of the world should be happy to oblige, were Cuba's cheerful promoters. The pair of youngsters operating Croatia's kiosk seemed bravely oblivious to Dubrovnik and Sarajevo blowing up behind them, not to mention the horrors of towns with names like Srebrenica or Zepa; they smilingly pushed forward brochures of topless beach bunnies on the Adriatic coast. When they spoke to me of their touristic wonders, there was no hint of irony or embarrassment or self-consciousness.

Everybody either wants to be a tourist, or wants tourists to come to their country to enrich it. But the blessing is mixed, the bargain often Faustian. The prices paid are high, and they are too often exacted from the wrong sources, from people or communities who can't afford them, who receive minimal benefit.

Story by story the negative, damaging, dangerous side effects and detritus of this huge worldwide industry are being compiled. Hotel and resort developments are on collision courses with the environment and local peoples. Coral reefs have been dynamited to provide construction materials for hotels and airports in a hundred places—places such as Kenya, Tanzania, Mozambique, Madagascar, Réunion, Mauritius, the Seychelles, Sri Lanka, Malaysia, and Thailand. Mangrove swamps have been filled in, and hotels and restaurants built on top of them; village fishermen have been evicted from their lagoons, and beach sand has been shoveled into cement mixers. Places that have scarce water have diverted their meager supplies to the tourists. The south of Spain, an arid land where people have learned over the course of hundreds of years how carefully to conserve their water, now watches golf courses and swimming pools suck it up for the benefit of tourists. The arrival of tourism and cash-carrying tourists has destroyed intricate local barter economies and has turned religious ceremonies and pageants into curiosities. In remote passes of the Himalayas that happen to be along the trekker trail, the candy and soft drink handouts of well-meaning tourists has quadrupled the incidence of tooth decay among the Tibetan children.

When dictator Ne Win and his generals, who have ruled Burma since 1962, decided that tourism could both bring in foreign currency and modify the regime's harsh image in the rest of the world, they coined the slogan: "Visit Myanmar 1996." Western companies quickly responded, scrambling to get on board. "Burma offers the ultimate in luxury," trilled British Airways brochures. The Orient Express told its customers: "To find an unspoilt country today may seem impossible, but Burma is such a place. It has retained its charm, its fascinating traditions . . . its easy going ways are a tonic to the western traveller."

But critical observers saw the preparations for Burma's tourism—hidden from the visitor's eyes and ignored by the operators who so badly wanted to cooperate in setting up the systems there—as being as brutal as everything else in the Ne Win regime. *Manchester Guardian* journalist John Pilger wrote; "Last year the International Confederation of Free Trade Unions reported that a million people had been forced from their homes in Rangoon alone in preparation for tourism and foreign investment. Throughout Burma, perhaps 3 million people have been brutally swept aside and exiled to 'satellite zones' where they are compelled silently to serve Burma's new facade of 'economic growth'."

One such satellite zone was cobbled together outside Pagan, Burma's ancient capital. Only guides and the staffs of the string of planned new hotels were to be permitted to stay in the old city which, with its temples and colossal standing Buddhas, is one of the last remaining wonders of the ancient world. 4,000 peasants saw their homes bulldozed, and then they were marched at gunpoint to a dismal, barren place and told to build themselves a new village. "Those villagers who objected were sent out on to the barren plain, or beaten, or taken away in the night."

Grim fact follows grim fact. Since the days of marauding barbarians and invading armies, sex has been closely associated with travel. In parts of the world today, the sex-tour business has come to operate on an almost industrial scale. Japanese men, since the 1960s and 1970s, have flocked to Taiwan and South Korea, and more recently to the Philippines and Thailand on junkets organized expressly around procuring sex with inexpensive and willing prostitutes. Morocco, Bombay (Mumbai), Vietnam, and Melbourne, Australia, are newer destinations to join a growing list. In Bombay, the customers, usually Arabs from the Middle East, have developed an elaborate ruse to disguise the true nature of their trip. Inexpensive medical treatment for a variety of ailments is a common excuse for the hop across the Arabian Sea. But once there, the sheiks find that brothels exist, conveniently, next to their hospitals and clinics. The true purpose for the junket falls miraculously into place; for anywhere from a hundred to a thousand dollars, the visitor can forget about his ailment and join a dancing girl on a sumptuous bed of flowers to act out a mock Hindi marriage ritual.

The role of sex as an integral part of tourism has long been winked at; as *Time* magazine pointed out in a June 1993 cover story, "If 100,000 German men a year choose to visit Thailand on package sex tours, who is to object?" But then it was discovered that of Thailand's two million prostitutes, a huge proportion were minors, many of them young girls who had been sold by impoverished parents into an indentured sex slavery. More adolescents had been kidnapped and transported to Bangkok from rural villages in neighboring Burma, Laos, or southern China. The United Nations Children's Fund estimates there are 300,000 underage prostitutes in India; the Organization to End Child Prostitution in Asian Tourism believes there are over a million youngsters in prostitution in Asia as a whole.

Little girls in Thailand become prostitutes for the visiting sex junkets; the artifacts of the pyramids of Egypt and the temples of the Mayans are tramped upon, pried loose, and spirited off in visitors' duffel bags. Street crime and hustling has taken over whole islands such as Jamaica. Beaches, from the Caribbean to Southeast Asia, are being rapidly spoiled both by the small trash dropped by individuals and the big pollution left by unregulated hotel development. Traditional, thousand-year-old cultures are squeezed and changed, if not forced to move out altogether because their lands suddenly become more lucrative in the hands of politically well connected operators and developers. The world is a mess, and the insistent pressure of tourism is one of the reasons. But what can happen? Tourism has a gigantic momentum, in both our culture and in the world economy. To make substantial changes will be like altering the course of a huge ocean liner while it is traveling at full steam on seas that the majority of the crew believe to be calm. Few perceive the hidden shoals. Can it be possible, one wonders, to save either the world, or tourism? Can an industry built so much on the quick realization of maximium profit, that trades so largely on hedonism, self-indulgence, and self-absorption, be turned around?

11

Can Tourism Be Made Responsible? Can Tourism Save the World?

During twenty years as a planner and consultant, Louis D'Amore peddled tourism advice to a variety of clients, private corporations, and public governments, including the government of Canada. With a degree in business from the Wharton School, he was an expert in the forefront of an exciting field, helping to define a whole new industry whose growth potential seemed limitless. He and other colleagues like him were busy trying to get government officials to change their ways of thinking. They wanted them to shift their understanding of tourism from a hobby or a pastime at the periphery of human experience to an industry that could become central to the national economy. Louis D'Amore was on the cutting edge. He was excited, and he thought about tourism and its possibilities all the time, day and night. Whenever he met with clients, he saw a fresh opportunity to bend their minds in a new way, to get them excited about new possibilities.

For a long time, his work was the stuff of standard pragmatic models; defining a new area of the economy, pushing considerations about job creation and marketing and crossovers and taxation. D'Amore could tell a government official how many new jobs a hundred thousand or a million dollars of investment or grant or tax relief would predictably translate into. He could explain to a hotel company how to go about convincing public officials that their new resort development was just as critical to a local or a national economy as a new automobile manufacturing plant might be. Tourism and travel businesses needed experts like

D'Amore to help turn them from simply businesses into the industry they have become recognized as today.

But at some point, Louis D'Amore's thinking took an interesting turn, and he started to look at his field in a totally different way. He became reflective, philosophical, and he started to realize a virtue and a potential that nobody else was talking about very much, if at all. Acting on his new ideas, he abruptly changed what he was doing; he stopped being an advisor trying to lubricate the needs of the systems and the institutions. He formed an organization called the International Institute for Peace Through Tourism (IIPT). He became a crusader, an evangelist. When Louis D'Amore thinks about tourism now, he does so as a man who sees it as one of our age's great opportunities; not just for pleasure or economic return, but for education and peace. As a result, this short, balding, sixty-year-old man finds himself at the forefront of an original movement.

I met Louis D'Amore at one of the conferences he now designs and to which he brings hundreds of people from all over the world and from all walks of the tourism business. This particular conference, held in Montreal, had the title "Building A Sustainable World Through Tourism," but Louis D'Amore didn't think it ostentatious or pretentious in the least, and appeared to sense no irony. He was too busy scurrying about the glassed-in halls of Montreal's civic convention center in his rumpled black suit, handling the hundred and one details like a good conference organizer, making sure all his plenaries and seminars with titles like, "Creating Sustainable Tourism in Rural and Resort Communities," or "Visitor and Community Involvement in the Protection of Natural Habitats," or "Sustainable Tourism in Southeast Asia," or "The Greening of the Hotel Industry" were functioning smoothly.

D'Amore was never simply an ordinary planner; he is one of those thinkers who isn't abashed to call himself a "futurist." He is a dreamer with the kind of restless intelligence that doesn't want to stay locked too long in the status quo. He is also a religious man, motivated to leave the world a better place. Through his work he wants to "do good"; with his talents he says he wants to achieve something of larger purpose. So, in the course of his consulting labors for the tourism industry, it was natural for him to start to think hard about the possibilities of that tourism and to confront its best possibilities.

Tourism, and everything that goes with it, is undoubtedly changing the world. But when Louis D'Amore opened his organization's small headquarter office in Montreal, he decided to be one of the first to ask the intriguing question: "Might it not possibly change the world for the better?" Tourism, in becoming vastly popular, had hit a kind of lowest common denominator; the "three Ss" of sun, sand, and sex seemed to have taken over the mentality of holiday travelers. But could he not create some room for the higher motivations of learning, of crosscultural education, of bridge building? Could he push the masses to return to the spirit of the questing travelers of earlier times? Where the stampeding money and greed of conventional tourism was despoiling beaches, frightening wild fauna, threatening historic sites and artifacts, laying waste to environments, and throwing local cultures and economies into chaos, might he not persuade the industry to become sustainable? Might he not persuade the gigantic industry to use its economic power and its influence to build and develop in responsible, lasting ways? His first cause was peace.

The world certainly was not peaceful in the mid-1980s. It was still possible then to conceive of a nuclear war erupting between the Soviet Union and the United States, the world's two bipolar superpowers. In 1986 political terrorists managed to sneak in and plant a bomb at Rome's Leonardo da Vinci Airport, throwing the system and travelers into fear-filled chaos. The chaos rippled like a flu virus right through the industry; people responded by canceling airline reservations the world over. International travel dropped by a third, which underlined for the travel industry how precarious its position was and how much its business and economic health depended on the whim of world events and the world mood. The moment seemed right for D'Amore to commence his project.

D'Amore believed that the visiting and the learning and the exchange that should be part of ideal tourism had a huge potential for building understanding among common people and easing world tensions. "Initially, when I started, people thought it was kind of airy fairy," he admits, shrugging a little shyly. "But with things like the international terrorism, people in the industry realized that without peace, there could be no travel. And people who liked to travel to other countries could relate. Learning about other people and other cultures was a primary motivation of many of them. As people travel, they see how much they share with one another, and the walls, where there are walls, begin to come down. With world peace it made particular sense. When you travel, you meet people, and you don't then want to send your sons and daughters off to kill those people." He believed he could work with people's best instincts, and from there his thinking expanded; how could tourism become a force for crosscultural education? Could it become a factor in the protection of the Earth's environment? Could all the things that were identified as negative be turned around? Could tourism become responsible?

Louis D'Amore is not a crackpot. He's shy, he's a little rumpled; he's the kind of man you might underestimate on first impression. But the power of his convictions and the single-mindedness of his energy are infectious. After you have talked with him, you would feel foolish if you disagreed with him, somehow smaller. So when he calls conventions to discuss things like peace through tourism or building a sustainable world through tourism, the Prime Minister of Canada sends him greetings. Queen Noor, wife of King Hussein of Jordan, will show up to be honorary chair. Busy people like Maurice Strong, Chairman of the Earth Council, and Dr. Noel Brown, Director of the United Nations Environmental Programme, will find time to come and give speeches.

But it is an uphill battle. Organizations such as the IIPT and true believers such as Louis D'Amore have a long way to go to make a dent in the general perception of what mass tourism means in our world. For a wide variety of reasons, images that are largely negative have become deeply ingrained. A host of negative stereotypes about travelers pervade popular thinking: the outspoken, ethnocentric, dollar-dispensing "ugly American"; the loutish, pushy German; the persistent, camcorder-toting Japanese. Our general perception of tourism in the grand scale of things, therefore, might make it difficult for us to take it seriously as a force for education, understanding, world peace, and progress.

Tourism is more often portrayed as farce or a comedy of errors. Newspapers delight in carrying accounts of the silly things tourists do, like the man from California who voiced his disappointment after a visit to London's Buckingham Palace on the first day it was open to the public in the summer of 1994. "We're disappointed the Queen wasn't there," he complained. "When we go to Disneyland, Mickey's there." Then there was the tourist who asked the Anchorage Alaska Visitors and Convention Bureau when he should expect the Northern Lights to be switched on and where should he stand for the best view. Another tourist in Juneau inquired about who mows the tundra. Can people like Louis D'Amore manage to make a true change? Can some sanity be injected into the business, some justice, some sustainability? Can the world even survive tourism, let alone see it re-made into a force for positive good?

A place to start is by trying to understand not just tourism's size and numbers, but the complexity of the interests that work together to make it happen, and the tensions that shiver between them. Louis D'Amore and other futurist planning types like to use terms such as "stakeholders" or "partners." In this way, they are acknowledging that inside complicated systems more than one activity is going on at any given moment. There are competitions and conflicts, and elaborate cooperation is required; more than one body has an interest, and more than one body's happiness needs to be considered. Tourism is not monolithic, but there are interests that are competitive, and sometimes they diverge sharply. These are the stakeholders, or the players. Broadly speaking, the world of tourism has four main groups of stakeholders or players, each of them and their interests critical to the long-term game plan, the long-term health of worldwide travel and tourism.

The first group of these critical players are the tourists themselves. As mentioned, in the developed world, travel for pleasure is the third largest household expense after food and housing. Those of us who live in that world increasingly believe that our right to travel is sacred. We undertake it with zeal, and we welcome increases both in our disposable income that we can put toward travel and in the expanding capacity of the travel industry to accommodate us. We do not want limits placed on our right or our potential to travel, to go anywhere we wish. We take for granted the fact that we can get anywhere in the world within twenty-four hours, and we believe in our right to act on that ability. We want borders to be open, we want our travels to be safe, we want to be served and treated well upon arrival, and we hope our traveling can be ever less and less expensive. We are important, because it is our motivation that makes it happen, and it is our pocketbooks that pay the bill. Without us none of it would happen.

The second group of important players comprise the industry that has been built around tourism. This is the business: all the hotels, the tour companies, the agencies, the airlines, and the financiers. Many of these players are huge multinational conglomerates; many of them intersect and overlap. The industry is, by and large, knowledgeable and efficient. But the most important thing to remember about it is that it is a commercial industry, a money-making industry. This is capitalism. The industry that surrounds tourism is competitive and profit oriented. It will do whatever it needs to to stay afloat; it is exploitive when it needs to be, and cost cutting when it needs to be. The bottom line is ever present and constantly worried over. Capitalism, put simplistically as we might remember from our basic university economics courses, needs profits and flourishes on growth. The tourism industry, growing in leaps and bounds with, until now, almost endless frontiers, has been a near perfect example of this. The momentum of the industry, consequently, is huge. It is virtually unstoppable in its movement, and its direction not easy to shift.

The third group of players with a substantial interest are the countries and governments, the national economies that court tourism as an important component in their structures. These are not just small Caribbean islands for whom tourism is their monoculture crop and their main foreign exchange earner. Established western countries, too, are increasingly aware of and jealous of the role tourism plays in their economies. Tourism in France, for example, is worth $30 billion a year. Tourism in Britain is worth more than $35 billion. Therefore, governments everywhere in the last decade have made tourism central to their economic master plans. In countries such as Kenya and Cuba, tourism is commonly recognized as the main ticket for foreign exchange earnings; if they want to have money for any other sort of trade they have to keep tourists coming and tourism healthy. But in many other places it plays a critical role in national employment. Tourism in Britain supports 1.5 million jobs. The growth among those who are self-employed in tourism-related industries in Britain grew by 18 percent between 1981 and 1991. All over the world, tourism is a sizable player in nations' economies and thus wields enormous clout and leverage.

The last remaining group of players with a legitimate interest are the visited, the people and places that are the destinations of tourism. This includes the island beaches, the European cathedrals, the ancient temple ruins, and all the people who live near them who are being asked to share the temples and cathedrals and beaches and wild animals that have been part of their lives for centuries with visitors. Thai or Kenyan or Guatemalan villagers and the environments they inhabit must put up with tourism and tourists. They are not necessarily the direct economic beneficiaries of this tourism, yet they have no choice but to live in its onslaught and its wake. These, of all the players of tourism, have the smallest voice; they usually must struggle for attention even from their own government representatives.

To find the balance among the complexities of these competing interests is tourism's great challenge, a challenge of which it is becoming

more and more conscious. It is what people like Louis D'Amore refer to
as tourism's bottom line. Thus far it hasn't been highly successful; the
four interest areas are badly out of balance, the four players not nearly
equal to one another in strength. But as the voices for each interest area
become more articulate and more assertive, finding an acceptable, useful, happy, productive equilibrium will be the test of tourism's and perhaps even the world's ability to survive.

In 1987 the International Brundtland Commission, headed by Norway's Prime Minister, Gro Harlem Brundtland, helped place a new word
into the vogue of the world's vocabulary: "sustainability." "Sustainable
development," the Brundtland Commission defined for the world, is
"development that meets the needs of the present without compromis-
ing the ability of future generations to meet theirs." Simple societies of
people such as peasant farmers and fishermen and foresters had understood this concept for centuries: they had built their lives and their practices and even many of their ceremonies and rituals around the fact that
they could behave only in ways that would conserve for future generations. Many North American Indian tribes commonly operated on the
principle of "the seventh generation," taking into account the well-
being of children seven generations into the future in every important
decision. But for the modern industrial world, this way of thinking has
been long lost. So the idea of sustainability came like a bolt of lightning,
heralding something that had never occurred to us before. It was the answer to our growing environmental anxiety, so, like a mantra, the term
suddenly became attached as a prefix to every enterprise going. Including tourism. Every industry, not only to continue creating the greatest
good for its vested interests but also to survive into any but the most immediate future, would have to adopt the principles and meet the criteria
of sustainability. This was not altruistic; rather it was in every industry's
most astute self-interest. International mass tourism, therefore, would be
not the least of the industries that would have to adopt the sustainable
approach. So its leaders started to think in that way and, in its best quarters, they started to look for ways that the rights and health of its four
main players could be brought into a more happy balance.

Tourism's "visited," though they are continually growing in size and
number, are, at the moment, the least powerful and the most vulnerable
of the four players. In some places they are not in very good shape at all.
In countries where the national governments have abandoned all re-
straints in favor of hooking their future economies to tourism—as in

parts of Africa, the Caribbean, Malaysia, Thailand—the dismal expectation is that local life, environments, languages, cultures, economies, and aesthetics will all go to hell. The interests of these people and places are not, however, without their champions. There are now not only tourism ministries and junket operators interested, for example, in the huge travel into Southeast Asia, but there are also corresponding (though fledgeling) organizations to support the rights and the well-being of the young girls whose prostitution is part of the lure for sizable numbers of those junkets. There are Centers for Responsible Tourism headquartered in California, Ecumenical Coalitions on Third World Tourism based in Thailand, and World Ecotourism Societies in Virginia. An organization called Tourism Concern operates in Britain, with the aim of reducing the negative impact of tourism on local communities and the environment. The Centre for the Advancement of Responsive Travel, headquartered in Kent, aims to help people travel with sensitivity and, to that end, has published the *Credo for the Caring Traveller* and the *Responsive Traveller's Handbook*. An ecumenical church-run Coalition to End Child Prostitution in Asian Tourism is headquartered in Toronto. The need to protect the visited is one of the fastest-growing areas of concern in tourism. Implied are several kinds of protection: to protect vulnerable people, such as children who might become prostitutes, from harm and exploitation; to protect the natural environment they live in; and to protect things such as indigenous animals and historic or cultural or artistic artifacts from being destroyed by the visiting hordes, even though they profess to love them and to be so very interested in them. The pyramids of Egypt, the cathedrals of Europe, the art galleries of Florence, the animals and village life of Africa, and the streets of the village of Sarlat-la-Caneda— all need to be protected lest they be loved to death by the tourists.

If the interests of the visited can be protected and enhanced within the actions of tourism, this will truly change the world. But it is a delicate, complex task. It won't be achieved through the monitoring and policing activities of foreign watchdogs alone; it will happen more thoroughly when the benefits of tourism make it all the way down and are deposited more securely in the hands of the visited. We have seen that in Zimbabwe rural small farmers became tolerant of the wild animals that were nuisances to their crops and sometimes their lives only when some direct benefit appeared to come from those animals to the people and their families. They can be expected to look in the same manner at the nuisance created in their lives by tourists.

In Kenya, tourism, in 1987, passed coffee and tea as the main earner of foreign exchange. As far as the interests of that nation are concerned, tourism became then more than simply a critical industry: it is now almost a lifeline. But the other player in Kenya, ordinary people, have yet to agree. Paul Omondi is a professor at Moi University in Nairobi, specializing in tourism impact research. Tourism employs 110,000 people in Kenya, 8.3 percent of the country's wage earners. When Omondi, a tall intense man with round, steel-rimmed glasses, studied the industry in his country, he found the appreciation of tourism's value limited to those who had a very direct connection to its benefits. People who had relatives working in tourist lodges, for example, were very tolerant of tourists. They were also sympathetic to wildlife presumably because they understand the connection between wildlife conservation and the livelihood of their immediate relatives. But for the rest of Kenyans, these connections were not made. To Omondi, it was understandable; they saw no personal or family benefit, only nuisance.

Even if you work in the tourism industry, the question of benefit in places such as Kenya is a debatable one. The vast majority of those 110,000 people employed in tourism and tourist-related industries are waiters, chambermaids, gardeners, drivers, desk clerks, travel agents, and guards. A tourist spends on average $250 per day during his visit to Kenya. How much of that goes home with the Kenyan chambermaid? Alas, very little. Most of the money either leaves the country—to airlines, tour companies, hotel chains that are based elsewhere—or ends up in the pockets of a class one person described to me as the "vampire elite," the corrupt, over-rich, upper political echelons that plague too much of the Third World, certainly too much of Africa. Author Raymond Bonner charges that in Kenya corrupt officials siphoned off as much as 40 percent of the game park entrance fees paid by the 100,000 tourists visiting the Masai Mara. He also charged that despite warnings of environmentalists that the Mara was overloaded, more hotels and lodges were allowed to be built after appropriate officials were "paid off." "Some of the large lodges also routinely under-reported the number of guests by about 20 percent" in order to reduce the bed-night tax they have to submit, he wrote.

The money that comes into a country through tourism and then immediately departs is called "leakage." The gentleness of this term rather quaintly belies the depth of bitterness felt toward the phenomenon. But the phraseology is not totally benign; too much leakage, as we all know, can sink a ship. There are complex formulae to determine leakage as a percentage of gross income, but be assured, the percentage is more often large than small. The most modest figure comes from officials in the industry. Robert Burns, an American who has been the chairman of an industry association, the World Travel and Tourism Council, is adamant that leakage is only about 10 percent of expenditure, which, he says, is the profit margin of his international hotels and tour companies. But critics scorn this low figure. Third World tourism analyst Kreg Lindberg says "you must use my numbers cautiously," but he then puts them very high: 70 percent in Nepal, 60 percent in Thailand, 55 percent for the typical developing country, 45 percent in Costa Rica. An astonishing fact and a critical matter is that the worst leakage may occur at what is supposed to be tourism's best, most responsible end. According to some of Lindberg's studies, "more than 90 percent of tourism spending is thought to leak away from communities near most ecotourism sites." What gives?

It would perplex most tourists to know how much of the money dropped in a place such as Kenya promptly turns around and flies back to America or Britain or wherever it is the tourist has come from. This is the bane of tourism economics throughout the developing or Third World. Local people are stuck against their will, with no participation in making the decisions about the ways tourism will affect their lives and their communities. Leakage takes away their financial compensation, both that which might go to them directly as individuals or families and that which, in a more general way, would develop their country. Paul Omondi from Kenya explained, "We are told wildlife brings tourists, which gives money to the government. But the local people don't see that money, so they become even more hostile." Presumably and understandably they become hostile toward the tourists as well. Tourism economies that are rife with leakage do no favors whatsoever to developing countries and will probably, in the end, blow up in the face of all concerned. They bring nuisance and cost to the doorsteps of local people, but not enough benefit.

In Belize, person after person griped about leakage. In the island town of San Pedro, because of the massive foreign and non–San Pedro ownership of hotels, restaurants, and tour companies, very little of the money the tourists spend actually passes by the villagers. The visitors book tickets in the United States or Canada, pay in the United States or Canada, and the money stays in the United States or Canada. Of the $3,000 or so it cost me to spend two weeks in San Pedro, probably only about a third, if that, stayed in the country. The money that stayed was for the meals I ate, the wages of the hotel employees, (the maid and the desk clerk didn't get close to the $1,249 price of our fourteen nights), a few assorted local transportation tickets: that was it. The big items went out of the country: my trip was arranged through a Canadian company, the airline I flew on was Mexican, the hotel was owned by an American consortium. In some respects I might have done the people of Belize a bigger favor by staying home. The franchises of foreign-owned hotels in Belize, I was told, operate on overdrafts, which means basically that Belize comes into the picture only if and when there is a problem. When operations are successful, the profits leave; if they go belly up, it becomes a local, in this case a Belize, problem.

Property development schemes, particularly the ones with either direct or implicit government support or participation, turn local people into cynics and drive deep wedges in tourism. Local people may be poor, but they are seldom stupid (though sometimes their governments are). In scenario after scenario, citizens have watched naive or overeager governments persuaded to invest public money in hotel or resort projects. They do this either through direct investment, through offering tax breaks, or by providing public money for construction of the required roads, waterworks, sewers, or airports. But the smart lawyers seem hardly ever to be on the government side, and the deck in such ventures often seems stacked against locals and their governments.

If developers have enough clout to influence politics or taxes or zoning, even the minimum benefits to a Third World country can disappear. In Belize in 1993, on the north end of Ambergris Cay, an American-owned consortium from Mississippi optioned 22,000 acres, three quarters of the island, promising a massive tourism development. The locals in the town of San Pedro were both frightened and highly critical. They wanted to fight it, or at least have all safeguards ensured. Celi McCorkle, the local Belizian businesswoman who was the first tourist operator in the town thirty years ago, explained, however, that when it was pointed out to government officials that the "master development plan" for the island opposed such a development, the politicians reacted by shelving the master plan.

The seduction of tourism, however, is hard to resist. Tourism, especially in developing countries, pushes all the right buttons. It is sexy, and it is labor intensive. A foreign-owned company holds out prospects of an injection of foreign capital that will create something that will employ local people and that will flatter the country by trading on an appreciation of local natural or cultural or historic attractions. Politicians, bent under burdens of unemployment and underdevelopment, find this tempting and scramble to find ways to be of assistance, doing what they can to make the path for any such development smoother. There is lots of room in this, if either the company or the politicians are corrupt, to add some grease to guarantee the process. But even when everyone is honest and everything is aboveboard, a kind of seduction kicks in. Tourism ventures are still considered more sexy than, say, an auto parts plant or a pineapple plantation. The governments fall in line, and if the tourism developer has any negotiating skills at all, huge concessions can be wrung out of the politicians.

Patrick Blednick, in his book *Another Day in Paradise*, describes in detail the negotiations between Club Med chairman, Gilbert Trigano, and the government of the tiny Caribbean Turks and Caicos Islands in the early 1980s when Club Med wished to build its Turkoise Village on Providenciales. According to Blednick, by the time Club Med had completed construction of their 490-bed resort, Turks and Caicos, backed grudgingly by taxpayers back in Britain of whom Turks and Caicos was still a protectorate, had forked out over $12 million to build roads, water and sewage systems, and an elaborately expensive new airport (the third such airstrip capable of handling large international carriers in a jurisdiction that had only 10,000 local citizens). Due to the all-too-usual types of inflations and cost overruns, they had watched helplessly as the initial estimate of £3.9 million swelled to almost double. As well as the outlay of that cash, they had agreed to the gift of a twenty-year exemption for the developer for taxes on profits and property.

During the process the British government sponsored a study that, when it examined the impact the Club Med venture would have on housing, employment, education, medical services, the environment, and numerous other concerns, advised against the development. It would, said the report by John Harrison, a social-development advisor to the British Development Division in the Caribbean, upset the labor balance on the island where unemployment was, in fact, already very low; the small hotels operating there already believed Club Med would steal their staffs from them. They also feared it would drive property values into a radical inflation. It would damage other things as well: "the very things that make Provo appealing to visitors—the wonderful clean environment, the birds and animals, and the beautiful beaches—would be severely affected by the onslaught of large scale tourism." Even in the face of this study, the development won out and secured the whopping subsidy of public expenditure. Club Med uses the slogan "Happiness Is Our Business." The Provo deal might well have fulfilled that aphorism; at least it must have left Club Med happy. A skilled developer, through a combination of bluff and bluster, can successfully bully either an unsophisticated or a corrupt local government. Development happens, but who wins? Are the local people happier or more prosperous? When, if ever, will the local governments, under such terms, start to show a benefit in their ledgers?

The environmental movement's prophet Rachel Carson, in her book *The Sea Around Us,* lamented the fate she witnessed happening to South Pacific islands. "In a reasonable world, men would have treated these islands as precious possessions, as natural museums filled with beautiful and curious works of creation, valuable beyond price, because nowhere in the world are they duplicated," she wrote. But, alas, it seemed not to be a reasonable world. The attitude that back in 1950 had despoiled the South Sea Islands has been all too prevalent in tourism. The credo "See it before it's spoiled," for instance, has been tossed around thoughtlessly by tourists and within tourism seemingly without any idea that things could be different. It is probably the single most dangerous slogan coined by the business. Its assumption, taken so cavalierly by all of us so often over the years, is the very antithesis of sustainability. Clearly that will have to change. Critics believe profound changes are required both in the ways tourism business is carried out, and in the ways we, the public, think about tourism. Responsible and sustainable tourism means tourism that does not and cannot continue as "business as usual." Everywhere throughout the world there are examples of ways in which things must change and the pressures, from within or without, that will force the change. So many of tourism's most hopeful projects and most standard approaches are blowing up in the faces of their authors or those who count on them, or on the conventional wisdom, that a huge sea change is in the offing.

Some observers believe imposing quotas and then strictly enforcing them is what is required to preserve both individual locations and the tourism industry. Analyst Kreg Lindberg, from his studies of Belize, argues forcefully for the principle of selectivity. "Belize," he told me, "is not and probably never will be a suitable destination for mass tourism."

Mass tourism to Belize, in fact, would work against the country's best attractions and possibilities, its natural appeal for serious ecological and nature devotees. Therefore it must protect those assets and find the best ways to get the maximum financial return from the visitors it does have.

Tourists may feel their holidays are expensive, but from the standpoint of the visited country, the tourists frequently get virtually a free ride. Not just Belize, but country after country, according to Lindberg, is woefully low on the taxes and entry fees exacted from visitors to main attraction sites. "In Latin America, entrance fees tend to be low or nonexistent. The funds that are collected go to central government treasuries, with no direct benefit to the protected areas themselves." Even when countries raise fees, as Costa Rica has done, they are still low—about $1.40. Even in the higher-fee places such as Kenya, where they average about $10, such fees account for a pitifully small part of a tourist's total expenditures. With low entry fees and low taxes, the Third World country is in fact subsidizing the visitor's holiday rather than the other way around. A rather extreme exception to this might be tiny Bhutan, landlocked between Tibet, Nepal, and Bangladesh, which has instituted a tourist day charge of $450. This certainly must discourage all but the most serious visitors, but it's hard to know if enough people go to Bhutan for the high fees to provide actually much of a financial return. The answer for sustainability is to be aware of limits on both sides, and to restrict the number of visitors to any site to the number that will do no damage, while charging a substantial enough fee to offset costs and pay for further conservation.

Limiting tourism, it goes without saying, would require decisiveness and acts of political will. "It appears Belize has reached a point," writes Kreg Lindberg, "at which it must decide which market or markets to pursue and then take actions consistent with that decision." In fragile situations, whether those are fragile ecosystems or fragile cultural systems, limits on visitors might soon become mandatory. Stonehenge gets 700,000 visitors a year, a mass of tourists who, in the heavy seasons, clog up the roads for miles around. The English Lake District has fourteen million tourists each summer. How can tourist havens such as these survive such numbers? Quotas may indeed be the salvation for heavily pressured places; but can they be made fair to the visitors? The city of Venice, sinking under the weight of its history and rising waters, is considering a lottery as a fair way to choose the limited number of tourists it can handle. Many museums all over the world operate on an appoint-

ment system—first in line, first served—and the pressures of numbers
are thus managed. Those who argue in favor of quotas make the point
that quotas don't discriminate among visitors, whereas high entry fees
do. Bhutan's $450 per day visitor fees exclude all but the rich. The
Andaman Islands in the Bay of Bengal issue 1,000 visitor permits per
year. If you are 999 in line, you get in. If you are 1,001, it won't matter if
you are rich or not, you're out of luck.

In some places where the risks are too high and there is no way to
mitigate damage, there should probably be no tourism. Period. Travel
journalist Wallace Immen, writing in Toronto's *Globe and Mail*, recalled a
trip among forty other tourists to a mummified ancient forest on Axel
Heiberg Island in Canada's high Arctic. "In just one afternoon, we
changed the look of the island's fragile environment forever as our footprints created a crisscross of trails in the soft earth. The trails will become
deeper with subsequent erosion. The forest was a stunning sight, yet I
left wondering whether our seeing it was worth the cost to the pristine
habitat."

It is important to remember that tourism is not a panacea for a developing place, and it is important not to treat it as such. It is very easy, says
Lindberg, for expectations to outpace tourism's ability to generate benefits. The limitations of tourism should always be kept in mind. But it can
be an incredibly important resource if handled sustainably. One approach, very much in vogue with the right thinkers, is ecotourism. At
times it suffers from a fuzzy definition; it can be, sometimes, whatever
the person using the word wants it to be. It suffers, also, from a kind of
"holier than thou" self-appointment. An elite who deign themselves at
the apex of the traveler hierarchy perpetually seem to be looking down
their noses at their unwashed, polyester-clad cousins. But under its most
generous definition, ecotourism's practices of emphasizing the educational, of leaving sites as close to possible the way they were found
("take only photographs, leave only footprints"), and of trying to leave
as much benefit as possible in the local visited area come closest to a sustainable model. The Ecotourism Society, headquartered in Alexandria,
Virginia, has also become an avid watchdog, keeping tab on the sins and
shortcomings of the tourism industry. The fact that the term "ecotourism" has entered the lexicon is telling in itself. Travel, it suggests, is
a privilege, not a right.

Ecotourism is the traveler becoming aware of sustainability and
changing his or her practices, often with the encouragement of the vis-

ited. The approach of the big players of the tourism industry to sustainability is another thing. In 1994 the big players in the international tourism industry made a gesture toward sustainability on the environmental side when they instituted a program called the "Green Globe." The World Travel and Tourism Council (WTTC) invented a system of incentives where, at the highest CEO levels, the giants of the world tourism industry—the airlines, hotel chains, and tour companies—promised to build environmental improvement into every aspect of their company's activities. They promised to police themselves and vowed even to go beyond government-imposed guidelines. They said they would instruct governments to make tougher guidelines. "Were governments to be tougher on developers," said Robert Burns, then chairman of the WTTC, "that wouldn't scare us off." He said he was concerned, rather, "that we take care not to spoil what has made us prosperous."

The skeptics remained skeptical; people in organizations such as the Ecotourism Society remained hard to please. When I asked Megan Epler Wood, that organization's president, about Green Globe, she scoffed and called it simply a public relations strategy, a smokescreen while an unremitting wave of new concrete was being poured around the world, often landing on top of fragile ecosystems. Others were more generous. People such as Louis D'Amore, who had done a great deal of lobbying toward instituting the program, called it a genuine movement in the right direction. John Elkington and Julia Hailes in their guide to greener holidays, *Holidays That Don't Cost the Earth*, say "the situation is not all bad," though they point out that hotel developments could go a long way toward sustainability simply by committing themselves to using more local products, from their construction materials to the items on their menu. They credit the Inter-Continental Hotel Group, however, with assiduously looking after energy management and minimizing environmental impacts in their hotel developments around the world. ITT Sheraton's Africa and Indian Ocean division asked guests to leave donations that the hotels would forward to green causes, and found that 86 percent of the guests complied. When the Canadian chain of CP Hotels made the decision consciously to become an environmentally responsible enterprise, 85 percent of their employees offered to volunteer their own time to help. Louis D'Amore points out that in 1979, when he told a tourism association they should look at environmentalists as their long-term quality-control allies, he was scoffed at. "But now there is a generally accepted environmentalist-tourism alliance." D'Amore quotes environmentalists who credit tourism as being a critical factor in maintaining the biodiversity belt around the equator. When tourists visit, awareness develops. The combination of education, moral pressure, and economic pressure is yielding results.

It is hard to fault anything that makes gestures in the right direction, even if they are incomplete or only a start. Yet it goes without saying that a sustainable approach to tourism in general is a long way from a universally accomplished fact. Sustainability has to encompass more than an ecological definition: not polluting the water, or using only renewable forms of energy. Sustainability has to be extended to the economies and the cultures of host villages. There can't be economic or cultural hit-and-runs any more than there can be ecological ones. The idea of sustainability points to the end for the flavor-of-the-month destinations. The concept also holds out the possibility for better experiences for visitors. "Sustainable" means you don't exhaust a location, but you don't exhaust a tourist either. It might imply much more in the way of return and repeat visiting. Visiting would take on some depth; relationships would be established between visitors and hosts, within which true exchange could happen instead of the McDonald's drive-through model—grab, eat, throw away, move on—that has fashioned so much of mass tourism up to now.

As tourism moves into the future, much will change. If we listen to Louis D'Amore, much will change for the better. The destinations will demand better treatment and better travelers, and travelers will demand better treatment and better destinations. The people whose countries and communities are the hosts for tourist visitors will not suffer exploitation quietly. They will demand a broader benefit from all the people coming into their world, and they will demand more sensitivity on the part of those visitors. They will demand that their countries and environments and cultural treasures not be dismissed or damaged, disparaged or destroyed. They will demand more control, and lower levels of leakage.

Mass tourism has become such a huge and such a pervasive phenomenon that, according to Louis D'Amore, it is "no longer even an industry, but is a sub-system of our society and culture, inter-connected and inter-dependent with many other things." At the business end, hotel chains, airlines, and car-rental systems understand how intricately inter-dependent they are and have taken the steps to make sure they interconnect. But well beyond business, tourism is becoming woven into the fabric of our entire culture.

Travel and tourism more and more exist not as something on their own but in ongoing and growing dynamic tension with other aspects of our "culture", with education, with entertainment, with the arts. In Thomas Cook's day a trip was a respite, a diversion, an adventure. In the first sixty years of this century it was treated in pretty much the same way. The big change now, says Louis D'Amore, is in the integration, and in the fact that tourism is "vision driven rather than market driven." Tourism has grown up.

Travelers, too, are growing up. They are going to become more discriminating. They will tolerate less and less a system that treats them like so many cattle herded on a barge. Within this new world, one of the most important jobs will be that of the travel agent. Traditionally a low-paying career where harried, poorly trained clerks scramble to broker destinations with carriers and accommodations and financing all for the lowest possible price for a finicky public, this job has vast possibilities in the future world. The travel agent in the future might be someone more like a professor or a university department head, setting a course for eager students in the school of life, offering options and discussing their implications. Travel agents, enlightened, enthused, motivated, could be like your "good life planner," the key to bringing the traveler, the destination, the industry, and the people who live at the destination together and making it all work.

In an ideal world where tourism plays its ideal role, there will be reciprocation and exchange. In a distant corner of rural Zimbabwe, in a village on the edge of a great national park where North Americans and Europeans go to stay in lodges among herds of elephants and giraffes, a young boy of about twelve was minding his mother's store. The store was not much more than a roadside stand that sold chewing gum and warm soda pop, soap and not-absolutely-current newspapers. Most of the customers were local villagers, but occasionally a foreigner, driving by in a rental car on the way to the park and the lodge, would stop. The boy, who was poor, in ragged shorts, and a clean but well-worn tee shirt, was nevertheless bright, curious, friendly. We exchanged the kind of half-teasing pleasantries you do when you encounter a twelve-year-old you like. He was in the fourth year at his village school. He knew where America was and associated it with Michael Jordan. He liked to read, but said he was also good at mathematics. I looked around at the meager store he was minding. A couple of much smaller children, his sisters, played behind the lean-to with a dirty plastic pail, dumping water and steering it through a little trench they had made in the sand. Across the road, well in front of the lush green hills that marked the place where the national park began, was a hodgepodge of cottages and shanties that was the village or town where my new friend lived. I was about to move on to the lodge, to fulfill my plans to see elephants, but I paused for a moment curious as to what his future might be, the future of a boy as bright and as curious and as engaging as anyone you might want to meet in London or Vancouver or Atlanta. What, I wondered, did he want to be when he grew up? He didn't hestitate. He looked straight at me with a happy grin of optimism. "A tourist," he answered.

Endnotes

Chapter 1

between 1932 and 1938, tourism doubled. Witold Rybczynski, *Waiting for the Weekend* (New York: Penguin Books, 1991), p. 148.

would be a sign of lower social status. Jack Kugelmass, "The Rites of the Tribe: American Jewish Tourism in Poland," an essay included in *Museums and Communities: The Politics of Public Culture*, edited by Ivan Karp, Christine Mullen Kreamer, and Steven Lavine (Washington and London: Smithsonian Institution Press, 1992), p. 385.

fragments into unified experience. Dean MacCannell, quoted by Jack Kugelmass, "The Rites of the Tribe," p. 385.

the sleazy god of ritual conformity. John Dunn, "Daring To Leave The Beaten Track," *Globe and Mail* (Toronto, October 25, 1990).

enjoyment of leisure required some justification. Edmund Swinglehurst, *Cook's Tours: The Story of Popular Travel* (Poole, Dorset, U.K.: Blandford Press, 1982), p. 183.

behaves differently than an undisturbed cheetah. David Quammen, "The Economy of Nature," *Outside* (February 1992), p. 26.

selling themselves into a new slavery. V.S. Naipaul, *The Middle Passage,* quoted by Mark Kurlansky, *A Continent of Islands* (Reading, Massachusetts: Addison-Wesley, 1992), p. 22.

People go to see what they already know is there. Daniel Boorstin, quoted by John Dunn, *Globe & Mail* (October 25, 1990).

photo of me wearing my straw hat. Kurlansky, *A Continent of Islands,* p. 20.

Chapter 2

the realization of Utopia in America. Quoted from Richard O'Connor, *The German Americans* (Boston, Toronto, London: Little Brown, 1968), p. 101.

Navigare necesse est, vivere non est necesse. O'Connor, *The German Americans*, p. 102.

the handles of the doors are glass. Descriptions of mid and late 19th century sailing vessels plying the Atlantic between Bremen or Le Havre and New York and the comparisons of conditions in first class and steerage. Ibid, p. 100–105.

drawing the corks. Ibid, p. 104.

totally open to the North Atlantic gales. Ibid, p. 104.

and $5,709 in first class. "Is This Worth Ten Times the Price of Coach? *Conde Nast Traveler* (March 1993) had writer Graham Boynton test and compare service, facilities, and prices among classes on thirteen different airlines.

we make our way to cities such as Lagos, Mexico City, Lima. Russell Banks, "Primal Dreams: Can You Still Find the Native Planet in Florida?" *Conde Nast Traveler* (September 1994), p. 127.

Chapter 3

would lead to the bridging of the social gap as well. Swinglehurst, *Cook's Tours*, p. 34.

they have never dreamed of aspiring at home. Ibid, p. 48.

lengthened lives and pulpit and pastoral efficiency. Thomas Cook quoted by Swinglehurst, *Cook's Tours*, p. 34.

wouldn't know what to do with it. Patrick Blednick, *Another Day in Paradise: The Real Club Med Story* (Toronto: Macmillan of Canada, 1988), p. 187.

each country's indigenous atmosphere. Club Med corporate Fact Sheet.

the Mediterranean of Durrell, Douglas, and Lawrence sigh with despair. Swinglehurst, *Cook's Tours*, p. 185.

Chapter 4

It is all but uninhabitable. Aldous Huxley quoted by Paul Glassman, *Belize Guide* (Champlain, NY: Passport Press, 1992), p. 2.

a refreshing breeze usually blows through. Ibid, p. 67.

Tourism is going to be the best performing sector of the economy. Nuala Byrne, "Building The Economy, Preserving The Environment," *Fortune* (February 22, 1993), presented as an advertising feature, then reprinted, *The Belize Times* (March 28, 1993), p. 8.

Chapter 5

people in the business are committed to preserving it. Ibid, p. 21.

now being explored by an ever-expanding number of eco-tourists. Tom Barry, *Inside Belize* (Albuquerque NM: Inter-Hemispheric Education Resource Center, 1992), p. 134.

protection against hurricane losses. Ibid, p. 134.

it's a travesty and a curse. Quammen, "The Economy of Nature," p. 26.

Ecotourism is not beer and Pringles in the rainforest. Quammen, "The Economy of Nature," p. 26.

nature and culture in an exciting and responsible way. from a subscription ad for *EcoTraveler.*

and/or reduced domestic consumption. Kreg Lindberg and Jeremy Enriquez, *An Analysis of Ecotourism's Economic Contribution to Conservation and Development in Belize* (World Wildlife Fund and Ministry of Tourism and the Environment (Belize), 1994), p. 25.

Chapter 6

the three sister Graces of our moral being. Edward Rice, *Captain Sir Richard Francis Burton* (New York: Charles Scribner's Sons, 1990), p. 278.

forward you will be lucky to make forty in the same time. Winston S. Churchill, *My African Journey* (London: Holland Press, 1908), p. 86.

almost as remote and strange as outer space is today. Alan Moorehead, *The White Nile* (London: Hamish Hamilton, 1960), p. 16.

its botany, geology and meteorology. Ibid, p. 27.

the craven preference for comfort over dignity. Evelyn Waugh, *A Tourist In Africa* (London: Chapman & Hall Ltd., 1960), p. 67.

slung on long poles and carried by two men at a time. Rice, *Captain Sir Richard Francis Burton,* p. 290.

and abundant squabbling. Ibid, p. 292.

regions unvisited by their own colour. Ibid, p. 291.

retired before he could be punished. Ibid, p. 260–261. These accounts are from Burton's notes and diaries, recounted by Rice.

beyond balancing ourselves upon our donkeys. Ibid, p. 294.

inflicted a visit of unbearable length upon my kind hosts. Waugh, *A Tourist In Africa,* p. 73.

political and scientific inventions were unthinkable then. Moorehead, *The White Nile.*

we wait patiently for his reappearance, but he reappears not. Rice, *Captain Sir Richard Francis Burton,* p. 287.

or want of skill, with the rifle. Churchill, *My African Journey,* p. 7.

every kind of small deer and gazelle. Ibid, p. 6.

the vultures have already begun to whirl. Ibid, p. 11–12.

eventually to inflame the passions of the Chinese. Waugh, *A Tourist In Africa,* p. 68.

a higher level of economic utility. Churchill, *My African Journey,* p. 21.

complete a grotesque and indecorous picture. Ibid, p. 20.

from the cramped and unsanitary jungle-slums of Europe. Ibid, p. 38.

ornamented leather works, brilliant shirts, huge hats. Waugh, *A Tourist In Africa,* p. 109.

odd tribute from the Defender of the Faith. Ibid, p. 77.

asking our host to turn off the wireless. Ibid, p. 104.

tame the jungle—more jungles than one. Churchill, *My African Journey,* p. 53.

tables made to look rather like beer barrels. Waugh, *A Tourist In Africa,* p. 117.

state 'sex of wife'. Ibid, p. 115.

the native races are not yet far enough advanced. Ibid, p. 116.

Chapter 7

the continent's under-development and poverty. Raymond Bonner, *At the Hand of Man: Peril and Hope for Africa's Wildlife* (New York: Alfred A. Knopf, 1993), p. 93.

roughly the same as Belgium and its ten million people. Lance Morrow, "Africa: The Scramble for Existence," *Time* (September 7, 1992), p. 28.

106 percent of gross domestic product. "Africa, Out in the Cold", editorial in the *New York Times* (January 2, 1994).

and perfected them in peace within a lasting community. Georges Louis Leclerc, compte de Buffon, quoted by John Berger, "Why Look At Animals?" *About Looking* (New York: Pantheon Books, 1980), p. 19.

a monument to the impossibility of such encounters. Berger, "Why Look At Animals?" *About Looking,* p. 19.

without disturbing the domestic life of a single catfish. Beryl Markham, *West With The Night* (Boston: Houghton Mifflin, 1942, reprinted San Francisco: North Point Press, 1983), p. 205.

only the wealthy can afford it. Ibid, p. 211.

however preposterous the proposition might seem on first examination. Bonner, *At The Hand Of Man*, p. 243.

disappointed, if not angry, with the driver of the van. Ibid, p. 245.

either outcome deprives the cheetah of its meal. Ibid, p. 244.

telling the inhabitants to fend for themselves. Graham Boynton, "In The Valley of Death: Wildlife Poaching In Africa," *Conde Nast Traveler* (October 1995), p. 192.

involved in revenue sharing in only a limited way. Costas Christ, "Report on Community Wildlife Service of the Kenyan Wildlife Service (KWS) to the Ecotourism Society," reported in *The Ecotourism Society Newsletter* (Vol. 4, No. 1, Winter 1994).

the something caged comes festooned with zoom lenses. Jeremy Ferguson. *Globe and Mail* (Toronto, Aug 6, 1994).

Chapter 8

The town had no center. It had been eaten by shopping malls. Bill Bryson, *The Lost Continent: Travels In Small Town America* (London: Secker & Warburg, 1989), p. 41.

Chapter 9

The anarchists, as always, are the 'gentlement of the road'. Bruce Chatwin, *The Songlines* (New York: Viking, 1987), p. 271.

and take the opportunity of times, places, seasons. Ibid, p. 169. He quotes Robert Burton, *The Anatomy of Melancholy*. Robert Burton lived from 1577 to 1640. *The Anatomy of Melancholy* was most recently printed by Dent, London, in 1973.

that we should ever be in motion. Ibid, p. 169.

if one just keeps on walking, everything will be all right. Chatwin, *The Songlines*, p. 171, quoting Soren Kierkegaard, letter to Jette (1847).

I have not told half of what I saw. Marco Polo quoted by Richard J. Walsh, editor, *The Adventures of Marco Polo* (New York: The John Day Company, 1948), p. xii.

not liking much of anything. Sallie Tisdale, "Never Let the Locals See Your Map: Why Most Travel Writers Should Stay Home," *Harper's* (September 1995), p. 67.

silly or inappropriate or just not cool. Ibid, p. 74.

a map unfolded on the street corner, lost again. Ibid, p. 74.

willingness to play the fool for awhile. Ibid, p. 68.

we do not take a trip, a trip takes us. John Steinbeck, *Travels with Charley* (New York: Penguin Books, 1962), p. 4.

Chapter 10

perhaps only for two weeks at a time, is beside the point. John Elkington and Julia Hailes, *Holidays That Don't Cost The Earth: The Guide To Greener Holidays* (London: Victor Gollancz Ltd., 1992).

lives upon tourists who, if they are not beloved, are welcome. Moorehead quoting Reade, *The White Nile*, p. 154.

carved right out of walls as souvenirs. Swinglehurst, *Cook's Tours*, p. 95.

worst experience in more than thirty years of annual visits to France. Brian MacArthur, "Is Fake France Better than the Real Thing?" *London Times* (Weekend Section, August 27, 1994), p. 1.

a town of real beauty is being destroyed by tourism and tourists. Ibid, p. 1.

Civil War Fort. Andrew Cockburn, "Making A Stand: The Fight Against Disney's Theme Park in Virginia," *Conde Nast Traveler* (September 1994), p. 150.

It was pretty boring. Andrew Cockburn, Ibid.

Can the world sustain so much tourism? MacArthur, "Is Fake France Better than the Real Thing?", p. 3.

Burma's new facade of 'economic growth'. John Pilger, "Brutal Facts Lay Bare a Land of Fear," *Guardian Weekly* (May 12, 1996), p. 22.

beaten, or taken away in the night. Ibid, p. 22.

Thailand on package sex tours, who is to object? Margot Hornblower, "The Skin Trade," *Time* (June 21, 1993), p. 18.

Chapter 11

in order to reduce the bed-night tax they have to submit. Bonner, *At the Hand of Man*, p. 135–136.

leak away from communities near most ecotourism sites. Lindberg and Enriquez, *An Analysis of Ecotourism's Economic Contribution to Conservation and Development in Belize*, p. 47.

by the onslaught of large scale tourism. Blednick, *Another Day In Paradise*, p. 148.

because nowhere in the world are they duplicated. Rachel Carson, *The Sea Around Us* (New York: Oxford University Press, 1951).

take actions consistent with that decision. Lindberg and Enriquez, *An Analysis of Ecotourism's Economic Contribution to Conservation and Development in Belize.*

whether our seeing it was worth the cost to the pristine habitat. Wallace Immen, "We Need To Limit Tourism While There Is Something Left To See," *Globe and Mail* (Toronto, April 13, 1994).

Selected Bibliography

Books

Austen, Jane. *Emma*. London: John Murray, 1816.

Barry, Tom. *Inside Belize*. Albuquerque, NM: Inter-Hemispheric Education Resource Center, 1992.

Blednick, Patrick. *Another Day In Paradise: The real Club Med story*. Toronto: MacMillan of Canada, 1988.

Blunt, Wilfrid. *The Dream King*. London: Hamish Hamilton, 1970.

Bonner, Raymond. *At the Hand of Man: Peril and Hope for Africa's Wildlife*. New York: Alfred A. Knopf, 1993.

Bryson, Bill. *The Lost Continent: Travels In Small Town America*. London: Secker & Warburg, 1989.

Chatwin, Bruce. *The Songlines*. New York: Viking, 1987.

Churchill, Winston S. *My African Journey*. London: Holland Press, 1908.

Elkington, John, and Hailes, Julia. *Holidays That Don't Cost the Earth; The Guide to Greener Holidays*. London: Victor Gollancz Ltd., 1992.

Fussell, Paul, ed. *The Norton Book of Travel*. New York, London: W. W. Norton, 1987.

Glassman, Paul. *Belize Guide*. Champlain, NY: Passport Press, 1992.

Kurlansky, Mark. *A Continent of Islands*. Reading, Massachusetts: Addison-Wesley, 1992.

Marco Polo. *The Adventures of Marco Polo*. Edited Richard J. Walsh. New York: The John Day Company, 1948.

Markham, Beryl. *West With The Night*. Boston: Houghton Mifflin, 1942; San Francisco: North Point Press, 1983.

Moorehead, Alan. *The White Nile*. London: Hamish Hamilton, 1960.

O'Connor, Richard. *The German Americans: An Informal History*. Boston and Toronto: Little, Brown, 1968.

Rice, Edward. *Captain Sir Richard Francis Burton*. New York: Charles Scribner's Sons, 1990.

Rybczynski, Witold. *Waiting for the Weekend*. New York: Penguin, 1991.

Steinbeck, John. *Travels with Charley: In Search of America*. New York: Penguin, 1962.

Swinglehurst, Edmund. *Cook's Tours, The Story of Popular Travel*. Poole, Dorset: Blandford Press, 1982; distributed in the U.S. by Sterling Publishers, New York.

Waugh, Evelyn. *A Tourist In Africa*. London: Chapman & Hall Ltd., 1960.

Articles and Reports

Banks, Russell. "Primal Dreams: Can You Still Find the Native Planet in Florida?" *Conde Nast Traveler* 29, no. 9 (September 1994): 126.

Boynton, Graham. "In The Valley Of Death." *Conde Nast Traveler* 30, no. 10 (October 1995): 182.

Boynton, Graham. "Is This Worth Ten Times the Price of Coach? We're Talking Business Class" *Conde Nast Traveler* 28, no. 3 (March 1993): 182.

Cockburn, Andrew. "Making A Stand" *Conde Nast Traveler* 29, no. 9 (September 1994): 146.

Kugelmass, Jack. "The Rites of the Tribe: American Jewish Tourism in Poland." In *Museums and Communities, the Politics of Public Culture* edited by Ivan Karp, Christine Mullen Kreamer, and Steven Lavine. Washington and London: Smithsonian Institution Press, 1992.

Lindberg, Kreg. "Policies For Maximizing Nature Tourism's Ecological and Economic Benefits." Washington DC: World Resources Institute, 1991.

Lindberg, Kreg, and Jeremy Enriquez. "An Analysis of Ecotourism's Economic Contribution to Conservation and Development in Belize." A report prepared for the World Wildlife Fund (U.S.) and the Ministry of Tourism and the Environment (Belize), 1994.

Quammen, David. "The Economy of Nature." *Outside* (February 1992): 25.

Sas-Rolfes, Michael 't. "Rhinos: Conservation, Economics and Trade-Offs." London: Institute For Economic Affairs Studies on the Environment, 1995.

Tisdale, Sallie. "Never Let The Locals See Your Map; Why Most Travel Writers Should Stay Home." *Harper's* 29, no. 1744 (September 1995): 66.

"United States Travel and Tourism: A New Economic Perspective." World Travel & Tourism Council. Brussels, London, New York, Hong Kong. March 1995.